Youth Work and Islam

Youth Work and Islam

A Leap of Faith for Young People

Edited by

Brian Belton
Sadek Hamid
YMCA George Williams College, London, UK

SENSE PUBLISHERS
ROTTERDAM/BOSTON/TAIPEI

A C.I.P. record for this book is available from the Library of Congress.

ISBN: 978-94-6091-634-2 (paperback)
ISBN: 978-94-6091-635-9 (hardback)
ISBN: 978-94-6091-636-6 (e-book)

Published by: Sense Publishers,
P.O. Box 21858,
3001 AW Rotterdam,
The Netherlands
www.sensepublishers.com

Printed on acid-free paper

CONTENTS

CONTENTS

INTRODUCTION

This book has an eclectic focus, emanating from the duel inspirations presented by its title. Through the perspective and voice of practitioners, it considers how youth work can be informed by Islam, but at the same time looks to demonstrate how practice can be pertinent to young Muslims, their community and relationship with wider society. But more broadly it also does something to demonstrate how an understanding of Islam can enhance and develop youth work practice across the horizon of the discipline, providing a much needed impetus to theory and ideas, many of which have ceased to be relevant or are coming close to being passed their sell by date.

This ground breaking collection has, for the first time, brought together a range of voices and views to elaborate and celebrate the relationship between young British Muslims, Islam and youth work. By creating a discursive space to inform, debate and share experiences, it is hoped, that this volume will be of interest to professional and voluntary youth workers, policy makers and anyone with a stake in the welfare of Muslim youth. As a whole, the book questions the bifurcation usually proposed (or proclaimed) by the media, and that is sometimes implied in policy, which purports that the imagined homogenous Muslim population and the rest of society (apparently taken to be anything but the heterogeneous conglomeration that it is) are separate and often divergent entities. Moreover it challenges the myth that young Muslims (and perhaps the young generally) are a kind of sub-species within this dichotomic fantasy.

The chapters that follow are timely as, particularly in the European context, Muslims are being effectively ostracised for being who they are, in a way that would be deemed as unacceptable from any civilised or liberal standpoint. Under the diaphanous camouflage of the weakening of 'collective identity', in Munich, on February 2011, as the English Defence League, which has been accused of Islamophobia, being understood by many to disgorge a clearly anti-Muslim vocabulary as the spine of their organisational logic, held a mass rally in Luton, British Tory Prime Minister, David Cameron told the world in a speech, which ostensibly focused on terrorism (mentioning the words 'Muslim' or 'Islam' 36 times and 'extremism/ist' 23 times);

In our communities, groups and organisations led by young, dynamic leaders promote separatism by encouraging Muslims to define themselves solely in terms of their religion.

He went on to declare;

...organisations that seek to present themselves as a gateway to the Muslim community are showered with public money despite doing little to combat extremism

This qualifies as a gross and flagrant misrepresentation of the vast majority of young Muslims and of Muslim organisations; many of the latter receive no public funding whatsoever.

But even worse than this, the tenor and ethos of the this speech marks out Muslims, and particularly young Muslims, as a dangerous threat to European populations;

...this threat comes in Europe overwhelmingly from young men who follow a completely perverse, warped interpretation of Islam... young men find it hard to identify with the traditional Islam practiced at home by their parents, whose customs can seem staid when transplanted to modern Western countries

This kind of rhetoric, at a time of economic recession, smacks of the language of pogrom, and echoes Cameron's Tory predecessor Enoch Powell's 1968 warning (also a period of recession) of 'Rivers of Blood' that served as a shot in the arm for the National Front, an earlier incarnation of British National Party.

In the face of this type of insensitive, undistinguished, hurtful and apparently purposely divisive onslaught (not even the most foolish Politian, which Cameron is not, could believe this type drum beating would not have the power to fuel the fires of hatred) of all professionals, youth workers, as long-time self proclaimed 'advocates of young people' need to make a response.

Perhaps the most authoritative rejoinder to such decided hyperbolic anamorphosis is to demonstrate how Islam and Muslims have augmented, and continue to contribute, inform, increase the integrity of and refresh valuable work, which potentially and actually impacts on all young people. In this cause, *Youth Work and Islam* brings together Muslim and non-Muslim youth practitioners and academics in a project that demonstrates how Islamic understanding and the presence of Muslim youth workers has enhanced and continues to enrich British culture and the life of young people of this country, promoting a fairer, more just and humane society. However, perhaps contrary to the distorted pastiche of Islam that has become popularised in the European context, what the reader will be left with on engagement with this book is the vigour Islam offers to encourage dialogue and so questioning. It is this which can give rise to action and ideas that are able generate an ethos that might be the closest we can come to experiencing democracy, not just as a word but as a field effect. This provides a means to connect and meld a nation, which is being systematically and violently broken up into distinct human categories, into a functioning society, that can be energised by its rich diversity.

Youth work arises out of the society that fosters it, while playing a part in maintaining and creating that society. As such, youth work, influenced by Islam or effecting young Muslims, shapes and is shaped by the same. However, the product and process of this symbiosis is hardly understood because it has more or less remained unexamined. Indeed, most of the time and energy given to considering the actual or potential relationship between Islam and youth work tends to see one element (Islam) as a target of the other (youth work). Anyone who has any understanding of either Islam or youth work will, with consideration, recognise this to be at least unrealistic and perhaps a ridiculous point of view. Even if it seems to make sense on paper, in practice the delivery of youth work hardly ever achieves the kind of cultural hygiene that policy makers might wish for. At its best youth work tends to melt into its context and become at one with it. As a secondary effect, particular incarnations of practice have a propensity to bleed into the whole, reforming the general nature of the field (youth work is a field and not a discipline – its plasticity and tendency to metamorphose dictates this).

This understanding guides the purpose of what follows; youth work and Islam are not approached as separate considerations affecting or infecting each other; we do not want to put youth work into Islam, nor veneer youth work with Islam; we see youth work and Islam as complimentary in terms of a values, hopes and ambitions. This is something more than fabricating a notion of complementary systems of thinking and acting, it is effectively the pointing out, for what the most part has historically been, a hidden seam of precious synchronicity; a synthesis of ethics, attitudes and ways of being.

This approach produces much more than a straightforward view of theologically informed practice, it presents a broad and humane understanding of the character and possibilities of youth work practice. Centrally, while, taken as a whole, the book demonstrates how Islam and Muslims have been and are part of the development of youth work, it also puts forward ideas and standpoints that demonstrate how Islam can continue to enlighten, augment and direct practice, while adding to and enlivening (perhaps helping to resuscitate) the traditionally humanitarian spirit of youth work. This can only make our endeavours amongst, with and alongside the young people we serve more effective.

The book starts out with chapters by Brian Belton and Tahir Alam, who provide introductory explorations of the relevance of Islamic values to youth work, demonstrating how professional practice can be enriched by these principles, benefiting both Muslim and non-Muslim young people. This may surprise some people in this age of anxiety about the alleged failures of multiculturalism; however the fact of our societal diversity is not going to be wished away. Those who resist societal pluralism would do well to remember that human interdependence is necessary to create civilised co-existence. Besides, there has not been a point for the best part of 3,000 when the islands that make up Britain have been anything else other than pluralist, ethnically, culturally or religiously[1]. So it's not so much about getting used to it, it's about getting with it!

The context and pathologised representations of young British Muslims are analysed in detail in the first section by Sughra Ahmed and Tahir Abbas. Muslim young people, they argue, cannot be reduced to a homogeneous 'problem' that needs to be 'fixed'. However, this is not to deny that young people are encountering unique tensions within the communities they live in and wider society. Particularly troubling is the ongoing securitised framing of Muslim youth, which looks set to continue under the current coalition government. In reality there is much more to Muslim young people's lives than just 'preventing violent extremism'. Like their non-Muslim friends, their social well being can be disadvantaged by poverty, educational underachievement, unemployment, the further reduction of youth and recreational services and in some cases threatened by gang warfare, knife and gun crime.

The second section explains how delivering effective, high quality youth work, informed by Islamic perspectives, can help to provide skills and experiences to deal with these challenges. A distinctive approach to working with Muslim youth is necessary and demonstrated in the good practice discussed by Julie Griffith. However, as Sadek Hamid argues, faith based youth work can create counter productive trends that need alternative models of practice, a theme enthusiastically taken up by Maurice Coles in his framework for youth participation.

The final third of this anthology is devoted to the reflections of youth workers engaged in work with Muslim youth from across the UK. Each contributor, having different stand points and experiences, provide rich insights into the diverse ways of engaging young people and the challenges they encounter. The anonymous autobiographical reflection on growing up as a Muslim and becoming a youth worker is a refreshingly honest example of the dilemmas of trying to successfully negotiate multiple identities. In a concise but intricate analysis Firzana Khan, narrates some of the impacts of marginalisation, categorisation and the 'weak power' encompassed in the same, while Irfan Shah assesses the problematic nature of the recent Prevention of Violent Extremism (PVE) agenda and its repercussions on work with young people. Mark Roberts and Zoey Williams respectively explore the relevance of the key concepts of education, community and Ummah in relation to youth work theory. These contributions, which share underlying themes, should be read in sequence. In the next chapter Brian Belton looks at the place of mercy in youth work and how this sentiment links and confirms some of our common needs with our unity via and across faith boundaries. Andrew Smith demonstrates how positive relations can be fostered between Christian and Muslim youth, and how this can cultivate open discussion, maintain integrity and avoid both polemics and apologetics.

Brian Belton's final chapter relates fragments of his own intellectual and spiritual journey and the centrality of action, echoing a core Islamic teaching of the indispensable link between faith and practice; this provides a fitting conclusion to the book.

All the above accounts powerfully vindicate, communicate and commemorate the necessity of faith and cultural competence as an eminent path to integrity of practice; all emphasise the centrality of the well being and growth of those we work with and amongst. As such, as a collection the book champions the best traditions of youth work, within a theme of developmental and critical practice.

We, the writers who have come together with our words and ideas, do not seek to sentimentalise religious belief, which can in certain ideological forms encourage prejudice and violence. However, in our experience the ideals and ethics of the Muslim faith can offer wisdom and new directions which enhance the quality of youth work with Muslim young people and those with different religious backgrounds. This message of solidarity is critical at a time when young people, your and our children, seek meaning, belonging and direction in a confusing, fast changing world. These viewpoints cannot remain feel good rhetoric in situations where young people are demanding urgent positive change. So the task remains to convert theory into practice; we hope we have offered a few useful signposts for this journey.

NOTES

[1] Until the sea levels rose following the most recent ice age (the Devensian glaciation) about 8,000 years ago, Britain was part of the European land mass. As such, before that point in time there was no barrier to the exchange and intermingling of populations, beliefs, cultures and even between 'subspecies' (Neanderthals were still knocking around in Europe around 30,000 years ago) from across and beyond the European land mass. Incidentally, as Britain became cut off from Europe we have no idea of the skin colour of the people of the newly formed island; there is no reason to suggest it was white for instance.

CONTEXT

BRIAN BELTON

1. YOUTH WORK AND ISLAM – A GROWING TRADITION

Dr Brian Belton was born and brought up in Newham and is a Senior Lecturer at YMCA George Williams College in East London. He has nearly 40 years experience in youth work; as a field worker and an academic he as experience in Africa, Canada, the USA, Iceland, Sweden, Greece, China, the Falkland Islands and Eastern Europe, He has recently been involved in the professionalization of youth work in Malaysia and across south-east Asia. However, his practice and personal roots are in London's East End communities, which of course has included Muslim contexts. Recently Brian took a lead in developing a pre-graduate course at the George Williams College for youth workers involved in Islamic contexts, looking to lay a path for this group to enter undergraduate studies. He has written close to 50 books looking at identity, social history, race, ethnicity and sport.

INTRODUCTION

The Prophet said, 'He is not of us who does not have mercy on young children

Al-Tirmidhi Hadith

The following seeks to generate a sense of the development of youth work with young Muslims in North and East London over the last 40 years via autobiographical and narrative research, but also to demonstrate something of how an awareness of Islam can enrich and enliven practice. It includes analysis of the life-stories of Muslims who grew up in the area, their encounters with youth provision and how they moved on to become youth workers. I believe their contribution exemplifies the influence of Muslims in youth work over the years, but also shows the relevance of Islam to the field in the contemporary period.

Overall, this chapter looks to draw attention to the relatively long history of the relationship Muslims have had with youth work provision in these areas of London and generate an analysis of the impact this has had on those concerned. This is achieved by highlighting how Islam has influenced the sphere of practice of particular workers and the way in which insights drawn from Islamic teachings and ways of

B. Belton and S. Hamid (eds), Youth Work and Islam:
A leao of faith for young people, 3–27.

'being' can inform contemporary practice on a generic basis, while often proving more relevant and appropriate than some of the deficit oriented philosophy/theory that can be found in the literature surrounding the practice of informal education and youth work.

I should say at the outset that I am not, by any stretch of imagination or metaphor and scholar of Islam. My Arabic is as limited as the reader's imagination might allow and mostly self-taught with the aid of one or two more learned, more linguistically aware friends. For these shortcomings I apologise in advance, but my first hope is that you can hear what I have to say in the spirit of Islamic theory of knowledge. This said, I have been involved in youth work for the best part of 40 years, much of this working alongside Muslim colleagues and with Muslim clients. My second hope is that this will be seen worthy enough to serve as a foundation of my position.

MUSLIMS AND YOUTH WORK

Any attempt to portray the general experience of an eclectic population such as Muslims feels bound to fail to do very much more than generate vague stereotypes in order to produce an image that has no real use and even less authenticity.

There is no 'one type' of Muslim. Most people know of that there are Sunni and Shia Muslims. However, just looking at Sunni Islam, within that grouping there are different schools of law and belief (Ash'ari, Maturidi, Murji'ah, Mu'tazili, Athari and Zahiri. Within Shia there are the Zaidiyyah, Alaw and Alevi).

However, Islam also encompasses Kharijite Islam, Sufism and Ahmadiyya Muslims, as well as Liberal, Qur'aniyoon and Heterodox groups, such as Mahdavism, Moorish Science, Nation of Islam, Submitters, Druze and Ahl-e Haqq. Added to this are different cultural, national, tribal/clan, district, regional and even familial interpretations, understandings (and misunderstandings), translations, traditions, habits and customs. Many understand Islam to be united in the Arabic language, but Arab dialects can be almost languages in themselves and it can't be taken that a rural Bangladeshi farmer will understand the Arabic used by a middle-class Egyptian.

As might be predicted, not everyone within this diverse mixture of people will agree that all those included above are 'real' Muslims.

For all this, for most of its history the investigation of faith based youth work has ignored the participation and contribution of individual Muslims and the general influence of Islam. In saying this I invite, probably understandably, defensive responses; I have experienced some of the same over the last few years, both from Muslims and non-Muslims. These include variations of;
– 'Muslims haven't played much of a part in faith based youth work until relatively recently'
– 'There is no mainstream Islamic youth work'

– 'Muslims don't have any time for anything other than formal education'
Such rejoinders, as is pretty obvious, come from people who believe they are able
to speak for all Muslims over time and place. However, at the same time, such
views also seem to make the point that Muslims have been and are people who
play no significant part in conventional youth work.

YOUTH WORK AS A MUSLIM TRADITION

For me, a comment of a young Bangladeshi man (his family had come from what
was in the mid-1960s still East Pakistan) named Naeem, with whom I worked in
Bethnal Green (East London) in the early 1970s, summed this attitude up and as
such it has stuck in my mind:

We (Muslims) *have been invisible in youth work because what we do hasn't
been seen as youth work. I organise a football match and I sort of disappear; it's
as if it organised itself! Then all that anyone sees it the football match. They don't
see the before and after of it; what it's like getting parents to agree, getting the
kids to agree! I want to swear but I don't swear. Because after what is a great big
work of diplomacy, negotiation, decision making, trying all the time to be
democratic and fair, keeping everyone involved, stopping fights, arguments,
getting people to see both sides, all anyone sees is the game! I think I am just
taken as one of the kids or something.*

This refusal to see Muslim youth workers, that gives rise the stereotypical
comments detailed above, I believe to be lazily myopic more than an effort to be
purposely untruthful.

Youth work, as Naeem understood, does not have a mainstream as such. The
discipline continues to be what it has always been, an eclectic and evolving
response to young people, delivered in an almost overwhelming range of forms,
in an apparently endless series of locations, deploying a continually growing
array of techniques and approaches, which are motivated by a superfluity of
motivations, policies and beliefs. Over time, because youth work practice has
taken place in such a range of situations, it has been delivered under so many
guises (currently often under the auspices of 'childcare services') and via a
plethora of methods (including informal, non-formal, social, political education)
adhering to a shifting, hardly ever definite philosophy. As such the idea of a typical
or archetypal form of youth work is fanciful.

This point is exemplified by Hala Saeed, a Muslim woman, who was born in
Somalia and migrated to the UK in 1995. She is the youngest child of the Saeed
Abdiqader family and was raised, along with her four siblings, by her mother.
She now has a young daughter herself, Fatima. Hala's involvement in youth
work is much more recent than Naeem's. She gained her professional
qualification in youth work in 2009 from the YMCA College in East London,
and has been involved with several projects in the London borough of

Hounslow, including the Hounslow Youth Offending Service. She is also a Family Program Leader, working with vulnerable Somali parents. She has recently qualified to Teach English as a Foreign Language (TEFL) at Kingston University.

For some years Hala has been involved with community action, often being an advocate for the Somali community in Hounslow and beyond. At the time of writing she was setting up a private community interests company, aimed at supporting Muslims families, while volunteering as a teaching assistant, focusing on Somali refugee children in West London. She hopes to move forward with her teaching career and studies with a Masters degree in Education.

Hala sees youth work and Islam coming together quite logically. For her it would be unreasonable to expect people to successfully meet the responsibilities that come as adulthood dawns without people who have moved beyond that stage being willing to walk with young people as they enter this new phase of their lives;

In Islam, puberty marks the entry to the challenges and responsibilities of life. As such it is described as the age of 'taklif', or legal obligation. From this time onwards a young person is obliged to perform the religious duties as an adult Muslim.

For Muslims, their first reference point is the Qur'an, which describes itself as "... a guide and a healing to those who believe" (S.41: V. 44). This plays a significant role in satisfying physical as well as spiritual needs. We as Muslims, and as adults, have an ethical, religious and moral duty make ourselves helpful to young people as they enter the process that taklif involves.

Islam teaches a code of behaviour, social values and gives meaning for our existence. Of particular value during the adolescent transition is its guidance towards toleration and developing adaptive capacities in the face of stressful life events. It can also act as a means of developing a sense of self-respect, while offering teaching about the virtues of family life, and the need to work towards a cohesive society, via a sense of relatedness.

My faith incorporates a comprehensive set of values, ethics and code of behaviour in techniques of social learning, which I believe can provide young people with the opportunity to use their influence and find their personal authority on individual, local community and Ummatic levels. I feel this is what youth work is about.

Traditionally a central consideration of youth work has been justice. The Qur'an shares this concern.

O ye who believe! Stand out firmly for justice, as witnesses to Allah, even as against yourselves, or your parents, or your kin, and whether it be (against) *rich or poor: for Allah can best protect both. Follow not the lusts* (of your hearts), *lest ye swerve, and if ye distort* (justice) *or decline to do justice, verily Allah is well-acquainted with all that ye do.* [An-Nisa 4:35]

Hala has a deep commitment to this kind of sentiment in her work, but in particular with young women (of course anti-sexism has been a basic principal of modern youth work);

Somalis coming to England have gained greater independence, not born of expectation, but necessity. Many arrived in the 1990s as single parents, with several children to support, their husbands killed in the civil war. But the public voice of the Somali community continues to be male. Those unfamiliar with Somali culture perceive women as being in the background, mostly focused on homemaking and raising children.

The reason women's rights in Islam need special concern is because of the position of women in some Muslim countries. What adds insult to injury is the justification of this oppression of women in the name of 'Islam'. How can these societies be 'healed', in the sense that the Qur'an puts it, unless Muslims live up to the ideals of their faith, which teaches them to honour women and ensure that their rights, which are given to them by God, are secured?

In Islam, men and women are asked to equally submit to God, and both are ennobled by the Creator. Despite some stereotypical images and representations of Muslim women as repressed and oppressed, many Muslim women today are actively affirming the rights and responsibilities that they believe the Qur'an affords to them. They are affirming that men and women are created from one soul, to be partners to each other; that males and females have the same religious responsibilities.

The discussion of Muslim women and their roles is an important one for every Muslim, firstly because it's an area in which there are many misconceptions by non-Muslims, which need to be corrected, and secondly some Muslims treat women unjustly in the name of Islam. However, their actions are often a result of cultural or tribal customs and not connected to the religion.

While the role of motherhood is among the highest states a believer can achieve, being a mother and a wife are not the only roles open to a Muslim woman. Islam, amongst other things, permits the women to perform Hajj (pilgrimage), *to exercise the vote, engage in politics, to take up employment and run her own business.*

In Islam females are associated with 'rehmat' (mercy) *fortune and joy. As a wife one is the companion to man (and the man is her companion) in all social, physical and economic endeavours and should not be subjugated in any way. Muslim women have traditionally played a crucial part in their communities, not just in customary roles. Historically women took part in teaching, scholarship, medicine and other significant activities. They were a long way from being subjugated to the men as they were valued for both their courage and wisdom. Within Islam religion is understood as a guide to living and life; it provides a structure and boundaries within which women are held in high regard, with as much potential to be respected and followed as a role model within her community and wider society as men.*

At least from the time of Naeem's entry into the field to Hala's involvement, Muslims have been part of youth work, as participants and facilitators. As such, Islam has stimulated and informed youth work practice ever since its birth as a national, generic service phenomenon in the 1960s. There was also a Muslim presence before this, in some of the numerous enclaves of missionary, religious, instructional, moral and disciplinary attention to young people from the 19th Century onwards that some historians mistakenly propose as straightforwardly the direct progenitors of today's practice. In the 18th and 19th Centuries the influence of Islam was strong enough to attract converts amongst the English upper classes.

For all this, it is probably enough to say that Muslims, and thus Islam, have been part of youth work in the UK at least as long as living memory. The following pages, in a small way, are, added to the other aims of the chapter, an effort to engender some recognition and understanding of this.

'ILM' AND YOUTH WORK

The term used for knowledge in Arabic is *'ilm*, which has a much wider connotation than its synonyms in English and other Western languages. 'Knowledge' falls short of expressing all the aspects of *'ilm*. Knowledge in the West is often taken to mean information about something, divine or corporeal, while *'ilm* is an all-embracing term covering theory, action and education; it gives these activities a distinctive shape. It has been argued that this type of comprehension is of supreme value for Muslims and indeed, *'ilm* is Islam, in that Islam is the path of 'knowledge'.

Outside of Islam it is arguable if any other religion or ideology puts so much emphasis on the importance of *'ilm*. Each of us, being the creations of Allah (the first educator and the absolute guide of humanity) no matter how humble or even ill informed, has the potential to access and add to *'ilm*; attempting to understand and listen to our fellow humans (not necessarily agreeing with them). This can be understood as one of the basic precepts of *'ilm* and it is why (I think) *'ilm* is at least one of the pillars of youth work and as such necessary to the thoughtful practice of the same.

This perspective is, in my experience, part of the treasure that many Muslim youth workers have brought to their practice. However, this kind of contribution has gone largely unacknowledged, partially because when we talk of the conjoining of youth work and Islam we understand it, as an expression, as a relatively recent aspect of the wider field of practice, and partly because it has been carried into youth work as part of a 'Muslim package' that has been delivered, in the main, quite unselfconsciously. By that I mean that most effective youth workers bring facets of themselves to their practice and it is the resultant heterogeneity of response that makes youth work a uniquely responsive and eclectic discipline. At times, in certain places, *'ilm,* as an aspect of Islamic identity

8

and culture, has been infused into youth work practice in a pleasingly informal way and much of what follows will relate to this.

Naeem described how youth work can be recognised as '*ilm*

You can only really teach so much and perhaps certain things; you can pass on information and guidance and kids can remember all that, and that might be thought of as knowledge. But people need something more than just being taught or instructed. People have the means within them, a sort of light, which can illuminate understanding. At the same time that is a gateway that allows awareness to sort of happen. No one can do that for someone, although shutting kids up and cutting them off can do a lot to stop it. But experience, action, going out and doing things in the world provides the sparks. That is what I want to do as a youth worker, and I grow from it too.

How do I know this? Well, the Qur'an tells you this. It encourages people to come together, care for each other, teach each other, be tolerant, listen, collaborate and that is how things happen and how people become more than what they are. No matter how frustrating youth work can be, it's being able to make some room for all that to happen which makes it worthwhile...more than worthwhile for me – it expresses what I am as a Muslim and a human being!
Yes, you can be taught, but in the end you can't be taught everything by someone else, you have to do the learning for yourself – you can get people to teach you, but that is no good unless you are going to learn. But we have it in us to do that, working and living with others.

ISLAM, SCIENCE AND YOUTH WORK

My first job as a professionally qualified youth worker took me to Tower Hamlets and the Arnold Circus, Brick Lane district. From my agency in Virginia Road I undertook a number of projects with young Muslims, in liaison the now legendary 'Avenues Unlimited', on the Chiksand Estate. Much of this work was relatively instinctive, you kind of learnt as you went along. Looking back, the kids we worked with must have been very patient or perhaps felt sorry for us; they probably worked more with us than we did with them. However, in the last few years there has been a growing consciousness of the need to think about youth work in Muslim contexts. More recently perhaps there has been a few of us who have been endeavouring to bring attention to how the teachings and traditions of Islam can and do contribute to our efforts to serve young people from a range of backgrounds, regardless of religious affinities. This being the case, in this chapter I want to highlight a sense of the development of youth work influenced by Islam. I will argue that this has a history of at least half a century, although the dynamics of what might be called the 'Islamic world-historic legacy' underpin the nature and conduct of practice just as law, education, medicine and the foundation of the achievements of Occidental science have significant roots in Islamic heritage.

Amongst the very first things a trainee youth worker is taught (in one way or another) is the skills of observation; how to look at/inspect things and people. This is usually followed by the recording of these observations. These recordings are forms of evidence that work has taken place and perhaps information about the trajectory of particular pieces of practice and/or agency direction over time. But they can also prove to be a means of analysis of what has happened and/or been accomplished; what people do when things are done, how individuals and groups undertake tasks and why they might be motivated to act in certain ways. This process is undertaken firstly to provide a record of events, when and who was involved, but the 'why' question takes the procedure into another 'diagnostic' realm; it is at that crossroads that youth work meets with science. The resultant awareness of what has happened can be used to predict future events;

If this thing happened, with these people involved, in this way, then it is likely that, given similar circumstances, much the same thing will happen the next time those people do those things, in that way.

This provides the potential either to seek to replicate situations, change personnel or environments, to alter outcomes. In short, this is doing what science seeks to do; manage or control what seemed to be (without observation, recording and analysis) random, unpredictable and uncontrollable events or circumstances – 'truth from proof' – not 'the' truth, but the pursuit of the same, or as Arab philosopher Al Kindi, wrote, '...nothing should be dearer to the seeker of truth than the truth itself' (*Tabaqat al-'itbia*, Ibn abi-Usiba's).

While science cannot be said to be solely the product of Muslim endeavour, the call of Islam to seek knowledge, in the broadest sense of the word, has had a profound effect on the development of scientific knowledge. According to the Prophet, seeking knowledge is an obligation upon every Muslim (cited in Siddiqui, 1990, 135–6).

The Arab 'Golden Age' of Baghdad, Persia, and Muslim Iberia, from 632 to 1258 AD, was the first of a sequence of 'golden ages' of Muslim thought, that encompassed a geographical and spiritual terrain from Shiite Iran to Mughal India, up to the 18th century. These waves of intellectual fervour represent great world wide endeavours and adventures (Sinbad, the fictional sailor from Basrah, might be thought of as a sort of metaphor relating to this period) on the part of Muslims to seek, collect and refine knowledge. This led to new discoveries and innovations. Scholars and researchers, working from Samarkand, in modern-day Uzbekistan, to Cordoba in Spain, advanced our understanding and application of (amongst other things):

– **Astronomy** - there is a vast crater on the moon named after Astronomer Al Manon

- **Chemistry, engineering** - the achievements of al-Jazari, a Turkish engineer of the 13th century, include the crank, the camshaft, and the reciprocating piston; the exiled Emir Abdal Rahman brought irrigation systems and unique architecture to Cordoba, Spain
- **Mathematics** - Musa al-Khwarizmi developed algebra in 9th century Baghdad, drawing on work by mathematicians in India - his invention of algorithms made cell phone technology possible, while Omar Khayyam, the admired poet of the Rubaiyat, was a mathematical genius who calculated the length of a year to be 365.242 days – atomic clocks agree with him to within millionths of a second
- **Medicine** - it was Syrian-born Al Nafis, who revealed that the blood flows from the heart, through the lungs, to the body and back again; ibn Sina, wrote the textbook *Canon of Medicine* that was a standard work in Europe's universities until the 1600s.
- **Philosophy** - as a corollary and precursor to all the above was taken to new heights.

As I'm making a list I must also mention Al Ma'mun, who founded Baghdad's international House of Wisdom from which came foundations for modern mathematics, astronomy, chemistry, medicine, and literature.

These achievements are just exemplars of a sophisticated culture and civilization that was based on belief in God – as such what is known as the 'Dark Ages' can be seen to be something of a European misnomer, as it was during this period that a vast, extended debate took place between scientists, philosophers and theologians on the nature of physical reality and limits to human reason. Indeed, it seems the very basics of the Arabic language were formed out of the need to express mathematical principles. As such, one can confidently claim that early Muslim culture set the foundation for the Renaissance in Europe and for nearly every aspect of the modern world. It is this basis on which youth work stands as a potentially civilising discipline.

DIALECTIC

However, this cultural flowering was also a means of developing the overriding conclusion that was to arise out of the 'gathering of knowledge' that the Golden Age was. This was a protracted era of concentrated and multifaceted dialectic, under the Islamic auspices, which grew out of a consciousness that violent (violating) force can hardly ever positively resolve issues of the spirit or soul with regard to individuals, groups, communities or societies. The awareness that this search confirmed was that the path to whatever we might achieve as human beings lies in the honing of knowledge and understanding through the commitment to dialectical relations between people. This dialectic (not simplistic dialogue - chatting) is for me is the rock on which the practice of youth work stands.

At the same time it is a product of Islamic culture, a means to acquire and comprehend '*ilm*.

This means both teacher and learner need to be aiming to promote 'dialectic'. This, straightforwardly, is a situation wherein ideas can shared and so developed in order to promote new ideas and insights. The diagram below outlines this process:

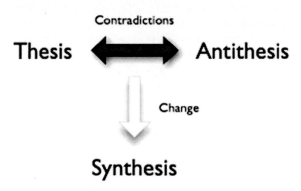

Here you can see that one person starts of with an idea (Thesis). This demands to be met with ideas that might challenge or enlarge that idea (Antithesis). This brings about a new understanding (the two perspectives coming together – the Synthesis)

A similar graphic illustrates this as a sort of 'intellectual pathway' for developing our understanding of reality (it is a plain helix, but it reminds us of the DNA structure that lies at the core of each of us and all living things):

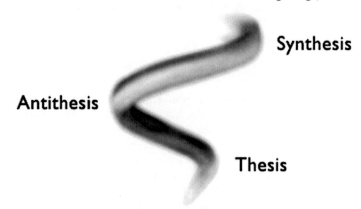

As you can see, this is a leap forward from simplistic dialogue, which can become pretty much aimless (or sometimes more destructively degenerate into gossip) or a give rise to a situation wherein it is all too easy for the teacher to dominate the process via their aims to educate. This said, the dialectical process of mutual discovery can be understood as the sort of interaction one might aim for following the establishment of dialogue. Dialectic may arise out of dialogue to generate mutual insight that can be expressed. This contrasts to what might be thought of as a 'stationary dialogue', wherein reciprocal insight is not necessarily engendered and as such remain be unexpressed.

The above coil might be thought of as potentially eternal rather than the picture of a whole journey, as the dialectic is never fully resolved, returning as it does to the start of the of the literal voyage of discovery (dialogue).

For all this, the point is for both parties involved (although more than two people might be implicated) in the dialect to develop insight, understanding and awareness. It is a different process to that premised on the aim that the student should somehow simply learn from or be educated by the teacher. This would in fact not be education at all; at best it is advice giving, instruction or confessional (perhaps encompassing symbolic or actual absolution and penitence) at worse it could be understood as indoctrination, domination or colonization.

Some readers may have been aware of some or all of the above, but in terms of this chapter it had to be stated because it is the sort of runway on which the tradition of Islamic education lands on the British youth work scene; it is just a hint of the cultural foundation of the Islamic influence in education.

'UMMAH' - THE INFLUENCE OF ISLAM

I can't truly say that there was a moment in my own life when I first felt the influence of Islam on my direction in life. I was born and brought up in Newham in East London, which for my first dozen or so years was East and West Ham. I was an inhabitant of the latter, less prosperous of the two then different boroughs. At the age of 11 I was consigned to Burke Secondary Modern School. This was very much the dustbin of West Ham's low achievers and juvenile miscreants, for whom education was as much a joke as it was an imposition. At the time the borough languished in the deepest depths of poor achievement in secondary education in Britain, during a period when the UK slithered around the bottom echelon of secondary educational attainment in Western Europe. Hence I can boast that I attended, what was probably at the time, the worst school in Western Europe!

My behaviour at primary school had led to my expulsion from Greengate School in Plaistow, so I never actually took the 11-plus examinations that decided which part of the then tripartite system one would be sentenced to, but my former head made sure I was set nicely in the very lowest stream at Burke after telling me, 'Belton, you are headed nowhere but prison'; did I detect a subtle hint of pessimism about my future?

On my first day in secondary education I found myself being one of two English speakers in my class. That first day was less than 20 years after the Partition of India, at a point in time when the effects of then recent civil war in Cyprus were still being dealt with and, as a consequence, although I had very little awareness of this at the time, the majority of my peers were Muslims. Our teacher was Mr Said, a gentle but firm Pakistani Muslim. He was one of the many teachers who had come to Burke from across the world. The school also boasted American, Canadian, Indian, South African, Ugandan, Kenyan, Hong Kong Chinese and Russian teachers, not a few of whom had come to the East End, some via Oxford, Cambridge and Harvard, to hone their skill in a challenging environment. Indeed, an American teacher, Mr Wilson, told me, 'if you can teach at Burke you can teach anywhere'. Hence we also attracted more than our share of well meaning but ill prepared young men and women carrying a missionary zeal, who at other times, not long before, East Enders would have, without question, considered their social 'betters'. As it was, at that point in history, Union activity and the concomitant class consciousness was blowing through the Docklands like a mighty wind and our teachers put up with an awful lot from Burke's reluctant scholars, but it has to be said, they had an impact. However, as my first teacher, none had the same influence as Mr Said and it was he who taught me his understanding of 'ummah' (أمة) but, probably more importantly, a way to activate the spirit of this concept.

Unlike the notion of 'community', which is often seen as its equivalent, ummah embodies a potentially all embracing inclusiveness (*ummatun wahidah* in the Qur'an refers to whole of the Islamic world unified). The meaning of community encompasses both sameness and difference; it defines some people as 'inside' and others as 'outside'. As such, community is effectively a means of discrimination; the tighter a community boundary is, the less likely it is that it will interact with other communities. In such situations communities become isolated, introverted and inward looking; they tend to be arenas were little knowledge comes in or goes out; hence they are contrary to the ethos of Islam as they become pools of ignorance and as such are inherently prone to prejudice (pre-judging). This may partly explain why Islamic rulers in the classical period encouraged and welcomed Jewish and Christian scholarship.

Contrary to the negative effects of community, the Qu'ranic precepts concerning '*ilm* (the living out of ummah) provide pragmatic means to avoid the development of prejudice, which tend to arise out of the propagation/sharing/promotion of ignorance. While ummah can be understood to refer specifically to Islam, Islam does not preclude people by birth, creed, colour, education, race, ethnicity, culture, neighbourhood, wealth, poverty, intellectual or political leanings etc. in the way that community does. If you think about it, it is very hard to either enter or extract yourself from community. In fact, often when people leave relatively tightly bound communities they are seen to have 'sold out' or be 'traitors'. On the other hand those attempting to enter communities will usually have to deal with allegations of being 'outsiders' and/or 'deserters' from another community. I, as a West Ham supporter, would find it difficult to enter into the 'Arsenal' community. I will never cease to be a former West Ham community member. Likewise, all the other 'faithful' West Ham supporters will see me as irredeemably a defector and turncoat.

This process, I believe, is the antithesis of ummah, in that you, me, everybody on earth, have the capacity to accept and be accepted by everyone else by way of the duty to accept those who enter into ummah; ummah is a sacred destiny of humanity in oneness, while community is the purposeful carving up of people into discreet categories and as such a form of violence. In ummah there is 'collectiveness' and 'connectiveness'; we are all football supporters. The differences between West Ham and Arsenal are comparable only to the dissimilarities between a pear and an apple and as such representative of the wonderful diversities that make life worth living, in that we can appreciate the qualities of each without one precluding us from the other (up the 'Ammers!).

MUSLIMUN

Mr Said also taught me another retrospective lesson. *Muslimun* is the plural form of Muslim, meaning, 'those who have peacefully submitted' i.e., the believers of Islam. This collective submission might be thought of as part of the creation of the connection or wholeness between those within the faith (potentially all humanity). For me, this bond reflects something of the nature of Islam, promoting as it does a concept that human beings are born with the capacity to be integrated and become part of a collective and connective expression of being.

In much the same way aspects of our shared and individual life, religious, political or educational, need not be regarded as separate spheres, as they are expressions of the wholeness/connectivity/collectivity that we prospectively embody. To separate my education from my faith, or from the rest of who I am, rather than making room for or allowing the same to coalesce, is yet another violent act; symbolically or metaphorically similar to cutting off a limb and examining it as if it had only a tangential relationship to the rest of my body. At the same time, this severance can create division between me and others. The possibility to share our 'whole selves' is undermined as individuals compartmentalize different aspects themselves. Instead of the whole 'me' connecting with the whole 'you', we will need to find the bits of us that can meet, but in such a process we will identify that which cannot be accept by the other. Unless we are individually integrated how might we coagulate with that which everyone else is or might be (particularly if every self is similarly split)?

To me, this violation of self separation is exacerbated by the effort to dissect education into formal and informal elements (as is the habit in much youth work training). The good teacher (or the enlightened youth worker) like Mr. Said,

15

will use what others might recognise as informal and formal methods interchangeably (and even both at the same time!). But for my first secondary school teacher there would be no dichotomy, as his efforts were integrated into an educational enterprise that was about my realisation of myself as an integrated individual and as potentially part of ummah. He once told us;

...isn't my behaviour saying a lot about who I am, how I live, how I want to live, how I want to treat others and how I might expect to be treated myself? Surely my behaviour is not a separate thing that is nothing to do with me? Is my behaviour what I make seen of myelf in the world? Do others conclude, probably quite rightly, that I am doing whatever it is I do for a reason?

That, as my father used to say, is quite a 'straightener'. Mr. Said, in the space taken up by four short questions about himself (not statements or instructions about 'you') for the listener, reason replaces excuses, as consequences are realised. In the process the ground is prepared whereon one might become aware and so responsible. Part of the foundation of wisdom must surely be a sense of my own responsibility, my impact on the world, as this is intimately tied an awareness of the consequences (for me an others) of my actions.

As such, now more than 40 years on, I can recognise the influence on and inspiration of this kind of response on my practice, both as a youth worker and lecturer, while, in the spirit of ummah and *'ilm,* I pass this on to the people I work with, for and amongst.

MODELS OF GOOD PRACTICE

Mr Said was a good educator, which included being a teacher, but he did more than teach. He was prepared to be taught by us! He was, seemingly, endlessly interested in us, his pupils, and asked as many questions of us as we asked of him (probably more). Often bad behaviour was exposed to his genuine curiosity. 'Why did you do that?' The answer was always met with another question. For example;

'Because I wanted to'

'And why did you want to?'

The overall effect of this was most of us couldn't be bothered to act up in his class because of the third degree consequences, which obliged us to look at ourselves and our motivations, and often the consequences of the same; 'What effect do you think that had?' 'How do you feel about it now?' This was hard work as one thing most East Enders of my generation could not help doing, in common with my Indian, Cypriot, Turkish and Pakistani class mates it seemed, was answer any question asked of us. I think Mr Said understood this; it was something he had learnt about us. Of course, when someone takes the trouble to learn about you, you find yourself learning about them; learning, if it is learning, is hardly ever a one way process.

So, Mr Said was not just a teacher, in that he was a social educator and a social critic, constantly involved in his own social education. I now understand that he was also a youth worker; a person who literally worked with, cared and learnt about, taught, talked and listened to youth.

SOCIAL KINDNESS

So youth work practice is and has been carried out by Muslims in all sorts of contexts and ways. Over the years I have collected many examples of these as part of an effort to discern how Islam can benefit and broaden our response to young people. Mostly they are instances in practice where a socialisation within Islam can be seen to have had an impact, but what makes them fascinating for me is how this influence is largely unselfconscious; to this extent it is natural or instinctual, thus it flows from people, and so it is gentle. I would suggest that the overall authority is as such a sort of social kindness in an atmosphere that has been given some very sharp edges by Western capitalism (most youth work has been funded, directly or indirectly, by the state, which as I write is waging illegal wars that have been sanctioned by no one outside a corporate/political elite).

MUZAFFER

Muzaffer arrived in Britain in the late 1950s from Turkey at the age of 3. His parents were observant Sunni Muslims. He was brought up in Brighton, where his father worked in the catering industry. His mum found employment, first as a cleaner and then as an administrator in a big Hotel.

The family came to live in North London. As a 17 year old Muzaffer got a job, like his dad, working in the catering industry. He was married in 1977 to Aisha, a student (who ultimately became a primary school teacher). Her family had fled Uganda and the persecution of Idi Amin in 1972. The couple had two children and faith was an important part of family life.

It was through the children's attendance at a youth club that Muzaffer became involved in youth work. By 2000 he had nearly 15 years experience working with young people, firstly as a football coach and then, after gaining a string of part-time qualifications, a detached youth worker. He told me he would certainly have done the work for nothing, although could not have devoted as much time to it as he did as a paid worker. His faith has been a constant source of inspiration and reflection in his youth work practice.

At first I didn't have a clue how to work with young people. I just did what come naturally and did the best I could. It was not until I started to work with others that I became a little bit critical of what I saw. I had always seen kids as being basically good. When they were a naughty there was nearly always a reason and once you sorted that out things were generally ok. So when I first went to meetings with youth workers it felt slightly uncomfortable, because they seemed to all agree that the kids they were working with 'had problems'; it was as if there was something wrong with them, like as individuals. They either were 'unable to concentrate' or 'lacked self esteem' or were covered by an expression I never understood – they 'had issues'.

But the Qu'ran asks 'Why do they not reflect on themselves?' It is too easy just to point out what someone else does, especially someone who is young, and say, 'the reason they're bad is that they are bad'. If I look to myself, 'What is it about me that is not helping this person to be good?' Then I think you tend to get a lot further with the person you are working with.

This attitude is in alignment with the position that Sufism attributes to Muhammad;

Happy are those who find fault with themselves instead of finding fault with others. Abu al Qusim (Muhammad)

MODELS OF DEFICIT

What Muzaffer has seen in operation was the 'deficit model' of young people that runs through youth work practice and related literature. This perspective depicts those we work with as lacking something in themselves; the attitude that lower achievement is due to a problem with the individual rather than considering the role of institutions (such as schools) instructional practices, organisational structures, etc. Deficit is often ascribed to individuals using a lexicon of vague terms, mostly drawn from the overlap between psychotherapy and psychoanalysis, that include 'attention seeking' (who does not seek attention and if someone was seeking it why wouldn't we give it to them?) and 'lack of self–esteem' - although this estimate hardly ever provides what this lack is being compared to; people who have 'just enough' self-esteem perhaps? At the same time the person making such a statement tends to neglect telling us how or by what criteria they are measuring self-esteem, or in what way they are qualified to undertake this measurement.

The likes of William Ayers (2005, 2006, with Ford 2008, with Quinn and Stovall 2009, with Alexander-Tanner 2010) is the latest in a long line of thinkers that have written about the effects of young people's experience of being treated as 'lacking', the consequences of the same and possible strategies to avoid the blithe (and often blind) application of deficit labels (see Berg 1972, Holt 1964 and Kohl 1991 for example). This apart, you can probably think of many examples of this kind of amateur psychiatry based on the premise (and generally bald assumption) of another's lack. However, in the main, a prognosis of this type suggests that the person being referred to is suffering from some personal malady/pathology. It is in fact much less common to hear workers look to political, economic, environmental and/or situational influences on behaviour, and it is even rarer to find youth workers, as an initial response, who like Muzaffer, look at how they themselves might have elicited or invited the seemingly negative, but perhaps rational, response of a young person.

THE 'RIGHT WORD'

From an Islamic perspective largely unsubstantiated assumptions about young people's psychological state, or 'uneducated' guesses about people's disposition/personality, are not acceptable

O you who believe! Keep your duty to Allah and fear Him, and speak always the right word [Surah Al-Ahzab (33): ayat 70]

The 'right word' is not some handy expression that seems to fit a particular moment or response. To find the 'right word' we need to at the very least look at a range of possible motivations. If we neglect this investigation those of us in the professional realm have failed to use our professional judgement. But whoever one might be, the progeny of such negligence is prejudice; we become pre-judges, setting ourselves up above others (young people) based on what we believe to be our superior experience or insight. At this point the worker has allowed the resource of personal humility to slip through their fingers, and as The Prophet Muhammad said; *Whoever is humble to men for God's sake, may God exalt his eminence.* (Al-Mamum Al-Suhrawardy Allama Sir Abdullah. 1954 p12) That humility is an acknowledgement just how little we actually know about the complex character of any individual (a creation of God no less) let alone those we might see for a few hours in one particular context in any given week.

ELENA

From my earliest days as a youth worker I was involved with Gypsy, Traveller and Roma young people. This was chiefly related to my own background, but from the late-1960s through to the mid-1970s I was involved in the lively and, at times, brutal politics arising out of what was nothing less than the persecution of the nomadic people of Britain. It was at this time that I met Elena, whose parents had come to London from Bulgaria just after the Second World War. Elena, a Sufi Muslim, had been involved with Travellers from the late-1940s, motivated in part by the response to the threat to her family (labelled as 'Pomaks'[1]) under Nazi and then Communist influence during and after World War Two.

After losing touch with her religion for a few years in her 20s and becoming a single parent, politics did much to fill the vacuum. But later Elena found a new rigor for her faith and, over the years, had become something of a student of Islam. This, she told me, tongue in cheek, worried her parents almost as much as her previous wandering away from with her beliefs.

At the time I knew Elena she was part of the growing Human Rights movement. Her son, who she brought up in Islam, was very much the centre of her existence, but her active interest in social justice and minority rights was an enduring preoccupation.

In a long conversation that went on through one cold January night, while observing police and bailiff behaviour at a prospective eviction (such a presence often meant that removals of caravans would be less brutal) Elena told me;

In Britain most institutions, legal, educational or whatever, were formed during the time of British colonialism and it would be surprising if they did not operate showing that influence and history. So youth workers and social workers are sent out into communities just as missionaries were sent to India and Africa to bring 'civilisation' and 'education' to the 'natives', which meant getting them to act according to the standards and values that were 'acceptable' to 'respectable' British people.

The idea was to make them 'good subjects' and useful to the Empire even if a lot of well meaning people didn't see this. That is also the purpose of education and welfare in Britain. It is not really education; it is not about 'helping others' or 'learning to question' – why would the government sponsor that? It is a form of colonisation that uses indoctrination and propaganda designed to produce relatively cheap, relatively flexible workers that are useful to capitalist enterprise. Of course not all teachers or social workers see this; else many of them would not want to do what it is they do. But we live in a capitalist state, what else could be the case?

Since this conversation I have grown to understand that while seeing people in deficit has an obscure lineage, its genesis in Britain is probably intrinsically linked to the age of colonialism. This was a time when the privileged of the Empire sought to bring their culture, religion and education to what they took to be those in deficit; the 'natives' of the subjugated territories. Of course, this was the social guise of control and domination, via forms of indoctrination, which were likely to have fooled the missionaries and servants of Empire as least as much as those they looked endow with the (questionable) benefits of European civilisation.

British institutions, education, law, government etc. were formed, shaped and defined and as a consequence of and so reflective of the colonial period. This being the case, these arms of the state are still imbrued with the culture of colonialism and as such propagate a deficit perspective of those they encompass, both functionaries and clients; the educator approaches the pupil or student not primarily with the motivation to learn about them, but with the view that they are more or less ignorant (they lack knowledge/awareness/ understanding).

For example, the moment one presents oneself to a medical practitioner one is treated as someone who lacks health; a person who is sick, not as an individual who is just not as healthy as they might be, one who has a level of health, but is experiencing a measure of discomfort or relative infirmity. Likewise, the educator approaches those they seek to educate with the assumption that they are ignorant and maybe they are in some respects, but they also have something valuable to teach the educator; this knowledge/information is the means to make the teacher a more effective educator.

I was reminded of Elena's position recently by a young Bektashi Islam woman[2], who originally came to the UK from Kosovo. Antigona, who a while ago was working as a volunteer with young people in the north of England, talked to me about an ambition that is often expressed in youth work circles; to 'instigate change';

Change from what to what? Who asked anyone to change them? When did anyone write to Council and ask for someone to come down here and change them? What's this change for? What is it that needs changing about people and who decides how much change and when the change might start happening and where it will end? I think we are talking about changing people to be more like the people that are looking for them to change...Let's change the neighbourhood; how we gonna know if the majority of the people living there want this change we are working at? What we gonna do, knock on people's doors and ask them what it is they want changing? That's gonna be a big job aint it!

I am so often struck how Islam is (despite what its media profile might suggest) a questioning faith; questions arise from the search (quest) for knowledge.

MUJAHADA (STRIVING)

For me, at that time, Elena's stance was a pretty radical and her outlook has continued to haunt my thinking up to the present, but she did not adopt the usual anti-colonial rhetoric or propose some sort of revolution. Her response to her perspective provided an insight into how her faith guided her practice;

Sufism has the something called 'mujahada' (I later found out this is related to jihad) *which is an intense determination to follow a spiritual life that the Prophet exemplified. The hardest conflict is the struggle with your physical self, which is morally more demanding than protesting against or fighting others, but produces something in the individual that is more permanent than just turning the oppressors into the oppressed by what looks like victory but is in fact the continuation of injustice.*

This stance reflects the position of the 14th century Persian Gnostic, Sayyid Haydar Amuli, that jihad, at the higher levels, becomes a struggle against the self and against the doubts and misgivings of the speculative intellect. There is also a famous hadith of the Prophet Muhammad relating to returning form the battle field where he told his followers, 'We return from the lesser struggle [jihad al-asghar] to the greater struggle [jihad al-akbar]. To which his followers asked, "what struggle can be greater than that of the battle field?" To which Muhammad replied, 'The battle of the soul [ruh] over the ego [nafs]."However, this can also be taken as a profoundly anti-colonial attitude, echoed by the likes of Steve Biko in his passionate assertion that as soon as one rejects the label of 'the oppressed' one is no longer oppressed. (Biko 1978, p 61-78). This change of perspective is not achieved primarily by a conflict with others, but by a struggle with self to overcome a perspective born out of persecution and domination. This means transplanting a more rational and autonomous view of self as first and foremost the glorious, complex and beautiful creation of God.

Elena's work was essentially built around learning about and being sensitive to the mujahada (the striving) of others; being able to identify with the inner travail this involves for the individual. Mujahada can be very informed and move on a solid trajectory, but for many of us, perhaps often for the young, this inner striving can have a confused direction and/or be guided by a not altogether rationalised purpose or clear motivation; it is not 'just there' it is something that 'becomes' over time and contexts. Like much of what makes us human, the spiritual, like the intellectual or the physical, is something in the process of growth and development (known in Arabic as, tazkiyyah, lit., 'self-purification'). This is what I, retrospectively, think Elena understood and had come to know how to work with. As she informed me;

Finding what we believe in is not about being told or even guided, although this might help. People need to go though their own struggles; those struggles belong to them and they are for them. Allah does not take away our tribulation but he has given us the means to face and overcome obstacles, and perhaps make them something we learn from. If we didn't have these things, if we did not have the challenges of life, how could we become more than what we are? How could we develop?

For me this has become a driving force in my work with others. Blame or bemoaning my misfortune is very much an easy exit and something that is profoundly 'anti-developmental'. As soon as I unload my situation as being caused by external forces I have shed responsibility for my own actions and claimed that there is a force that shifts my destiny, which in that shifting is greater than God. For sure, social factors have an influence on what I do and how I do it, but none of us are 'corks in a social sea'. We have our intellect and will, the sail and rudder, given to us by God. We also have the compass of His word and the teaching of His Prophets. We are not helpless or without the means to chart a root; we have a course to steer in life. Like Muzaffer, Elena's work was about developing her own consciousness of these assets within herself and others. This is also where I think Antigona was coming from;

The work is not, for me anyway, about changing others. It's about me changing in response to them; that's a skill I can develop and I'm getting good at that. And, if they want to change something, about themselves or where they live, I think they can do it without me needing to change them. But I can change my response, what I do, for

them to change themselves if they want to or, if they want, retain things about
themselves that others want to change...the 'change bullies'...ha ha!

COLONIAL MENTALITY

Franz Fanon (1965, 1967) generates similar sentiments to Elena, Muzaffer and
Antigona, arguing that colonised environments engender a sort of colonial
mentality wherein the colonised take on the values of the coloniser and measure
themselves according to those standards, although, as a colonised person, they
can never achieve these norms. This gives rise to hatred of self and at the same
time a hatred of the coloniser, so condemning the colonised to live in a neurotic
and toxic environment of hate and blame. The progressive initial response to
this is to somehow cast off the coloniser's categorisations in order to make
room for the development of a more humane and liberated understanding of
self. Once more, this requires the colonised to enter into a struggle with
themselves rather than adopt or be recruited by ill-defined notions of social
rebellion or revolution into forms of violence and by association self-
denigration. Such a path can lead to little more than the reversal of roles and the
continuance of hatred. Pol Pot's Cambodia and currently Zimbabwe might be
seen as cases in point.

THINGS CANNOT CHANGE UNLESS YOU CHANGE

But the situation is not confined to traditional areas of colonisation. Eldridge
Cleaver (1967) reflects on how the welfare system in America caused young
Blacks to see themselves as principally the recipients. His insistence (echoed by
Stokely Carmichael, 1967) was that Black people needed to reject the position
they had been assigned (and that they took on) by those who wished to exploit
them. At the same time Cleaver argued that Blacks needed to develop a different
notion of who they were and what it was they wanted to base their own values,
hopes and ambitions on.

What Cleaver was positing was that 'things cannot change unless you
change'. As much as environments can dictate the response of individuals,
individuals, collectively, can change environments by their response to them.
But people will not be able to alter environments via the efforts of
professionals, such as youth workers, to propagate a view of the individual as
pathological or 'lacking' something (deficit models). Cleaver, Carmichael, Biko
and Fanon all essentially confirm the process of *mujahada*; that people are
capable of, and we should expect them and ourselves to undertake, a disciplined
and determined examination of themselves in order that we might work towards
a world without colonisers or the colonised. In the words of the Prophet,

The most excellent jihad is that for the conquest of self; He who knoweth his own self, knoweth God (Bukhari Sharee)

This emphasis has always appealed to me as a means to carry out and a general aim of my work with young people. Overall it is very straightforward; the insistence on attempting to see those I work with in a positive light (the light of God?) as beings that hold within them all the potential of a creation of God, and working with them on projects, events and activities that might be part of that which causes them to embark on, continue and endure their own consistent and focused *mujahada*. In doing that I maintain my own *mujahada* and together we move towards an evermore liberated environment, as it is made up of evermore liberated individuals.

THE OFFERING OF SELF

Muzaffer, Naeem, Antigona, Mr Said and Elena, from different perspectives within Islam, had developed a sort of anti-deficit approach, but in each of them this was largely an unselfconscious response, not really something consciously worked for or against. If you like, it was in them, long before they got into the realm of youth and community work or education. Their immersion in Islam made their responses something of their nature; a gentle but nevertheless energetic emanation, coming from the people they were.

It is something quite difficult for people coming into training in youth work to really grasp that it is not doing things in this way or that which is seminal. The codes and commands of the books and websites devoted to informal education have a place, as must the policy and organisational demands placed on youth work. But the richness of the practice is the people who deliver the work and those that participate in the same as our clients. The most effective youth workers are those that are able to bring a little of their unique selves to what they do. We are at our best when we can offer this literal distinction while generating a genuine enthusiasm for those we work with to teach us about themselves. In this you might be able to detect something of a peaceful submission, in that it probably requires some humility and suspension of ego. Unless we do this how will we know those we work with, build associations with them or engender trust? If we do not know them, how can they know us? If we disallow them from teaching us about their wants or needs, their hopes, troubles and joys, how will we be able to work with them effectively?

This is what Elena, Naeem, Hala, Antigona and Muzaffer told me about; how they, as individuals, people who are Muslims, learnt about those they worked with and amongst, how they saw them as a resource more than whatever personal knowledge they as practitioners had. This is how they, personally, from themselves, interpreted their practice – it is that which made (and makes) their youth work distinctive, humane and effective; a fulfilling and fascinating *mujahada*.

FAITH BASED WORK

There has been a comparatively great deal of talk and writing about 'faith based practice' within youth work over the last decade or so, but I'm not sure there is a great deal of discernable commonality between or even within faith motivated practice. Some years ago I was talking to someone who worked for a Christian youth organisation. He and his colleagues would wander around a midlands city centre wearing Parker jackets with huge crosses emblazoned on the back. He told me about strolling up to a young man and, without introduction or any preamble, telling him, 'Jesus loves you'. He went on to claim that just making this statement changed this young person's life. I have found so called faith based work peppered with these sorts of claims and anecdotes. A few magic words start a palliative procedure that in turn fires-up a process of redemption.

This instance is not meant to exemplify Christian youth work, but it does ask the question if simplistic evangelical approaches, seemingly premised on a 'road to Damascus' principle, often motivated by the wish to play a saviour role, perhaps itself arising out of a lack of other practice options/direction, is wholly beneficial to either practitioner or client.

The YMCA, integration and mujahada

One of the biggest youth organisations in the world, the YMCA, does have evangelicalism as part of its historical underpinning, but I think the distinction that has evolved from practice is what the organisation asks of those that became part of it. The fulcrum of the movement has become the cultivation of mind, body and spirit; a kind of take on the 'three-in-one' notion recognisable as inherent in much of Christian belief.

Within this culture, an ethos similar to *muslimun*, human beings are seen as being integrated entities, in as much as it is taken as evident that:
– When you cultivate the spirit, it has an effect on mind and body
– When you nourish the mind this enriches the spirit and this will have influence on the body
– Nurture of the physical self will positively affect state of mind and the feeling of spiritual well being.
No line that makes up the YMCA's symbolic triangle exists independently of the whole; if it did there would be no triangle, just three separate lines.

But all this doesn't happen, or even start with a youth worker making a statement. It begins with the commitment of the individual, the giving of oneself to (a 'peaceful submission') which is premised on particular and definite set ideas, principles, beliefs and a faith. However, this faith is two way; it is faith in

God and in yourself as an expression of God. But there is a third line of faith that completes the triangle; faith in the young person having everything in them, that which is gifted them by God, to become all they can be. We need force nothing in, we only need to work with them to appreciate and so cultivate what it is that can bloom in and of them.

Such commitment requires constant effort and exercise of the will. It is not something that happens once and that's it. But if it is practiced (as we saw with, for example, Elena and Muzaffer) what is produced in response to others becomes something unselfconscious and natural.

Every day faith is challenged and the will to continue in the faith is more or less strong or weak. Faith, to be faith, needs to be energised and renewed. As doubt is part of modern human existence it is an element of contemporary faith. This situation makes demands of those of us who take on faith as something that permeates our work and our lives. If you are a person of faith and never experience such demands it might be fair to ask yourself if you are living in denial, because they are everywhere and consistent. Our faith may well have answers but there are, every minute, more questions for us and our faith to answer, so faith itself is questioning. As such a requirement of faith is the gaining of knowledge and understanding of the world, of others and like Mr Said asked of us, of ourselves.

You might be able to see parallels here between the character of the practice of Muslim youth workers I have presented and some of the spirit of areas of Christian, and perhaps faith based youth work in general.

CONCLUSION

In the relatively little space I have tried to respond to some big issues. I feel I have not really be able to express very much about my subject. But I hope what I have written provides you with an example of what has become a passion of mine; the idea that we have only really touched the tip of the iceberg in terms of how Islam can refresh and humanise some of the more mechanistic aspects of youth work practice. Much of youth work has become infested with what often seems like purely economic aims and as such it is sometimes transformed into something instrumental, attuned to outcomes that in effect dehumanise us and even more so, those we work with. This undermines the certainty that these people are not objects to be moulded or changed by what we might see as our superior knowledge or experience, but the wonderful and multifaceted creations of God, who, as such, have a destiny only He ultimately can judge.

NOTES

[1] A Muslim minority population of Bulgaria, whose members claim a variety of ethnic identities.
[2] Bektashism is a Sufi order that encompasses Shi'ite concepts while sharing much with
other Islamic mystical movements, e.g. the need for an experienced spiritual guide, the doctrine of
the four gates to be traversed: the Shari'ah (religious law), Tariqah (the spiritual path), Ma'rifah (true
knowledge), Haqiqah (reality). Bektashism places emphasis on the concept of *Wahdat-ul-Wujood*,
the 'Unity of Being' that was formulated by Ibn Arabi.

REFERENCES

Al-Mamun Al-Suhrawardy Allama Sir Abdullah (1954) *The Sayings of Muhammad* London: John Murray
Ayers, W. (2005). *Teaching toward freedom: Moral commitment and ethical action in the classsroom*. Beacon Press.
Ayers, W. (2006). *To become a teacher: Making a difference in children's Lives*. Teachers' College Press.
Ayers, W., & Alexander-Tanner, R. (2010). *To teach: The journey, in comics*. Teachers' College Press.
Ayers, W., & Ford, P. (2008). *City kids, city teachers: Reports from the front row*. The New Press.
Ayers, W., Quinn, T., & Stovall, D. (Eds.). (2009). *Handbook of social justice in education*. Routledge.
Berg, L. (1972). *Look at kids*. Penguin.
Biko, S. (1987). *I write what I like*. Heinemann International Literature & Textbooks.
Carmichael, S., & Hamilton, C. V. (1967). *Black power*. Random House.
Cleaver, E. *Soul on ice*. Bantam Doubleday Dell.
Fanon, F. (1965). *The wretched of the earth*. MacGibbon & Kee.
Fanon, F. (1967). *Black skin white masks*. Grove Press.
Foucault, M. (1973), The Birth of The Clinic, London:Tavistock Publications Limited
Foucault, M. (1969), The Archaeology of Knowledge, London: Routledge
Holt. J. (1964). *How children fail*. Pitman Publishing Corporation.
Kohl, H. (1991). *I won't learn from you*. The New Press.
Siddiqui, A. H. (1990) (Trans.), *Mishkat-ul-Masabih*, (Vol 1) New Delhi: Kitab Bhavan

TAHIR ALAM

2. ENHANCING YOUTH WORK PRACTICE THROUGH THE CONCEPTS OF ISLAMIC MORALITY AND EDUCATION

Tahir Alam was born in Bangladesh in a small village in Sylhet. After arriving in the UK at a young age, up to the age of 11 he lived in Windsor. However, his family fell into unfortunate financial circumstances with the failure of his father business. Losing everything the family moved back to Bangladesh and stayed there for three years, at which time Tahir studied Bengali until the end of high school. His family later moved back to the UK and took residency in the rough suburbs of London.

Tahir grew up in inner London at a time of racial tension, this alongside the experience of deprivation and poverty, was a stark contrast to his former life in Windsor. As a young person and an adult Tahir has seen many changes to the political and social landscape of London and has first hand experienced of the issues associated with inequality and discrimination. He has navigated his way through the many pitfalls that can trip up a young person on their journey through life and set them up for failure.

As well as working by way of what he sees as 'proactive engagement' as a youth worker in various locations across London for the last ten years, Tahir is also an occasional speaker at his local Islamic cultural centre and has written about current affairs, social and political.

Tahir is a Tutor and Supervisor for the YMCA George Williams College and works as an Adult Education Development Officer for local government. He is currently finishing a Masters degree in the Sociology of Education at the Institute of Education, University of London and also continuing his studies in the Islamic Sciences, focusing on Philosophy of Islamic law and Prophetic Traditions with Dr Akram Nadwi from Oxford University.

INTRODUCTION

Over recent years the religion of Islam has become a major actor in the global public domain. However, rather than its central teachings of peace, justice, tolerance and harmony, to the horror of most Muslims, the faith is commonly associated with injustice, intolerance and injury. This negative perception, given

B. Belton and S. Hamid (eds), Youth Work and Islam:
A leao of faith for young people, 29–37.

currency by groups of Muslims who claim to follow the Islamic message, continues to perpetuate in the general understanding of Islam. They have obscured the image of 'Islam', a word that in its Arabic derivation means to be 'at peace and to be safe' (Lane: 1984: Vol 1, p1412).

However, those who look into Islamic teachings with an open heart will find clarity, and an invitation to justice and harmony. In this chapter I want to look at a few of the traditional understandings of one of greatest aspects of the Islamic message, the ennobling of good character embodied in the personage of The Prophet of Islam, Muhammad, of whom God clearly states in the Qu'ran; *indeed your character is of a vast ethos* (Qu'ran:2003, 68:4). I want to show how these teachings speak to us as youth workers in contemporary society. I will be referring to traditional Islamic teachings and agreed upon sources after the Qu'ran and Sunnah[1], presenting not just a classical, orthodox view of Islam. I will also include a fusion of contemporary understanding of youth work, and consideration of current thoughts on its practice and values. Although the contemporary models of youth work in its many styles and forms of delivery has much to offer in their different approaches, I feel there is a level of underlying concern as to the integrity of many of the current models, which appear to be based on and regulated by the norms of consumer society. As a result there appears to be a loss of faith in a metaphorical sense. This being the case, I hope the models derived from Islamic teachings might be helpful in the enhancement of current practice.

ISLAM AND YOUTH WORK

Before *Youth Work and Islam* there is almost no literature that explores the Islamic moral, ethical, spiritual, educational frameworks that can be employed in both Muslim and non-Muslim youth work. However, this title should not be read as a dichotomy. It has to be remembered that Islamic teaching is holistic in character; life is not separated exclusively into particular areas. Ideas of education, politics and diet for example are considered in the greater context of faith; everything is an expression of and connected to the whole. So from this perspective youth work in Islam is an expression and part of Islam.

However, Islamic values have the potential to bring a different perspective to youth work, something that most youth workers might agree is helpful and could facilitate new insights and interpretations to many of the prevalent models, which generally are secular in character or influenced by Christian thought. Indeed, Islamic perspectives from the Qu'ran, Hadith/Prophetic traditions[2] or Islamic thought, can generally cater for the spread of understanding equanimity and harmony in human social interaction.

Throughout world history, across cultures and faiths people have valued the building of moral character and righteous conduct. Generations of philosophers, over thousands of years have sought to establish the nature of ethical behaviour amongst and between human beings. Within this there has been an enduring belief that education will motivate and promote 'the good' and work to inculcate high moral standards in human character. While atheists and agnostics have ascribed moral laws and ethical behaviour to intelligent human construction, most civilisations throughout the ages have, at the centre of their social systems, a belief in a supreme being or beings, a Creator God or gods. Indeed, it is difficult to argue that the foundations of moral law have not, as part of humanity's tradition and history, been founded on and laid down by religious doctrines, which have claimed divine authority and as such having a basis in infinite wisdom.

These essentially faith based principals, values and ideals have historically been transmitted and developed via intermediaries such as the Prophets, or as the manifestation of God as an embodiment of Christ or Avatars and framed within law. Muslims believe that moral laws and guidelines have been sent by God through the message of Islam and that there is no one who knows more about the affairs of the creation than our Creator. God says in the Qu'ran *In the Law of Equality there is Life to you, O people of understanding* (Qu'ran:2003, 02:179). This verse makes clear the divine nature of the law and how it is fundamental to life. Muslims do not doubt that there is similar guidance in other revealed scriptures of other faiths, but take the Qu'ranic law as being the primary guiding principles in personal and social affairs.

"IN THE NAME OF GOD THE MOST MERCIFUL, THE MOST COMPASSIONATE"[3]

Muslims repeatedly utter this phrase at the beginning of the day, when waking, eating, going out, buying, selling and generally starting something in the same way as God begins each chapter of the Qu'ran. As such this forms a sacred ritual in every day life. The words in Arabic *Ar-Rahmaan* (The Most Merciful) *Ar-Raheem* (The Most Compassionate, Qu'ran 1:1) are the superlative of the word *Rahma* or 'mercy', which are two attributes of God. Humans, it seems by necessity, want to imitate Godlike attributes, even if they only believe a notion of God as metaphor. 'Power', 'authority', 'domination', 'knowledge' all seem to be desirable to us in one way or another. However, as a whole we seem pay little heed to those attributes that seem to imply meekness in one's character, especially in this age of rampant individualism, which can be understood to be, *the negation of any principle higher than individuality* (Guenon:1999, p71). But attributes like love, mercy, compassion and honesty offer a sense of contentment and fulfilment that cannot be found in material wealth alone. However these considerations are probably harder to acquire than wealth because they often entail some measure of sacrifice, tolerance, acceptance and/or a level of self restraint and selflessness. They are also the product of self-reflection and consideration for others.

As human beings we seem to have a basic need to embrace and be embraced by these attributes. As youth workers we need to express these, what are seemingly inherently human, qualities if we are to be successful in our role as educators of and carers for young people. In fact, if you think about it, it would be hard to get anywhere with young people unless we were able to articulate these attributes effectively. I think it is more than a statement of faith to argue that the showing of care (for instance) to another has the potential to draw out care in those cared for. On a bland psychological level we do tend to mirror behaviour in relationships, so why not project our 'better self'? The engendering of these qualities exalts the status of our being and, in reciprocation, that of others. This thus leads me to one of the most fundamental aspects of The Prophet Muhammad about whom God said in the Qu'ran *We did not send you except as a Mercy to the whole of Creation* (Qu'ran:2003, 21:107) and He, The Prophet, said about himself that, *I was not sent except that I may perfect good character* (Malik: 1991, p382).

As such it can be understood that moral teaching is at the heart and core of the Islamic tradition and one of the defining attributes the Prophet Muhammad mentioned in the Qu'ran. As God says in one verse; *That indeed your character is of a great moral ethos* (Qu'ran:2003, 68:4). His teachings, through his words and actions, have much to say to us about the spiritual nature of ourselves and our interaction with the whole of humanity. According to Hamza Yusuf, an eminent American Muslim scholar,

The Prophet's words are as vital and relevant today as they were 1,400 years ago when they were first spoken. Whether you are a Muslim, a practitioner of another faith, or even someone who has no religious belief, these sayings have much to teach us. Sayings such as "A kind word is charity" and "Love for humanity what you love for yourself", speaks to us regardless of our personal creed; they speak to our shared essential nature." (Yusuf: 2005, p6)

COMMUNION

Human beings, throughout history, have found comfort, security and sanctity through communion and familiarity. Effective and caring communion requires a level of affection, acceptance, understanding, appreciation and sometimes tolerance. Communion offers a field effect of intimacy that invites us to be open and share our thoughts and feelings in sincere and giving manner;

Familiarization is a key ingredient in the cultivation of love. It is difficult to love someone you do not know (Shakir cited in Waley: 2007, p21)

The word 'love' has many meanings that imply different levels of affection. The love we have for a parent is different to the love we have for a friend or a spouse. Sometimes we say we love some material things, but this is not the level of love I might have for my child. But in our work we express the ethos of communion as care. The young people we work with share their time with us; they speak to us and, to a greater or lesser extent, let us into their lives. Often they find comfort and a sense of security in our very presence, sometimes coming by choice (although for many youth provisions it is often the best option amongst a number of not very favourable options). This is an expression of a level of confidence in us. As such, it seems important to take the time and the effort to try to understand this articulation of feeling. It also seems useful to explore such belief in us and ethically appropriate to demonstrate a reciprocal level of belief in those who we effectively serve. In the contemporary era it is not unusual to hear those we work with and amongst referred to as 'customers' or 'clients'; it is as if we are there to sell something them, or to 'fix' their lives. It is usual to hear young people defined as or as having some kind of problem or deficiency, but does this view really say more about our deficiencies? What makes us understand the complexity and wonder that is a young person as a form of deficit?

It seems to me that if we are unable to offer tangible expressions of care to young people (as people) that include an understanding of them as having the huge potential given to them as creations of God (rather than having an inherent lack) we provoke the wall of apathy (the great secret weapon/defence of youth) that many of us are so often confronted with. It is often claimed that youth workers are 'role models' and 'examples' to young people. This may or may not be true, but if we appear to young people as holding their contribution cheap, if we do not attend to them with a sense that we understand the honour that they give us by coming to us, we cannot really be surprised if they are defensive towards us, hold us and others in contempt or at least at keep us at arms length. The using of young people as a means to an end, to meet targets (youth workers so often talk about 'using' relationships) seems almost inherent in contemporary practice. But although we have to use the tools we are given and to some extent 'who pays the piper calls the tune', is it not our skill to humanise these instruments, to inject the life of communion into what we do that marks us out as 'professional' ? Practically this might be thought of as the use of professional judgement, spiritually it is perhaps the ability to see the light of God in those we work with.

KIND REGARD FOR OTHERS

The Islamic ideal is that when we meet others we should make the effort to draw affirmative regard from our first impressions (if you like, in the words of Johnny Mercer and Harold Arlen, as sung by Bing Crosby, we should 'accentuate the positive'). This might perhaps be even more the case when we meet people that others have undermined or criticised (we focus on giving the benefit of the doubt). The 'physics' of this response is quite simple; it seems likely that if we give up on others they will give up on us and themselves. According to Islamic teachings, fostering a bad opinion of people just for the sake of it is considered a malady of the heart; ...*people are innocent until shown guilty* (Yusuf:2004, p95). Even when someone is found guilty we might extend active forms of mercy, lend them a helping hand as Ibn Hazm says,

It is the height of injustice to deny a habitual wrongdoer the opportunity of doing an occasional good deed (Laylah: 1990, p137).

Islam teaches that when the self is moved to criticize others it is like a mirror in which you may be seeing reflections of your own shortcomings and as a human being, vulnerable to self deception, injustice and inequity, we can usefully try not look in distain at others.

Youth workers, and the literature surrounding the profession, often depict the young person as problematic and yet when we look back on our own youth, even youth workers realise that their behaviour and attitudes might have been similar to those they now regard as 'difficult'. It seems that as adults we develop a kind of hypocritical amnesia that historically it is usual for the young not to be able, or to just plain refuse to conform to what might be seen as the norms of 'adult society'. However, young people, more often than not, seem to need to learn by their own experience and not the warnings, counsel or advice of self proclaimed wiser adults.

Is it not part of the skill set of youth workers that we are able to embrace and even celebrate the non-conformist propensity of young people? Few (even the young) might disagree that we live in a society where we believe we can provide 'quick fix' solutions and put in place tough measures to prevent young people from making what we, as adults, determine to be errors and mistakes. This actually, quite ineffectively seeks to prevent young people treading similar learning routes that most of us have journeyed until we come to understand that we do not learn by our mistakes or even other people's blunders, and that in fact it is much more usual to make the same mistakes over and over again until a crisis causes us to change. It is only after that point that we look back and realize we only understood situations by going through them ourselves and often we don't understand the first time round. It is that understanding that we might see as an example of us practicing the mercy of God on ourselves. That we can go back; that we and others can rectify our behaviour based on our understanding is living the love of God. We tend to make lessons out of grief, fault, sorrow and crisis. As such they are not evils to avoid, but part of the course of our lives, experiences that can teach us that we are not perfect and so need to *look elsewhere for peace and perfection* (Eaton:2006, p37) . If we believe it is possible to avoid mistakes on the strength of advice and warnings from youth workers, we would either be mad or be setting ourselves up as gods, which of course is the most foolish of blasphemies. 'No one is perfect' only God , therefore we must live and work with the situation that has been part of life for millennia; young people (and adults) learn by taking risks, making errors of judgement along the way.

From an Islamic perspective, there is a time for condemnation and punishment, but mercy outweighs demands for retaliation and revenge; forgiveness overrides the urge for retribution. In the Qu'ran, God gives both options;

...tooth for tooth, and wounds equal for equal. But if any one remits the retaliation by way of charity, it is an act of atonement for himself (Qur'an:2003, 5:45).

This means that the act of forgiveness is a higher spiritual path to take and it reminds us that today's sinner may become tomorrow's saint. Many external factors threaten the human condition. The odds might be against us, and this is probably especially obvious to those of us who may need to experience life and view the lives of others in an effort to begin to understand the nature of reality. But one of greatest truths of our existence, one that causes us perhaps suitable humility before God, is the realisation that none of us will fully understand the nature of existence in our life times and that the best informed of us compared to the wisdom of God, know very little at all.

A profound lesson of living is that we need each other and it is in our best interests as individuals, groups, communities and society to strive to live in harmony and work to begin to see past our differences, shortcomings and biases. We need to experience all of these to be educated and to educate; education cannot by definition be a 'one way' process (else it is, at worse, brainwashing). In Islam we believe that God has created us as inherently good and the *sound heart is understood to be free of character defects and spiritual blemishes* (Yusuf: 2004, p1). That being the case, is it too much to ask or expect that we as youth workers try to resist seeing young people as 'problems', 'difficult' or by the light of some deficit model essentially created by remote authors, theorists, policy makers or academics? Can we see them as the glorious creations of God, with awe inspiring potential? I think we should be able at least to try to find and tread this path of rectitude naturally by listening to our hearts as well as those of others.

CONCLUSION

The above is not really advice or a means to 'develop relationships' with young people or people generally. Nor is it meant to be a means just to build 'meaningful associations' in the dealings of our social affairs. I have been writing about some moral qualities we might usefully pursue and aspire to perfect within our own selves. I firmly believe we need practice what we preach, and apply similar standards for ourselves and others. Doing otherwise defeats the object of honesty, integrity and trust that we as youth workers claim to build and spread amongst our fellow beings. The conduct of our character and the way we carry out our affairs rather than advice, warnings and endless questioning are the vehicles of change we have at our command. For Imam Ghazzali, the person seeking to be helpful cannot achieve this unless the *model himself is reliable, because the person with bad morals cannot be a good influence* (Usman: 1999, p9).

It may be us and not the labeled 'trouble making', 'problem' young person who suffers from a lack of morality in refusing to consider that young people are faced with a profusion of competing moral influences. We might try to develop an approach that allows us to consider not judging a young person who has made mistakes by their error. Indeed, if we talk to them we will likely find that they have many moral codes of conduct that regulate relationships between themselves and the adults in their lives. Some, perhaps many of these codes are at odds with more traditional values and morality, but we can make an effort for some sort of reconciliation between ourselves. We may be called upon to define a new way of being, introducing different sides to the human character that can encompass what the person we are working with and for believes is 'right' and the rules, regulations, child protection and safety procedures, society demands we follow. Once more, I believe this to be part of our necessary skill set, premised on professional judgement.

In such a complex society, when the acts of people are defined by organisational parameters, who do we hold responsible? Organisations act, *but they cannot be loved or blamed or touched* (Eaton: 2006, p24). So are we to conform and become mechanical in our outward actions, following rigid rules ? Although it can be said that structures are in place for our safety and well being, what is the cost of this? Does effectively suspending professional judgement, just merely doing as we are told risk a loss of our humanity, integrity, intimacy, our natural disposition to think, act and care?

Simple emotional physics might show us that unless we honour others we are unlikely get regard from them. A secondary consequence is that we will not get too far in our work with people. In honouring others we honour ourselves. The fulcrum of this is our own truthfulness, honesty and capacity for mercy. Appreciating and valuing others helps us avoid harming our own hearts and souls. We made the choice to be youth workers; to take up the sacred trust given us to care for other people's children, and our choices and influence on others will spread out, as ripples spread from the stones tossed into a pool. The young people and people around us will undergo some changes as we change.

NOTES

[1] In Arabic, the sunnah literally means 'trodden path'. Therefore the sunnah of the Prophet means 'the way of the prophet'. Terminologically, the word 'Sunnah' in Sunni Islam, means those religious actions that were instituted by the Prophet Muhammad during the 23 years of his ministry and which Muslims initially documented through consensus of companions.

[2] The most important teachings that govern the life of Muslims after the Qu'ran are the Prophetic traditions: Or what is known and referred to in the Arabic as 'Hadith'. The word 'hadith' literally means communication or narration. In the Islamic context it has come to denote the record of what the Prophet Muhammad said, did, or tacitly approved and also makes up the source of Islamic doctrine and law, after the Qur'an (www.eathalal.org/glossary.htm)

[3] (Qu'ran:2003, 01:01)

BIBLIOGRAPHY

Ali, S. N. (1974). *Some moral and religious teachings of Al-Ghazali.* Ashraf Press.
Asad, M. (2003). *Islam at the crossroads.* Kitab Bhaven Publishers.
Atkinson, P., Coffey, A., & Delamont, S. (2003). *Key themes in qualitative research.* Altamira Press.

Eaton, G. (2006). *King of the castle: Choice and responsibility in the modern World*. The Islamic Text Society.

Guenon, R. (1999). *The crisis of the modern World*. First Impression Publications.

Hadad, A. (1998). *The book of assistance*. The Quilliam Press.

Hashmi, S. H. (2002). *Islamic political ethics: Civil society, pluralism and conflict*. Princeton University Press.

Lane, E. W. (1984). *Arabic English Lexicon*. The Islamic Text Society.

Laylah, A. M. (1990). In *Pursuit of virtue*. Ta Ha Publishers.

Malik Ibn Anas. (1991). Al *Muwatta* (Translated from the Arabic by A. A. Bewley). Madinah Press.

Martyn, D. (1998). *The good research guide*. Buckingham: Open University Press.

May, T. (1997). *Social research: Issues, methods and processes* (2nd ed.). Open University Press.

Mazrui, A. A. (2005). *The content of character; Ethical sayings of the prophet Muhammad* (H. Yusuf, Trans.). Sandalla LLC Publications.

Muhammad ibn Ismail al-Bukhari. (1997). *Sahih Al-Bukhari* (Translated from the Arabic by Dr. M. M. Khan). Darussalam Publishers.

Muslim ibn Al-Hajjaj. (1990). *Sahih Muslim* (Translated from the Arabic by A. H. Siddiqi). Ashraf Islamic Publishers.

Payne, G., & Payne, J. (2004). *Key concepts in social research*. Sage Publications.

Qu'ran. (2003). *The message of the Qu'ran* (M. Asad, Trans.). The Book Foundation.

Shafi, M. (2004). *Ma'ariful Qur'an: A comprehensive commentary on the Holy Qu'ran*. Maktabe-e-Darul-UloomKarachi Publishers.

Silverman, D. (1997). *Qualitative research: Theory, method and practice*. Sage Publications.

Usmani, T. (1999). *Discourses on Islamic way of life*. Daruul Ishaat Publications.

Waley, I. (2007). *Educating the young child*. A.L.M Print.

Wehr, H. (1976). *Arabic-English dictionary*. New York: Library of Congress Cataloguing Publication.

Yusuf, H. (2004). *Purification of the heart*. Starlatch Press.

Yusuf, H., & Shakir, Z. (2007). *Agenda to change our condition*. Zaytuna Publications.

Web Link References

http://www.as-sidq.org/qurcomm.html: Cited on 25/02/08

http://www.chester.ac.uk/undergraduate/fd_muslim_youth_work.html: Cited on 12/02/08

http://www.altmuslim.com/a/a/n/2620/: Cited on 17/04/08

http://www1.wsvn.com/features/articles/medicalreports/MI15486/) Cited on 19/03/08

http://en.wikipedia.org/wiki/Ibn_Miskawayh: Cited on 07/04/08

http://www.islamictimes.co.uk/content/view/636/87/: Cited on 09/12/07

www.eathalal.org/glossary.htm: Cited on 26/01/09

SUGHRA AMED

3. YOUNG, BRITISH AND MUSLIM

Sughra Ahmed is a Research Fellow in the Policy Research Centre of the Islamic Foundation. Her current area of research is exploring the migratory and settlement experiences of first generation Muslim women and men in the UK. As well as this she has worked with a number of organisations to consider the issues young people face whilst growing up in the UK and the impact of this upon wider British communities and has published 'Seen and Not Heard: Voices of Young British Muslims'(2009). She previously co-ordinated the 'Women in Faith' interfaith project, training British Muslim women to take the lead in interfaith activity at a regional and national level.

Sughra is a Trustee of the Inter Faith Network UK, an advisor to the Muslim Youth Helpline, Trustee of the Leicester Council of Faiths and an advisor to FaithxChange, which is concerned with young people of faith who are engaged in civil society. Sughra has a BA (Hons) in English Language and Literature and an MA in Islamic Studies, she is a qualified Chaplain and holds a Diploma in Islamic Jurisprudence. She regularly contributes to debates in the media both locally and nationally.

INTRODUCTION

Sociologists find the word 'youth' has become problematic in that its definition appears to be negative, applying to a phase of life that is neither childhood nor adulthood. Furthermore, young people are often labelled in negative terms, as a group that present a problem for society (Department of Sociology, 2003). This becomes interesting when agencies speak about youth, once they have been essentialised into the 'other', as a delinquent group that doesn't contribute positively to society and undermines the safety of others. Society has in essence created barriers preventing engagement with young people as well as discouraging young people to engage with the rest of society/the population. This essentialisation often does not recognise colour, religion or creed; instead it feeds on stereotypes of hoodies, gangs and yobs, which are generalised to all young people across the UK.

It may be argued that the UK has experienced a rapid growth of subcultures which only young people are privy to. Sociologists, such as Brake (1990) argue that subcultures are not created as the antithesis of wider culture or opposition,

B. Belton and S. Hamid (eds), Youth Work and Islam:
A leao of faith for young people, 39–52.

but instead, as argued by Murdock and McCron (1976), subcultures are an expression and extension of the meaning of the dominant system, and are not deviant; they rarely become a counterculture (Brake, 1990). For example, the teenage entertainment industry is manifested in youth culture by young people choosing to express their teenage identity through fashion, lyrics, speech and their perception of the world around them. This does not mean they reject wider culture, but are part of a subculture, which they can identify with and feel comfortable being a part of. In time it may be that they find an alternative subculture, which suits their adult needs, but at this stage in their lives (youth) they create a subculture, which they can best relate to.

Often subcultures are created because young people find contradictions in the social structure which lead them to create a collective identity, one in which they will find like-minded peers, who will understand what are shared norms and values. This allows an exploration of their identity. Brake argues that this is an exploration of masculinity and therefore relates directly to young men; for girls it is emancipation from the cult of romance and marriage (Brake, 1990, p. ix) from highly developed historical traditions.

Given the nature of political events today, much attention around extremism and terrorism has been focused on Muslim communities of the UK. Research into Muslim communities and Islam has also focused heavily around issues of cohesion, integration, identity and disadvantage. Cities such as Bradford, Leeds and Leicester, as well as towns such as Oldham and Burnley have featured in numerous reports and academic writings.

Published material on Muslim youth has investigated the possible explanations for the disturbances of the summer or 2001 in northern towns and cities, for example reports by Cantle (2001) and Ouseley (2001). Ethnographic research also provides a rich background on Pakistani Muslims in Bradford and other Muslim communities – mainly Pakistani and Bangladeshi – by writers such as Alam (2006), Saeed et al (1999) and Jacobson (1998). Other research from religious studies, sociology of religion or history of religion perspective have looked at the development of British Muslim identity (Husain, 2004 and Malik, 2006) and some of the evolving debates within Muslim communities, often touching on the discourse surrounding young people (Lewis, 1994 and 2007).

Where research and other published material might need to make a more significant contribution is around the challenges young Muslims face and how government, statutory services and Muslim communities can engage better with Muslim youth culture. Some recent projects have contributed to such themes. These include Murtuja, (2006) where topics around Islam, education and identity were explored with young Muslims from Leeds. These people expressed their thoughts on subjects such as what 'fitting' into society means, and quite clearly saw themselves as integrated young people: "... as Muslims we have to be good citizens too, try to fit in but not go to extremes such as clubbing" (Murtuja, 2006, p. 25). Others explained how they felt about the incitement of religious hatred:

There is new legislation coming out to deport people who incite religious hatred. What are they going to do with the BNP? Because they also incite religious hatred. Where are they going to deport them? (Murtuja, 2006, p. 29)

Jawad (2008) conducted a similar peer-led project, which explored issues around identity, education and the relationships young people experience with parents.

More recently research has sought to explore Muslims in light of a post 7/7 world (Shibli, 2010, Gest, 2010) reflecting the sentiments of some Muslims back to society, some through personal narratives and others through formal research. Kundnani, (2009) is one of a handful of publications which has sought to consider the Prevent policy in all its complexities, while giving an overview of the British Muslim communities and the way they are understood through the lens of Prevent.

The implications in the study of Muslim youth seem to be that the problems are endemic, unique, and ultimately put us all in danger: 7/7 is the pinnacle of the problem. But is there really a unique 'Muslim problem'? The direction of much of the current public debate and commentary seems to be making the case in the affirmative.

YOUNG BRITISH MUSLIMS UNDER STRESS

The concerns young Muslims are grappling with require an in-depth exploration in order to appreciate the pressures under which Muslim youth are negotiating the challenges around identity, sexuality, religiosity and so forth. Addressing and working towards creating youth-led service provision has a direct impact on the local communities in which these young people reside. Major obstacles to successful employment, education, instilling and understanding culturally sensitive norms and values all play a part in a young person's life and if successful can give a young person direction and guidance at a time when they need it most.

In order to tackle such pressures a combination of youth provision to increase social and emotional literacy and a madrasah education[1], which looks to empower young people, should be directly linked to the schools' extended services strand, under the duty on schools to promote cohesion. Developing partnerships between local youth provision and madrasahs, as well as schools, will enable this joined-up thinking to look at young Muslims as a whole. It will allow clarity of thought and action in relation to how young Muslims are performing, where needs are being missed and primarily will provide constant and consistent care for each child. It will also reduce the likelihood of different messages coming from schools, which may go against the madrasah agenda and vice versa.

We know many issues challenge young people. According to a survey by Muslim Youth Helpline, the most prevalent challenges for young Muslims were mental health, relationships and religion (Muslim Youth Helpline, 2008). A further exploration of some of these topics is necessary which can be seen in Ahmed (2009) where young Muslims themselves have alluded to some of these issues.

Evidence shows that young people in the UK as a whole are increasingly suffering from social and emotional disorders.[2] The prevalence of such disorders is thought to be higher in particular family types. These include lone-parent families where emotional disorders are at 16 percent. This compares with 8 percent for two-parent families. But other figures are telling. Such disorders occur in 17 percent of families with no educational qualifications but in only 4 percent of those who have a degree-level qualification. In families living in low-income, high-unemployment areas the figure is 15 percent compared to 7 percent in affluent areas (Green et al, 2005).

Layard and Dunn (2009) based on *The Good Childhood Inquiry*, by The Children's Society, provide one of the most up-to-date studies on the subject of mental health and young people in Britain. In a survey (as part of the inquiry) of 8,000 14–16-year-olds, 27 percent of young people agreed with the statement 'I often feel depressed'. Many also said they felt under pressure to look good, with seven out of ten admitting they dieted some or all of the time (ibid.).

In a separate online vote, conducted by CBBC's *Newsround* for the inquiry, 78 percent of those who voted said they felt fine, good or really good about their health; however, a worrying 22 percent felt bad or really bad.

Many of the participants in the research expressed concern about the impact that poverty and social disadvantage has on mental health and well being. Refugee children, children in trouble with the law, children with disabilities and children at risk on the streets, whom The Children's Society works with on a daily basis, are among those most affected by these issues (Layard and Dunn 2009). A 'mylife microsite' was set up by the Children's Society in an attempt to understand young people by listening to "what's important to them, what problems they face and what changes would make things better" (ibid.).

MUSLIM YOUTH AND MENTAL HEALTH

Of course, mental health challenges are not only present in young people. Culturally sensitive support services are required from the statutory sector and community groups in order to attract those affected from a range of cultural groups. As we have seen, young people are becoming increasingly affected by emotional and social disorders including depression, feeling 'really bad' and pressurised to look different. This group seem to be undergoing a state of crisis and as a result are now more than ever in need of well-designed and targeted support from agencies that specialise in mental health, counselling, guidance and providing physical health care. Presently many such agencies are perceived as catering only for those who are under extreme and obvious pressures, such as people suffering from anorexia, bulimia, schizophrenia and drug or alcohol-related illnesses. Most young people would not classify themselves in these terms, but nevertheless are in need of support from such agencies. The idea that they are unable to turn to local authority-led service provision further exacerbates the problem for young people in particular communities.

Muslim youth also seem disinclined to approach statutory agencies in relation to such issues, this may partly be the case because they feel the service providers do not understand them, but it is also likely that they feel their religion will not be understood (Muslim Youth Helpline, 2008). Culture and other social demands that young Muslims are faced with within their own community structures on a daily basis may also create barriers.

Support services are deficient in the skills needed to address this situation. Hence they are often underused or ignored by young British Muslims, who can go on to either internalise issues and/or just are unable or refuse to recognise such conditions, which left untreated affect both the young person and the community around them.

Although precise figures for Muslims affected are hard to identify, the causative factors of mental health and its challenges seem to be becoming clearer.

SPACE TO GROW

Some young people in working-class communities spend time socialising with their peers on street corners rather than in their homes, usually because they don't want to smoke or converse in front of their parents; this was certainly the case of the young Muslims in the programme aired on BBC Radio Leicester's *Gangsters*, a documentary by BBC journalist Hasan Patel (Patel, 2007). The young Muslims explained in an interview that they needed to hang around on the streets of Highfields (a predominantly Muslim part of Leicester) because they didn't want to disrespect their parents by socialising at home. They didn't know where else they could spend time with their friends after college. The local youth centre had shut down four years earlier because of a lack of funding and as such they were left with little choice but to stand on the streets. Their sense of dress – casual and affordable – was different to their middle-class counterparts in another part of the city, Oadby, a middle-class and more affluent area. Young Muslims in the interviews felt 'hanging around' in groups meant that they were more at risk of being questioned by the local police than their white counterparts in Oadby. As one young man from the Spinney Hills part of Leicester put it:

There's no way you can have 10 men in your house... it's a family home... you get bored sitting at home, so you have to come here... the council don't help us out... if you see a group of 15 white people in Oadby they [police] won't see them as a gang but as a group of people, here there's five of us and they see us as drug dealers and in a gang.

This impression of stereotypes doesn't deal with the problem of young people spending time on the streets; instead it makes them feel like criminals and sociologically this risks resulting in a self-fulfilling prophecy. If young people feel ill at ease and are made to feel like delinquents or a threat to wider society, they could begin to behave in this way and increasingly become detached from mainstream society.

These young people were concerned about the reputation their presence on the streets might have been creating – they were seen as part of a gang culture because they wore hoodies and gathered together in groups of more than a few. However, they shared their thoughts on how their presence on the streets could change; they argued that young people in deprived parts of the country deserved more attention than they were currently receiving. They stressed that people should not judge them before they have had conversations with them and got to know them for who they are. They talked of the need for an increase in youth provision, which matched the needs of the local communities. In the case of Spinney Hills they argued that a youth centre was needed as a space for young men and women to spend time socialising with their peers without being perceived as threatening to the wider community (Patel, 2007).

SPATIAL DISTRIBUTION OF MUSLIM COMMUNITIES

In the UK statistics show just over half of Muslims currently reside in London. Other relatively big populations live in Birmingham and Greater Manchester (ONS, 2001). The Muslim communities often live in the most deprived parts of these cities. Those Muslims who have settled outside the largest cities tend to settle in clusters in areas like Bradford and Kirklees, etc., often in the most socio-economically deprived districts. The most deprived areas of Oldham, Blackburn and Burnley house significant Muslim communities.

Studies have shown the strong links between socio-economic deprivation, educational underachievement, poor housing and poor health – all of which directly impact the 3 percent Muslim population in the UK by virtue of the fact that an overwhelming majority of them live in these socio-economically deprived parts of the country. This directly impacts on the future of young people from these communities.

In response to the above, several organisations have sought to fill some of the gaps in youth provision. For example, the Muslim Youth Helpline (MYH) has grown rapidly since its inception (August 2001) and has tailored its operations around areas such as counselling – both via telephone and the internet – as well as campaigns like the 'Prison Campaign', supporting Muslim inmates during Ramadan, providing packs, usually sponsored by the Muslim community, that contained messages of support and encouragement to work towards a positive future. They also contained a prayer mat, sweets, a Qur'an, and an Eid card for prisoners to send to loved ones.

MYH offers a service which statistics show is in great demand; the MYH website is full of information on the situation of their young Muslim clients. However, the service is London-centric and a strong case can be made for a MYH in every major city in Britain.

Other responses to the current gaps in youth provision for Muslims include the Muslim Youth Work Foundation (MYWF), which operates from the National Youth Agency offices in Leicester. Since its inception in 2006, the MYWF provides e-newsletters, periodically advertising and raising awareness of youth-related projects, funding, courses and activities around the country.

The MYWF is currently working with young Muslims to reduce the gap between community need and service provision by enabling young people to take advantage of youth-led schemes, in particular exchanges and trips with young people of any background to help broaden the understanding of British youth of cultures and experiences outside Britain have been a feature on the MYWF e-newsletter.

As well as this Muslim Youth Skills strives to capacity build across Britain's communities by equipping individuals and organisations who work with young people and community groups to be competent and confident about their work. They provide consultancy and a range of training, workshops and seminars for individuals and organisations.

Schemes such as the Glasgow-based Youth Counselling Services Agency (YCSA) are grappling with a fast-paced environment in which they aim, "to enhance the capacity of young people, individuals and groups" in their communities.

This service caters for young people in and around Glasgow. Clients range from Pakistani to Chinese, Indian to the African-Caribbean communities and the range of issues they approach YCSA with are as diverse as the following demonstrates:

It could be anything from family problems to drugs-related problems to anger management, whatever it may be, religion in school, issues in school with their education, so for example someone from the drugs and alcohol team, they might get a young person come, and they will need support in counselling, the majority of drug and alcohol users need some level of counselling. On top of that they might not have something to do in the evening after school/college so we provide that service. On top of that they might have left school with pretty much no or very minimal education so no literacy and numeracy which would provide the basic skills required.

The YCSA is responsive to demands and offers support services, on-demand training and positive, friendly staff receptive to individual and organisational requirements. It specialises in youth work, counselling, support, learning and advocacy – which enables them to provide a holistic support service for their users.

Muhammad, a youth worker, explained the motivation behind YCSA:

There wasn't any counselling service targeting ethnic minorities or understanding their needs, so we set up from that, and there were a number of things that had happened around about the mid-nineties in our school that I think also had an effect on how people felt... There were things like a riot at the local secondary school involving quite a lot of ethnic minority young people, specifically Muslim young people, who basically raided this school for the death of Imran Khan, a young boy who was killed and the effect that had on [this community]...

However, an interview with Umar Ansari (Youth and Justice Services Manager) revealed that they are rarely able to meet the demand they have on their time and resources from the minority communities of Glasgow. Unfortunately due to a lack of funding they are unable to continue catering for their clients as effectively; recently they lost some funding and are unable to resource appropriately skilled staff and premises.

Projects such as the YCSA rely on local government funding as well as support from the local community – Muslim and otherwise. They explained that they were unable to take half a day away from work to attend an important meeting related to research on young Muslims as they had recently lost several members of staff and were under an immense amount of pressure.

A SHORT HISTORY OF FAITH BASED YOUTH WORK IN THE UK

A brief overview of Church (Anglican) youth provision notes that many dioceses have some sort of youth officer or youth adviser in addition to one or two other youth-related staff; however, it is still considered to be an area of decreasing investment for the Church. Currently there are approximately 7,000 full-time youth workers employed by the Church of England; this is set to increase to approximately 19,000 (full time, part time and voluntary) by 2011. This represents a highly significant investment in youth work given that in 2008 there were just over 6,200 full-time qualified youth workers or youth support workers in 120 local authorities surveyed by the National Youth Agency (NYA, 2009)[3].

When we consider the history of Christian youth work in the UK and its relationship with the State, it is easy to appreciate that despite the targets for the coming years Christian youth work is still playing 'catch up' with the issues young Christians are dealing with. However, some dioceses around the country have employed Directors of Youth Work in order to boost youth work provision and meet the needs of young people. The Diocese of Leicester has such an officer whose role involves developing innovative and creative ways of working with young Christians across the Diocese with his teams.

The Albemarle Report (Ministry of Education, 1960) was the first serious attempt at understanding youth and youth work; it looked at efforts to get disenfranchised young people back into the youth clubs during the 1940s and 1950s. After the Second World War, Sunday schools were created as a secondary educational measure and focused on how to teach young people to be morally upright when the schools were closed.

Today some Sunday schools have that educational ethos, but as the nature of education and religious tempo of the nation have changed, the Sunday schools have lost their traditional roles.

The madrasah system, through which many young Muslims attend a supplementary school for approximately two hours per day, Monday to Friday, could potentially alleviate some of the pressures facing youth workers and youth organisations. Many young British Muslims aged 5–13 years attend such schools to learn a rudimentary knowledge of Islam. Often this learning involves prayer and worship as well as learning to read the Qur'an by rote. Some of these supplementary schools are treated as childcare facilities where parents know their children are in a safe space for a couple of hours. Others take a more diligent interest in the child's learning and often support the young person in their learning at home also – similar to mainstream schooling.

Throughout Ahmed (2009) youth workers who were involved in such areas complained of the competition they faced for young people's attention, often losing out to computer games, hanging out with friends on local streets and generally being perceived as an 'un-cool' place, for teenagers particularly, to spend their social time. They commented on the organised structures in the Muslim community such as the madrasah system and its impact on the well being of young people during particularly difficult hours when young people tend to be out with their friends after school.

In policy terms, safe spaces such as the madrasah provide relief for the youth services as well as inculcating positive character and good behaviour in young Muslims. Discussions around 'good' character as well as the Big Society (although details of this are yet to unfold) have recently become interesting to government. The merits of policies and departments dedicated to such concepts in Canada have sparked curiosity in British policy makers. A good madrasah can enhance such debates by providing education centred on Islamic ethics and morality, all of which serve to enhance young British Muslims in the developing of 'good' character, supporting them to become 'good' citizens who can contribute to their local communities in a positive way.

However, many madrasahs confine their role entirely too formal and religiously based pursuits. Muslim communities might usefully recognise the potential which lies in the institution of the Mosque. Should structured and focused syllabi, which aim to instil more than basic reading of the text and prayer, be used across madrasahs it could help to alleviate some of the serious social challenges young British Muslims are now facing.

FAITH AND YOUTH WORK: DIVERGENT POINTS OF VIEW

Many grassroots organisations work with young people by way of community projects, away days, summer camps, study programmes and various sports-related activities throughout towns and cities in Britain, some local and others national. Groups such as the Dawatul Islam Youth Group and the Young Muslims UK (YMUK) are examples of Muslim organisations that deliver projects and offer opportunities for volunteering throughout Britain.

YMUK was founded in 1984. It aims to provide young Muslims with the space to learn about, understand and practise their faith, with an emphasis on the British context. It relies heavily on volunteers. Its offers sports programmes and opportunities for raising money for charities, conferences, regional camps across England and Scotland and the use of new media to link members nationally. The organisation seeks to provide a reliable source of information on subjects related to faith, identity, citizenship and education. The organisation also provides relatively safe places to explore topics of this kind in relaxed environments, while mixing with other young British people.

These groups, although working actively with young Muslims, do not necessarily undertake what might recognise as conventional youth work. The lack of capacity, training and resources mean that they are usually restricted to providing general, relatively structure activities for young people. However, they are able to call on and bring together a range of professional skills from other sectors to voluntary services, thereby providing services without calling on state funding. Contact with these organisations reveals that although they see a need for youth work with Muslims, they recognise that they are not professional youth workers. However, they see themselves able to offer situations wherein young Muslims can explore and identify with their faith, while learn new skills through activities like outdoor experiences and education.

This type of work sometimes offers young Muslims the only contact they have with their faith peers from different parts of the country. At times it works as a means of spiritual invigoration but there are also opportunities for academic development and learning related to Islam in the British context.

However, given that most young Muslims will not be members of such organisations, so not taking advantage of services like these, there is an ample scope to develop approaches like those offered by YMUK.

Youth workers and academics such as Sadek Hamid, from University of Chester and Tafazal Mohammad Director of Muslim Youth Skills, reflecting on the challenges they feel are not currently being met in the landscape of youth work argue that there is a growing need for youth work in the Muslim communities.

Both Hamid and Mohammad make the case that Muslim youth workers are best able to fulfil this need as young Muslims face extra challenges, which require understanding and support beyond that which generic youth work provision can offer them.

A different view is held by Bea Foster, a youth worker in Burnley, who argues against faith based youth work (see Ahmed, 2009). For Foster the kind of approach promoted by Hamid and Mohammad isolates young Muslims even more than is currently the case.

Foster discusses the challenges of being a state youth worker. She is a practising Christian with experience working in the Black and minority ethnic communities. Following the disturbances in Burnley in 2001 she started working with Muslim groups in the Daneshouse and Stoneyholme district where she practiced until late 2009. Foster explains her approach to youth work:

Muslim young people are young people who are Muslim, not Muslim and then young people...I find Muslim young people feel very much under attack, and they feel very much that their identity is under attack, and that people want them to lose their identity as Muslims and want them to just become English and not have any of their own cultures... So as a result of that the Muslim young people are actually pushed into being Muslim first rather than young people...what happens then is workers work with the whole cultural stuff around Muslims and Islam and the culture and religion, rather than actually, first and foremost, working with that young person as a young person who has hopes, dreams, aspirations and needs to fulfil themselves in different ways. What is happening is that the work, youth work, is focusing on Muslim and Islamic stuff rather than the young person, [or being] *young person led.* (ibid.p.33)

This might be seen as illustrating the resistance by secular youth workers to faith sensitive approaches but what is immediately noticeable here is the Foster refers to what she thinks rather than the perceptions expressed by young people. For her, other layers to youth identity are secondary to one's identity as a youth, although what a 'youth' is in not decided by young people themselves but the society they live in, by way of state legislation etc. However, while Foster seems to have little notion of the lack of separation between faith and other facets of Islamic identity. She appears to recognise that young Muslims in Burnley feel that their identity has many layers and facets. While it is clear to Foster (not a young Muslim person) that the youth identity should be preeminent, it is hard to say how young Muslims in Burnley might see this.

Society, the state and the media undoubtedly play their part in causing particular groups, including Muslims and young Muslims, to understand themselves as being relatively different to the population as a whole. At the same time, these forces convince whatever might be considered as the 'majority population' to see these same groups as different to them. As Foster argues this feeds; "...the pre-conceived ideas and the prejudice of the indigenous community" (ibid.p.33).

Overall this essentialises these labelled groups as 'foreign beings'. However, it has to be pointed out that Foster herself feeds into the categorising process by her insistence on treating particular groups as 'young'; what is 'young' of course varies over time, place and culture, but in our society 'youth' also serves as a label of difference, often associated with problematic issues.

In line with notion of capturing hearts and minds, some youth workers consider their work as:

... made up of body, mind and soul, because that's what we're all made up of... the work that I do with young people is in some ways all those things. Around looking after the body, about being healthy, It is all that stuff around the drugs, the eating, the drinking, about how you abuse your body, or you don't and you look after it very much so. The mind is about education, it's about learning, it's about knowledge, it's about information. You know, your mind is learning all the time. And then your soul, it's about that spiritual aspect of life, which is around reflection, it's around thinking; it's around values and all of that sort of stuff. (ibid.)

While education is not just about learning, knowledge and information, this statement does helps us to think of young people as multi-dimensional so the strategy should be adapted to serve people from different religions, cultures, or from a background of no religion, etc. People are multifaceted and not any 'one' thing, although according to how they feel or want to be understood, they may be more one thing at times than they might be at others?

A former youth worker from Oldham expressed a serious issue of discrimination he had witnessed within the youth work sector:

There's lots of limitations...I actually had encountered some problems in terms of expressing my faith or practising my faith...the senior management structures in Oldham were very hostile to religion in general...it seemed Islam in particular...that's a pattern you may be aware of, an Islamophobic undercurrent, it's become more covert now but it's still there...when you're talking to young people and you're working with young people...it's been the case really since the late eighties, religion is a very important part of their lives whether they are practising or not it's a primary identity. (ibid. p34)

It is disquieting to learn that such issues exist within a sector that has been created to protect its constituents, particularly in the case of youth work. A strong sense of trust and reliability is required between youth workers and the young people they serve and any type of perception of discrimination makes it very difficult to build trust and loyalty. Youth work can have an extensive influence on a young person's life, and an effective youth worker is not only trusted by young people but is also a valuable resource for the local authority in creating a cohesive and harmonious community, although some might see this happening at the cost of compromising identity.

In support of this, Downes (1966) argues that subcultures emerge, "where there exists an effective interaction with one another, a number of actors with similar problems of adjustment for whom no effective solution as yet exists for a common, shared problem". Given this, Foster seemingly wanting people to some extent reformulate their identity formation is unrealistic, because that cohesion around identity has causes beyond just personal choice. This theory is applicable to young people across the world that have similar challenges of adjustment as we see in the case of young Muslims who struggle to understand their place in the world (as all young people do). But as well as this struggle, they try to grapple with negative notions and stereotypes of Islam and Muslims. They find themselves negotiating the personal world they inhabit as well as the dynamics of wider social interaction and engagement.

The challenges facing young Muslims often require frank and open discussions on topics which may seem controversial and possibly sensitive. Cultural taboos in particular may inhibit such discussions, which oblige young Muslims to either repress their experiences and concerns or speak to their peers who are sometimes not well equipped to deal with these challenges. Investment and support of all types is needed in order that young Muslims might, collectively and in collaboration with others, overcome some of the serious challenges that confront them.

Working-class communities and certainly the many British ethnic minority communities have a lot to offer which can make Britain a stronger, more energetic, multidimensional and resilient nation. In reality this potential lies in the hands of young people; without them there is literally no future, but logically the more of them that are involved in discovering their potential the brighter the future will be. An investment in the future of all our young people stands to serve everyone.

NOTES

[1] 'Madrasah' is the Arabic word for any type of educational institution, whether secular or religious (of any religion). It is variously transliterated as madrasah, madarasaa. In this instance it is referring to education in Muslim contexts
[2] Emotional disorders include separation anxiety, specific phobias, panic disorder, post traumatic stress disorder, obsessive compulsive disorder and depression. See Children's Society (2008).
[3] National Youth Agency (2009 England's Local Authority Youth Services: The NYA audit 2007–08. Leicester: National Youth Agency.

BIBLIOGRAPHY

Ahmed, S. (2009). *Seen and not heard: Voices of young British Muslims*. Policy Research Centre.
Alam, M. Y. (2006). *Made in Bradford*. Route Publishing.
Brake, M. (1990). *Comparative youth culture: The sociology of youth cultures and youth subcultures in America, Britain and Canada*. Routledge.
Cantle, T. (Chair) (2001). *Community cohesion report: A report of the independent review team*. Home Office.

Department of Sociology. (2003). *Sociological approaches to youth*. University of Bristol.

Downes, D. (1966). *The delinquent solution*. Routledge & Kegan Paul.

Gest, J. (2010). *Apart: Alienated and engaged Muslims in the West*. C Hurst & Co Publishers Ltd.

Green, H., McGinnity, A., Meltzer, H., Ford, T., & Goodman, R. (2005). *Mental health of children and young people in Great Britain*. Palgrave Macmillan. http://www.statistics.gov.uk/downloads/theme_health/GB2004.pdf

Husain, M. G. (2004). *Muslim youth and Madrasa Education*. Institute of Objective Studies.

Jacobson, J. (1998). *Islam in transition: Religion and identity among British Pakistani youth*. Routledge.

Jawad, H. (2008). *Forgotten voices: Developing more effective engagement with Muslim youth and communities*. Forward Thinking.

Kundnani, A. (2009). *Spooked! How not to prevent violent extremism*. Institute of Race Relations.

Layard, R., & Dunn, J. (2009). *A good childhood: Searching for values in a competitive age*. Penguin.

Lewis, P. (1994). *Islamic Britain: Religion, politics and identity among British Muslims: Bradford in the 1990s*. I. B. Tauris.

Lewis, P. (2007). *Young, British and Muslim*. Continuum International Publishing.

Malik, A. (2006). *The state we are in: Identity, terror and the law of Jihad*. Amal Press.

Murdock, G., & McCron, R. (1973). Scoobies, skin and contemporary pop. *New Society, 23*(247).

Murdock, G., & McCron, R. (1976). Consciousness of class and consciousness of generation. In S. Hall & T. Jefferson (Eds.), *Resistance through rituals*. Hutchinson.

Muslim Youth Helpline. (2008). *Issues*. Retrieved October 2008, from, www.myh.org.uk/information.php?id=2

Murtuja, B. (2006). *Muslim youth speak*. Hamara Centre.

National Youth Agency. (2009). *England's local authority youth services: The NYA audit 2007-08*. National Youth Agency.

ONS. (2001). *Census 2001*. Office for National Statistics. Retrieved July 14, 2008, from, www.statistics.gov.uk

Ouseley, H. (2001). *The Bradford district race review*. Bradford Vision.

Patel, H. (2007). *Radio programme on Gangsters*. BBC Radio Leicester. Retrieved December, 2007, from www.bbc.co.uk/leicester/local_radio/

Saeed, A., et al. (1999). New ethnic and national questions in Scotland: Post-British identities among Glasgow Pakistani teenagers. *Ethnic and Racial Studies, 22*(5).

Shibli, M. (2010). *7/7: Muslim perspectives*. Rabita Ltd.

The Children's Society. (2008, April 24). *UK failing to meet children's mental health and wellbeing needs*. Retrieved November 2008, from www.childrenssociety.org.uk/whats_happening/media_office/latest_news/7092_pr.html

The Children's Society. (2009). *Thinking about my life*. See http://sites.childrenssociety

TAHIR ABBAS

4. ISLAMOPHOBIA AND THE POLITICS OF YOUNG BRITISH MUSLIM ETHNO-RELIGIOUS IDENTITIES

*Tahir **ABBAS** BSc (Econ) MSocSc PhD is currently Associate Professor of Sociology at Fatih University, Istanbul. He is the author and editor of numerous books including, Islamic Radicalism and Multicultural Politics (Routledge, 2011); Islam and Education (Routledge, 2010, 4-volume, edited); Honour, Violence, Women and Islam (Routledge, 2010, co-edited, with MM Idriss); Islamic Political Radicalism (Edinburgh UP, edited, 2007); Immigration and Race Relations (IB Tauris, co-edited, with F Reeves, 2007); Muslim Britain (Zed, 2005, edited); and The Education of British South Asians (Palgrave-Macmillan, 2004). He has written, edited or contributed to 28 books, has over 30 (co)authored scientific publications and has delivered more than 100 lectures in over 25 countries. He is also the (co)author of a series of articles, reviews and op-eds in specialist collections and online publications, ranging from Ethnic & Racial Studies, Journal of Ethnic & Migration Studies, Social Identities, Social Epistemology, Gender & Education and Work Employment & Society, to Guardian Comment is Free, Islamonline.net, Open Democracy and Quantra.de. He has been a Fellow of the Royal Society of Arts since 2006, and has recently been Visiting Fellow at the University of Oxford Centre for Islamic Studies (2007-2008), Fellow of the University of Birmingham Centre for Studies in Security and Diplomacy (2007-2009), Honorary University Fellow of the University of Exeter Centre for Ethno-Politics (2009-2011) and Visiting Professor at the Hebrew University in Jerusalem (2011).*

To understand the place of youth work in Muslim contexts it is important to grasp the environment within which young Muslims live and situate, perpetuate and create their personal and collective identity. This also provides a means to understand the issues facing youth work with young Muslims and Muslim youth workers in contemporary Western Society. In this chapter Tahir Abbas provides an analysis of the political and social milieu that encompasses youth work and Islam

INTRODUCTION

In the current period, the focus on new Muslim youth identities has become significant in the context of contemporary media and political debates. Concern has been on the nature of extremism, radicalism, intercuturalism, and its implications for

B. Belton and S. Hamid (eds), Youth Work and Islam:
A leao of faith for young people, 53–71.

ethno-national multiculturalism. While significant attention falls on group characteristics, less is discussed in relation to wider social issues impacting on young Muslims in Britain today. Moreover, the issue of Islamophobia in Britain has gained notoriety in recent periods with a number of social, cultural and political concerns generating a whole host of media, political and community interests and tensions. Primary among these experiences has been the return to a focus on the *niqab* – the face veil – seen by a vociferous few as the antithesis to a post-Enlightenment age, wherein individual choice, liberty and freedom are given primacy, with questions of nationhood, citizenship and identity at the fore (Meer, N., C. Dwyer and T. Modood, 2010).

Other important issues have been the impact of far-right groups that have sought to create negative associations between Muslims based on a supposed lack of desire to integrate into wider society and urban based Muslim communities being regarded as an observable but also menacing presence to society.

Internationally, populist political decisions in France with regard to the veil, Switzerland in relation to the building of minarets, and the rise of Geertz Wilder's *Party for Freedom* in the June 2010 Netherlands general election, appear to signal a deepening sense of cultural, social and political Islamophobia in wider Western European society. That is, an explicit fear or dread of Islam itself; the idea of not just the religion but also the perceived and actual cultural characteristics people of migrant origin bring, sustain or develop in their new (and often generationally established) home (Caldwell, C., 2009).

Many of these questions and the related discussions are often premised on dramatic and almost continuingly unfolding events, but it is helpful to present the historical antecedents to the problems experienced today in order to learn lessons from the past at a time of genuine world concerns. These anxieties are exacerbated by the global uncertainty following the international economic crisis, as nation-states grapple to determine resolute political and cultural identities in the context of devolution, Europeanisation and globalisation. At the same time some of the younger second and third generation Muslims in Europe are struggling with identity formation, which is subject to a range of interventions by interested parties in completely oppositional terms (Abbas, T., 2007). This is a challenge that ranges across individual identities, community interests and the confidence of nation-states to remain the bastions of the free world in an age of individualisation, financial uncertainty, conflict, globalisation and the evolution of alternative political dimensions across Islamic North Africa.

CONTEXTUAL FRAMEWORK

First, it is important to provide a contextual framework. Islamophobia did not emerge from thin air; rather there is a narrative that defines Islamophobia as phenomenon, one which has many centuries of history. The latter invites looking at the nature of the problems of education in relation to Muslims given these wider historical considerations. This informs and helps define the concept of Islamophobia as it is used today.

There are often dissenting voices who view Islamophobia as a ruse in order to mask deep-seated problems of cultural relativism and patriarchal norms. This perception is discussed below. Local and global debates in relation to identities in the context of diaspora communities are also elaborated upon.

In conclusion, I will argue that the lived experience in relation to Islamophobia is an observable reality, causing significant concerns among young British Muslims who feel beleaguered because of the workings of society, or who are on the receiving end of hostile thought and behaviour from those who seemingly reject their pre-modern indigenous identities becoming the subject of cultural absorption from an 'othered' minority. Yet, nationalists and fascists who purport to these views have a misguided sense of their own identities – sometimes based on an imagined, convoluted, reactionary and highly selective memory of what once was. Meanwhile, of the half a billion people on the move at any one point in time any where in the world, three-quarters are Muslim. With nearly 20 million Muslims in Western Europe and over two million in Britain alone, Muslims are an observable community with various manifestations of a European Islam taking their shape throughout the region. In many ways, because of local concerns, national political agendas and global political interests, in the context of more intensive competition for resources, Islamophobia in the West, however perceived or actualised, is likely to remain if not grow in the foreseeable future.

SETTING THE SCENE

It is well-documented that Islam has been in Britain for over a thousand years, but it is also true that the population has grown extensively over the last century (Ansari, H., 2004). Indeed, the demographic, social, cultural and political positions of British Muslims have developed more significantly in the post-war era (Nielsen, J.S., 1997).

As the British Empire became one of the mightiest in history it did so at the expense of a 'civilising mission'. This cause exploited the world's human and natural resources for the singular end of capitalist profiteering and the fulfilment of wealth and status aspirations. These ambitions became embedded in society in the wake of a European renaissance in the fifteenth and sixteenth centuries, culminating in the capitalist era.

One particular historical episode, the British Raj, exemplifies the shifting contours of initially building positive working relations, but then moving towards an overwhelming exploitative framework (Dalrymple, W., 2003).

In the post-war era, Britain, short of domestic labour, was forced to encourage the formally-colonised people of the Commonwealth to come to the 'mother country' to carry out the work that few of the indigenous population were willing to do (Fryer, P., 1984). Trapped in cycles of under-employment, unemployment and low pay in general, many of the South Asian Muslims who came to various parts of the UK during that period found themselves unable to escape from those very same locations. This situation persists today, over sixty years after the immediate post-war boom in immigration (Phillips, D., 2006). As a consequence of these early years of arrival and settlement, and as result of various (limited external and internal) approaches to integration into a non-Muslim society, including the important and often over-looked factor of culture, namely patriarchy, it has taken many decades for Muslims to begin to act as a meaningful political and cultural voice, and one that remains far from fully formed (Anwar, M., 2001).

It could be said that Muslim migration and settlement in Britain is effectively based on five phases. In the classic Islamic era, Muslims traded with English elites and co-operated with the monarchy when expedient to all parties. Offa of Mercia, a seventh-century English ruler, traded with Arabs and inscribed the *shahadah* (the declaration of the faith of Islam) on coins used in exchange with them (Gilliat-Ray, S., 2010). Queen Elizabeth I maintained positive associations with the Turkish Ottomans who played a key role in thwarting the efforts of the Spanish Armada, which was part of a doomed effort to restore England to direct loyalty to the papacy (Matar, N., 1998).

The next recognisable episode can be characterised as one relating to the time of the Raj. Muslims came to Britain as elites, embarking on training in medicine or to read law in the established higher educational institutions of the country. This experience largely catered for the needs of the privileged few, while the less fortunate could only hope for a meagre income, fuelling the furnaces of coal-fired steam ships that supported the needs of Empire and war.

The post-Second World War period saw the most rapid increase in the population of Muslims in Britain and the majority of British Muslims today can trace their heritage to this period. The fourth period relates to the wealthy Arabs who profited from the hiking in crude oil prices in the early 1970s, or the elite Iranians who moved to places such as London and New York before the socialist revolution became an Islamic revolution in Iran in 1979.

The current period is one in which primary immigration from Muslim lands has all but ended. It is family re-unification and marriage migration from parts of South Asia that adds to the increasing population, although conversion to Islam is a growing phenomenon in Britain.

In 2010, in relation to UK-Pakistan transnational communities, there were 1.5m journeys a year between these two countries alone, with about 10-15,000 Pakistani wives and husbands joining their spouses in the UK every year (UK Government source, *personal communication*, 25 March 2010). This recent period also includes those who have come to the country as 'refugees' and 'asylum seekers', whose positions in society are marked by various forms of state institutionalised practices that often reduce the needy immigrant to second-class citizen in all but name.

One of the most significant events in the history of British Muslims has been in relation to the issue of '7/7'. This heightened concerns in relation to extremism and identity politics across the social and political landscape. However, the historical origins of the process of viewing Muslims through the lens of religion and culture rather than ethnicity, and before that race, are much longer in the making.

Since the 1960s, governments in Britain have shaped policy and practice in relation to ethnic minority groups based on various strategies of anti-immigration and anti-discrimination legislation on the one hand, and with efforts to promote assimilation, integration and, most recently, multiculturalism on the other. In the 2000s, various attempts were made by outspoken political commentators to suggest that multiculturalism was both misguided and defunct, both in practice and conceptually. However, British Muslims have consistently and actively worked towards a civic engagement approach, which transcends the workings of the state or mosques. This has had the effect of motivating Muslims to participate in wider society.

In the period that necessitated the re-thinking multiculturalism, some Muslims identified a new reflexive space (Meer, N. and Modood. T., 2009). Others understand present-day Islamophobia to be produced precisely in opposition to Muslim identity claims on society – where the fear of Muslims is connected with the fear of multiculturalism in Western Europe (Marranci, G., 2004) and the incompatibility of such differences in places such as the USA (Semati, M., 2010). What permeates policy and practice is the underlying assumption concerning the inevitable assimilation of immigrant groups (Layton-Henry, Z., 1984). In relation to British Muslims, this has not occurred to the extent some may have envisaged. This might be understood in part as a function of racist hostility diminishing the potential of individuals and groups to positively integrate into the dominant economy and society. But it may also be the result of a lack of appreciation of the extent to which ethnic minorities have come to rely on class and ethnic community resources to mobilise what little economic and social development they can achieve. In effect, Muslims often have had little choice but to retreat into their communities. It is not through choice, but through a lack of choice that this occurs.

Even before the events of 9/11, British Muslim 'loyalty' to a national cultural identity (although this is something hard to envisage) was in question. The Rushdie Affair of 1989 placed the concerns of British South Asian Muslims firmly on the political and social map, with issues of civic engagement, multicultural philosophy, the nature and orientation of certain religio-cultural norms and values, and socio-economic exclusion and marginalisation dominating rhetoric, policy and practice throughout the 1990s (Weller, P., 2009). Combined with matters in relation to social and cultural hybridisation and the recognition of minority religions, the experience of and dominant attitudes towards British Muslims throughout the 1990s were reflective of the entire range of debates and discussions in this field (Modood, T., 1998).

These are just some of the many challenges facing British Muslims in the current period. While there has been considerable attention paid to questions of race, ethnicity, loyalty, belonging, and local and global identities, there remains a lack of appreciation of the nuance of the experience and its contextualisation in relation to physical space, region and, perhaps more importantly, its impact on policy and practice. One significant area is education.

EDUCATING MUSLIMS

There over two million Muslims in Britain, with around one-in-three under the age of 15. This means that a considerable proportion are in education. Given the geographical concentrations of Muslims found in certain parts of the country, many of the local primary schools in some areas are entirely made up of young people from Muslim backgrounds. However, they are relatively few state-funded and grant-maintained Muslim schools. The question often asked, given the perennial underachievement of Muslims in education in the UK, is what role can Islam play in educational settings to improve and develop a sense of responsibility, engagement and participation in society? How would such actions ameliorate the effects of historical problems of under-performance, outmoded curricula, biased teachers, a lack of role models and the disengagement of parents who simply presume the school will do all the educating and schooling?

In secondary schools, the under-achievement in primary schooling is reflected in the starting point of young Muslims at this level of education. The consequence of the latter is, sadly but predictably, limited progress over their school career. In some secondary schools Muslims make up the entire profile of students and yet there is little active recognition of their 'Muslimness' in the curriculum. Moreover, there are often issues that are not always resolved with some teachers presenting a negative view of Muslims and their parents in relation to education.

While the educational achievement profile and performance level of young Muslim women has increased in recent periods, young Muslim men find themselves likely to be excluded and they have consistently under-performed relative to other groups. Particularly affected are Somalis, Pakistanis and Bangladeshis. There is also a growing perspective that this group reflect a wider decline of masculinity, which (hardly surprisingly) affects young Muslim men in the same way that it affects their non-Muslim gender and age peers. It has been argued that regionalism and globalisation have rendered these young men impotent in the world-wide market for skills and employment, and in the context of rapid flows of capital and labour in an international arena.

At the other end of the educational spectrum, more and more Muslims entering universities, find it difficult to fit because of limitations to the social experience. Many young Muslims who go away to university for the first time find it difficult to cope with the pressures and strains of being young in secular, liberal situations and actively show disdain towards integration. Universities, on the other hand, are often unaware of the many tensions and concerns facing young Muslim students as they go about obtaining their education (Fosis, 2005). Certain social spaces are restricted while the air of Islamophobia and anti-Muslim racism in wider society permeates the university campus experience.

All this is compounded by the policies that have been spawned by the 'War on Terror', that effectively interprets the hats and beards of young Muslim men and hijabs and jilbabs of young Muslim woman as being signs of extremism, marking them out as suspicious persons. This creates further barriers that impact at a local level.

Young Muslims in education are affected across age groups, from the age of 5 onwards. This has implications for how schools and universities are organised and managed in relation to the incorporation of Islam and Muslims specifically, and more broadly faith groups in general. Clearly, in the post-9/11 and post-7/7 climate a number of pressing security and democracy concerns exist.

However, while the focus is on the idea of eliminating terrorism through proactive measures on military, security and political fronts, there is little recognition or appreciation of the importance or value given to the nature of the religion as a force for positive change. While Islam is seen as a 'problem' in certain circles, the idea of Islam as part of the solution is given considerably less weight. Moreover, the continuing focus on the negative seems only capable of making the situation worse, certainly as there are clearly a range of alienated, marginalised and disenchanted young people facing insecurities because of existing vulnerabilities and sensibilities. There is a need to appreciate the role of acute global challenges and how they impact on local area identity politics.

Thus, a fundamental sea change is needed. We need to move from viewing Islam and Muslims as a threat to understanding this population as an asset. In particular, the genuine application of citizenship education in relation to building dedicated, loyal and strong-minded believers, as a specific function of the workings of a non-Muslim state, has been missed altogether. In addition, a combined focus on wider aspects of Islamic values more explicitly – not making it a religious issue but a cultural matter, therefore fostering a more inclusive and open-ended attitude – has also been given little attention. While certain sections of the political and religious right focus on a variety of narrow values, notions of common global human values that bring everyone together under a world-wide umbrella of freedoms, liberties, aspirations and hopes for a embattled planet are also neglected.

Education is not just about the attainment of certain scholastic achievements – it is also concerned with the need to engender more rounded individuals, who have the skills to become capable of effective participants in society.

When the 'third way' school raged forwards in the political arena in the 1990s, hand-picking aspects of deliberative democracy, neo-liberal economics, state involvement in the public sphere and investment in education was growing in the UK. However, an emphasis on the marketisation of education resulted in notions of civic and citizenship education taking less of a role, even though it was essential to the 'third way' agenda. With the passing of Labour administration in 2010, there was hope that the ConDem government might resuscitate notions of common human values and the positive assets of all faiths that might make a reality of such hopes and ambitions. However, cuts in educational resources, the impact of government constraints placed on local authority spending and the knock on effects for voluntary organisations, gives little hope outside the vague notion of the 'Big Society' for any substantive developments in this respect.

Islam and Muslims have suffered immeasurably in relation persistent negative media and political discourses in the last few decades. However it is hard to feel optimistic about change in this respect given the increasingly obvious right-wing strategies of the coalition government at the time of writing. Education, with basic resources at every level decimated and university fees rocketing, for the vast majority of young people, looks to be more of a forlorn hope than an answer to despair.

DEFINING ISLAMOPHOBIA

Notions of cultural and social identification of the 'Muslim other' emerge from an appreciation and experience of imperialism and colonialism. This 'fear or dread of Islam or Muslims' was described by the Runnymede Trust in 1997 as 'Islamophobia'. Since the emergence of Islam in the year 622, the general representation of Muslims in Europe has been largely negative through ignorance, conflict and the demonisation of Islam (Bennett, C., 1992). But there have also been periods of learning and understanding (Hillenbrand, C., 1999). Throughout the history of Western European contact with Islam, it has been convenient for the established powers to portray Islam and Muslims in the least positive light – in effect to prevent conversions, but also to encourage Europeans to resist Muslim forces at their borders. So, traditionally, historically and conventionally, in the European context, Muslims have been portrayed as 'barbaric', 'ignorant', 'narrow-minded' or 'intolerant religious zealots'. This characterisation of Islam is still present today in the sometimes damaging representation and treatment of the 'Muslim other', which often exists as part of an effort to aggrandise established powers and, in the process, to legitimise existing modes of domination and subordination. As much as present-day Islamophobia relies on history for its stereotypes, the current fear of Islam and Muslims has its own idiosyncratic features that connect it with more recent experiences of colonialism, decolonisation, immigration and racism.

While Muslims are not an undifferentiated mass, there being many ethnic, theocratic, cultural, social, economic and political differences between individuals and groups, the above characterisation of Islamophobia remains prevalent. While discrimination, inequality and prejudice on the basis of 'race' continues (as racism), the anti-Muslim shift suggests markers of difference of a social and religio-culture nature. The social and religious foundations of Islam, as well as Muslims in general, have attained such a degree of notoriety that their visibility is immediately associated with entirely negative and detrimental frames of reference, exemplified of late by statements from the likes of the pointedly anti-Islamic English Defence League.

Since 7/7 the situation has both deteriorated and intensified. Islamophobia has gained a greater discursive prevalence to the extent that much of Western European society has become uncritically (and sometimes unconsciously) receptive to an array of negative images, perceptions, attitudes and behaviours in relation to Islam and Muslims.

This Islamophobia is found at the level of wider society, but also in relation to specific aspects of representation – for example, in the media in relation to 'the Muslim terrorist' in Hollywood films, before and after the events of 9/11 (Shaheen, J. G., 2009). In television news the language has altered substantially, with 'Islamic terrorism' and 'Muslim extremist' becoming part of everyday parlance. The portrayal of British Muslims in the current period is described as a 'new racist discourse' (Van Dijk, T., 2000), that was, in the first few days of February of 2011, fed into by British Prime Minister David Cameroon, following his, 'Stronger national identity' speech in Munich.

This new racism differs from the 'old' in that it is more subtle or less overt, but at the same time it is explicit in the direction it takes. In the post-9/11 era, some British parliamentarians have used the fears people have of Islam for their own ends; by focusing on the 'War on Terror' politicians used the existing anti-Muslim frame of reference, but replaced it with the idea of 'terror' - this is the *politics of fear* as described by Frank Furedi (2009). The reporting of events negatively associated with Muslims is compounded by a concentration on the 'enemy within' (a phrase last deployed in politics by Margaret Thatcher to demonise members of National Union of Miners, their families and their communities in 1984) or questioning the loyalty of young Muslims to Britain.

Reasons for the increase in these themes in news reporting are symptomatic of the increased fear of the 'Muslim terrorist' since the 9/11 attacks on New York (and subsequently 11 March 2004 in Madrid, 2 November 2004 in Amsterdam, 7 July 2005 in London and August 2007 in Glasgow). In UK television docu-dramas, there has been a negative trend: *The Hamburg Cell* (2004, Channel 4),

Dirty War (2004, BBC), *Yasmin* (2006, Channel 4), *The Road to Guantanamo* (2006, ITV) and *Britz* (2007, ITV) are all stylised visual projects. Even attempts at comedy cinema have their limitations when satire is used to convey an important message, but in the context of hurt and frustration caused by terrorism in the UK feelings are still raw. The UK films *Four Lions* (2010, d. Christopher Morris) and *The Infidel* (2010, d. Josh Appignanesi) are recent examples of comedies attempting to engage with a liberal audience, while the television dramas have conveyed a more authoritative drive to deliver a form of intellectual representation. Nevertheless, dramas in relation to the 'Muslim terrorist' have portrayed sophisticated and seemingly well integrated Muslims, of various national and ethnic origins, possessed with the single intent of destroying human and economic targets in the West. None contained positive Muslim characters. All these attempts at news reporting and media manufacturing, particularly in television news, could be described as 'weapons of mass distraction' (Rampton, S. and Stauber, J., 2003). The point being emphasised here is that media and politics are inextricably linked.

In effect, the role of media and politics in the framing of anti-Muslim representation go hand in hand. Muslims in Britain feel that part of the reason for their continued existence as an unaccepted and often-despised minority is based upon the presence of the 'evil demon': the media (after Akbar S Ahmed - Ahmed, A.S., 2004). There is a belief that (and a deal of evidence that confirms) media representation of Muslims is distorted and stereotypical, and that the images of Western secularism and materialism menacingly invade their homes (Akhtar, S., 1989). The media portrayal in 1979 of the Iranian Revolution, the last of the 'classical revolutions', with its images of two million Muslims on the streets of Tehran, was perhaps the first multi-media event to cause the West to begin to think hard and look closely at this body of people called 'Muslims' (Asari, F., 1989). Dressed in black, seemingly exhibiting violence and aggression, these Muslims were painted as 'radical', fanatical' and 'fundamentalist'.

In 1989, the Rushdie Affair was the first time Britain began to look at its own Muslim population in a critical but also sensationalist manner. With most British Muslims strongly opposing the publication of the novel, *The Satanic Verses*, the almost totemic headline of 'Book Burnings in Bradford' became a sort of mantra of the time. These British Muslims were presented as intolerant, bigoted, reactionary and regressive. This response questioned their loyalty to the state, as well as their rights and obligations. For Muslims involved in the burnings, theirs was a genuine act of frustration arising out of the feelings of hurt that the book had caused them. But to non-Muslim onlookers these scenes, as they were portrayed on national and international television, came to be largely regarded as symbols of the uncontrollable fury and hatred that Muslims had towards the West. Media reporting at the time was regarded as 'shallow and extravagant', partly because few Islamic experts were permitted to comment on the situation [although it may be true that, at the time, few were media savvy enough to get their messages across].

As such, the limits of the debate were defined by the liberal establishment in partnership with the media. Coverage was distorted, focusing only on events, with sound bites loaded with emotion and based on reference to death threats, the 'medieval fundamentalists' and their 'fanaticism' and 'militant wrath'. The Rushdie Affair of 1989 was in many ways a defining moment in the history of Muslims in Britain, demonstrating aptly the characteristics and nuances of the nature of Islamophobia.

CRITIQUING ISLAMOPHOBIA

There are however important caveats. Kenan Malik, political activist and social commentator, has rejected the notion of the widespread existence of Islamophobia in his influential essay, *The Islamophobia Myth* (Malik, K. 2005). For him, caution is needed when attributing Islamophobia as the primary reason behind any apparent anti-Muslim event, as accusations of Islamophobia could be used as a mechanism to stifle debate and criticism of certain negative Muslim cultural practices and their societies. Furthermore, according to Malik, anti-social behaviour and delinquency may be the cause of a number of events cited as being Islamophobic attacks. However, it is quite apparent that Islamophobia is not merely about figures relating to reported physical violence or the numbers of Muslims who have been stopped and searched by the police. There are wider, historically significant, culturally-embedded institutional practices and behaviours involved.

Contemporary Britain prides itself on its liberal outlook, encouraging multicultural integration, freedom of speech and equality of opportunity. The present Government persists with the view that Britain has moved away from its inherently assimilationist post-war principles, having developed an integrated society in which the term 'British' can simultaneously refer to all cultures. This is really quite a silly notion as it defines 'Britishness' as being anything and everything, and echoing Lewis Caroll's *Humpty Dumpty* in *Through the Looking Glass:*

When I use a word...it means just what I choose it to mean − *neither more nor less.*

That 'British' refers to anything culturally tangible or relevant to the majority of people living in the UK is questioned by the fact that over the past twenty years the population of Britain has lived with and underlying tension between these culture perspectives and, on several occasions, overt conflict, including protests in 1989 following the publication of *The Satanic Verses*, and, more recently, following the publication of several cartoons by Danish right-wing newspaper, *Jyllands-Posten*, negatively depicting the Prophet Muhammad (originally published in September 2005 and then again in February 2006). Many advocates of freedom of speech have presented the argument that the Muslim reaction to *The Satanic Verses* and the cartoon depictions of the Prophet Muhammad as clear examples of excessive political correctness that threaten to contravene freedom of speech. This seems to be a failure to realise the distinct difference between freedom of speech and the freedom to offend.

In the final analysis, Islamophobia is a lived experience; it is an attitude, a set of behaviours and series of outcomes. From negative reporting in the media, to misrepresentation in political life; from being spat at on the street, to having headscarves ripped off the heads of Muslim women; from being called 'Paki Taliban', to direct and indirect cultural racism in schools, hospitals and in relation to employment applications and outcomes; from individual attacks of violence, to mosques being attacked symbolically, as well as physically. All this exemplifies that Islamophobia is rife.

In wider Western Europe a pregnant Iraqi pharmacist was stabbed to death by the German man she accused of anti-Muslim racism, while her husband, who tried to rescue her, was shot by a policeman – all of this in a German court of law. The pharmacist is now known as the 'headscarf martyr' (Connolly, K. and Shenker, J., 2009). A shift in attitudes in parts of Denmark, France, Netherlands, France and Italy demonstrates that 'old Europe' is seeing an awaking of an anti-Muslim sentiment at a time of economic crisis and in the context of a wider 'global War on Terror' since the events of 9/11 and beyond.

One issue that certainly is a cultural problem that dominates an anti-religious rhetoric is honour-related violence. Peel away the layers and one finds a damaging and wide-ranging practice that severely impacts on the lives of young Muslim women. But it has nothing at all to do with Islam and everything to do with dominant Muslim male cultural practices (Idriss, M.M. and Abbas, T., 2010).

NEW POLITICAL SUBJECTS

The emergence of 'new racisms' has seen a move away from a concentration on structure towards culture (Mac an Ghaill, M., 1999). Muslims in Britain and the nature of Islamophobia are increasingly a feature of debates, characterised by 'a complex spectrum of racisms' and a 'resurgence of ethnic, cultural and religious differentiation' (Bulmer, M. and Solomos, J., 2004 p7). There are many demographic studies focusing on Muslims in Western Europe that highlight Muslim engagement in limited spheres of civil life and in relation to the nature of political and cultural organisations; for example, when seeking to establish mosques, when securing provision of halal meat in prisons, schools and hospitals and when lobbying for state-funded Islamic schools (Klausen, J.. 2005). The building of mosques is reflective of continuous public expression of Muslim life (Cesari, J., 2005). Certain Muslim beliefs and practices are, moreover, characteristic of local contexts in regions of the subcontinent. They are often reproduced by newcomers to Britain as accommodations within multi-ethnic nation-states (Amghar, S., A. Boubekeur and Emerson, M., 2007). These ongoing developments are useful in explaining how Muslims have sought to contain and reproduce certain practices associated with their faith in multicultural societies and at specific times in their settlement and community development. As Steve Vertovec and Ceri Peach (1997) have suggested,

...the development of Muslim social organisations in Europe has been quite rapid since the 1970s, doubtless linked with the reunion of immigrant families during this period [...] and thoughts of permanent settlement which, in turn, raised awareness of the need for a variety of forms of communal expression (p.24).

As young Muslims enter institutional life, seeking accommodation and continuation of practice and belief associated with their faith, they have also resisted it. Islamic revivalisms, it is argued, are in contrast to these efforts as they seek to assert a particular identity and recognition, often using language or slogans which are characteristically 'Islamic' in the face of injustices targeted at Muslim identity and culture. Islamic revivalisms are emancipatory social movements, manifested in urban Islamic culture as well as political protests, with the language of Islam used as the dominant mode of expression. These revivalisms are defined by the conscious recognition of an identity that stretches into new political imageries. Discussions on Islamic revivalisms emphasise the primacy of grievances, including barriers to social mobility, lack of political and legal freedoms, economic despair and the Palestine/Israel issue, as providing the impetus for such movements. The underlying assumptions are that these grievances are generated by socio-economic and political crises, however these grievance-based theories are incomplete; they expose the reasons for suffering, but they do not provide explanations for the range and set of variables that translate particular grievances into revivalist movements (Wiktorowicz, Q., 2004).

Fred Halliday analyses the role of these other factors and contexts that lead to 'anti-Muslimism' and the image of an 'Islamic threat' (Halliday, F., 2003 p107). Foremost is the idea that Islam is under threat and at risk of being corrupted (ibid., p. 120.). Muslims invoke Islam as a justification for political action. For Halliday, issues such as the intrusion of the state into everyday life, legislation perceived as specifically targeting Muslims, and the fact of external domination and strict immigration controls suggest that Muslim communities may feel that there are under constant threat (ibid). Halliday suggests that Islamic revivalisms are reflective of panic reactions by Muslims who fear a threat to their religion and identity: 'theirs is a defensive cry'. The Rushdie Affair was an example of Islam 'in danger', not so much from outside but, potentially, from the loss of belief within (ibid p127). For Halliday, at the societal level, Islamist movements have developed as a cultural and nationalist response to contemporary problems facing Muslim communities. It is the inability of the nation-state to meet the economic expectations or cultural aspirations of groups that provides the context for Islamic revivalisms to develop. Talal Asad (1990) argues that the response of the British

State to the anger expressed by Muslims in relation to the publication of *The Satanic Verses*,

...should be seen primarily as yet another symptom of British, post imperial identity in crisis, and not [...] as an unhappy instance of some immigrants with difficulties in adjusting to a new and more civilized world. (p.455-480)

GLOBAL CHALLENGES, LOCAL IMPACTS

The relationship between Islamic societies in the West, and the rise of what is called a 'global Muslim subjectivity', is seen as a conscious response to Western hegemony and as a defining feature of post-modernism. The idea that identity is consciously formed is also propounded by Paul Gilroy (2000). Using the example of the history of racial slavery and the modern African diaspora in the West to understand the workings of identity, Gilroy suggests that,

...work must be done to summon the particularity and feelings of identity that are so often experienced as though they are spontaneous or automatic consequences of some governing culture or tradition that specifies basic and absolute differences between people (p.100).

According to Gilroy, the 'interplay of consciousness, territory and place becomes a major theme' in the process of identity formation, which, is asserted,

...as an antidote to anxiety and uncertainty associated with economic and political crisis. (ibid.p.101)

Miri Song draws attention to how Muslims have to contend with negative dominant representations in the media and popular culture, i.e. 'Muslim fundamentalists', and how this plays a constitutive role in the formation of their identities in wider society. For Song, the formation of minority group identities are part of a wider interaction between 'assignments' which are imposed by others in wider society, and by 'assertion', which is a claim to ethnicity made by the groups themselves (Song, M.. 2003). Song suggests that with the increased interconnections of social life brought about by globalisation, people have the opportunity to be involved with more than one culture. Thus,

...people's sense of their ethnic identities and affiliations are said to be relativised and shaped by their greater consciousness of the interconnections of people and societies around the world. (Gilroy 2000, op. cit., p. 113).

Globalisation, therefore, has implications for the ways in which people experience identity. On the one hand, there are the constraints experienced through powerful homogenising forces at work. At the same time, globalisation, transnationalism and the diasporic communities associated with Muslims offer the option of negotiating and forming an 'identity', and, as Gilroy suggests, 'identity is an anchor in globalisation' (ibid., p. 107.).

Globalisation, however, has implications for the nation-state, which, in turn, has implications for ethnic-minority groups within particular borders. Migration, which is closely related to processes of globalisation, makes it increasingly difficult for states to control the flows of populations, settlements and cultural exchange (Castles, S., 2000). This is what Vertovec calls the 'container model' of the state (Vertovec, S., 2001). Multiculturalism, in its conventional form, entails an essentialised understanding of culture. It proposes, what Vertovec (ibid) refers to as a 'top-down discourse of multicultural unity', which involves the expectation that ethnic minorities take on a feeling of belonging to a host country of reception.

Here, it is important to note the historical continuation of this experience in contemporary multicultural societies and its role in (re)producing Islamic revivalisms. The exclusivist and differentialist notion of culture that multiculturalism entails proves problematic for the nation-states in how they perceive and subsequently manage their ethnic and religious minority communities.

In contemporary notions and applications of multiculturalism, it is possible to see how the nation-state offers ethnic and religious minorities a negotiated space, but what is distinctively marked out within the wider national public sphere is that minority groups are expected to adapt to a predetermined sense of belonging. It can be seen in the 'Idea of Europe' and the subsequent ethnocentric norms that have helped to buttress the concept and, in the process, produce chauvinist and racist outcomes. Individual cultures are homogenised and expected to assimilate into a wider multicultural citizenship within an existing national cultural framework, eventually leading to monoculturalism.

However, cultures are, in reality, open and porous formations; they interact with mainstream life at a variety of levels; and there should be sensitivity to these differences (Parekh Report, 2000, p.37). Muslims, with their transnational allegiances to their countries of origin and to the concept of *ummah,* potentially pose a problem for multicultural states, which can lead to a paradoxical effect. Global Islamic revivalist movements represented in events such as 9/11 and the resistance to occupation in places such as Iraq and Palestine, lead to objectification of popular assumptions and discourses of Muslims living as 'terrorists' or 'fundamentalists'. The stigmatising process results in forcing a retreat into communities and a continuation of the cycle of racism and revivalism.

Vertovec recognises how British Muslim successes in achieving institutional accommodations and modes of public recognition have led to a growth in Islamophobia and suggests that the rise in both these phenomena are interpreted 'through a kind of linked and circular operation (Vertovec, S., p32 2002). It is argued that this dilemma can also be understood as part of a wider analysis of Muslim citizens in Western European countries being more self-conscious and a 'diaspora identity', which, according to Gilroy, 'exists outside and sometimes in opposition to political forms and codes of modern citizenship'(Gilroy, 2000, op. cit., p. 124.).

THE BATTLES AHEAD AND CONCLUDING THOUGHTS

The problems of the representation and experiences of Muslims in Britain have been exacerbated by a lack of appreciation of the needs of Muslim minority communities in inner cities experiencing deepening economic marginalisation and widening social inequality. Public attention is focused away from structure and towards culture, enforcing a debate in relation to dress, language or identity. There is an attempt to transform cultural pluralism (or multiculturalism) into monoculturalism or (cultural imperialism).

The other facet of this debate is the focus on women: that is, somehow Muslim women are prevented from exercising the freedoms enjoyed by all other women per se. This argument is weakened when the evidence for Western female emancipation clearly suggests that there is still a need for greater equality of opportunity and equality of outcome across the board, although there have been significant gains in the last two decades.

Many Muslim women argue the uniformity of wearing the niqab provides is a source of freedom and empowerment before Allah, however ill-defined the notion of face-veils in relation to Muslim women is in the Qur'an itself. In many respects, the niqab is a 'symbol of separateness' to most communities in the West, Muslim and non-Muslim. For others, it is clear young Muslim women are taking matters into their own hands as a direct response to their own and wider Islamic identity struggles within the Diaspora and within the heart of the Islamic world itself (Afshar, H., R. Aitken and M. Franks 2005). Some politicians will support the idea that the niqab leads to 'segregated communities', 'parallel lives' or 'voluntary apartheid', but what voters forget is the extent of exclusion and alienation that many Muslim minorities already experience. Young Muslim women appropriating a certain religiously inspired garb is a reaction to an on-going onslaught for some, while for others it is an expression of defiance in the light of current hostile discourses (Afshar, H., 2008). At the same time, this discussion is necessary, as within Islam there is tremendous deliberation on what this means for integration into non-Muslim societies over time. This includes debates about how the veil is reignited as a sensitive political issue, particularly in places such as France, with its assertions that differences in public sphere are regarded intolerable (Bowen, J.R., 2007). This is happening even in Turkey, which seeks to modernise and secularise as part of efforts to enter into the European Union.

The charge of media bias needs to be taken seriously as the extent of coverage of 'extremist Muslims' and 'Islamic terrorism' has dramatically increased in recent periods and especially since the events of 9/11 and 7/7. The language used to describe Muslims is often violent, thereby inferring that Islam is also violent. Arabic words have been appropriated into universal journalistic vocabulary and invested with new meaning, which is generally exaggerated and aggressive. Jihad, for example, has been used to signify a military war waged by Islamists against the

West. The deeper Arabic meaning of the term is, in fact, far broader and refers more to the idea of a 'struggle' [where the struggle against the 'false ego' – nafs – is the highest of all jihads]. Words such as 'fundamentalist', 'extremist' and 'radical' are regularly used in apocalyptic headlines across all sectors of the British press.

Europe and Islam share a significant history where violence and conflict characterised the interaction, but there has also been an immense mutual appreciation. However, this is often forgotten. Over the centuries, Muslims have been colonised and then, when the colonial masters left, the once-slaves arrived later to eat the crumbs of the cake their forefathers effectively gathered the ingredients to bake. Islamophobia formed during these periods of contact and demonisation and, because of this experience, it has particular features that are remarkably resistant to change, given how that part of British social and economic history is still so important for its position and aspirations today.

With the global events in relation to Muslim lands dominating the geo-political landscape since the end of the Cold War, the Islamophobic discourse is found in politics, but also in television, film, comedy, school textbooks, in the civil service and even the academy. The Rushdie Affair of 1989 defined Islamophobia, and British society is living with the consequences of that period in history – a dividing of communities and the state in relation to religion and society. That rift grows wider over time.

In the current period, there is a certain degree of Islamophobia found in think tanks that have a key role to play in influencing the current ConDem governmental regime. The London-based *Centre for Social Cohesion*, *Policy Exchange* and the *Quilliam Foundation* have all determined that Islamism is wide-ranging and that it is *the* problem of our times – meanwhile, Muslim umbrella organisations are busy fighting with each other for authenticity, authority, influence and a seat at the table of the very same power that feeds its thinking from the wells of the very same right-wing think tanks and media-savvy politicos they seek to challenge. As to intellectual impact, policy development and the resultant action of these endeavours, little emerges save from extensive community engagement and limited hurried policy responses fine-tuned to appeal to the middle ground.

Islamophobia is individual, community, organisational and societal – to counter it, greater consciousness and action is needed. However, it will be difficult in the context of crippling public sector cuts and the problems of fragmenting youth identities in dominant but often poor and outcast white-English communities. Cases of racist attacks are on the rise, and with a particular anti-Muslim frame of reference for groups such as the English Defence League, Stop Islamisation of Europe and the British National Party, there remain particular risks going forward.

All of this is compounded by a sharper gaze, which is a function of globalisation, and in the context of a global 'War on Terror' which continues unabated, much to the consternation of many. It is apparent that Islamophobia is firmly on the map, what is less clear is to how fix the problem before it grows to become potentially insurmountable. The challenges are greater than the opportunities, and much needs to be done. The realm of education remains a significant opportunity, but one that will not be effectively realised unless there are more dramatic changes to ideology, delivery and practice. What room is there for the greater integration of Islam in society and young Muslims in education in David Cameron's Big Society remain a big question, although, given even an cursory look at history, the answer is perhaps all to easy to guess.

BIBLIOGRAPHY

Abbas, T. (2007). Muslim minorities in Britain: Integration, multiculturalism and radicalism in the post-7/7 period. *Journal of Intercultural Studies, 28*(3), 287–300.

Afshar, H., Aitken, R., & Franks, M. (2005). Feminisms, Islamophobia and Identities. *Political Studies, 53*(2), 262–283.

Afshar, H. (2008). Can I see your hair? Choice, agency and attitudes: The dilemma of faith and feminism for Muslim women who cover. *Ethnic and Racial Studies, 31*(2), 411–427.

Ahmed, A. S. (2004). *Post-modernism and Islam: Predicament and promise* (2nd ed.). Routledge.

Akhtar, S. (1989). *Be careful with Muhammad: The Salman Rushdie affair*. Bedlow.

Amghar, S., Boubekeur, A., & Emerson, M. (2007). *Islam: Challenges for society and public policy*. Centre for European Policy Studies.

Ansari, H. (2004). *The infidel within: The history of Muslims in Britain, 1800 to the present*. Hurst.

Anwar, M. (2001). The participation of ethnic minorities in British politics. *Journal of Ethnic and Migration Studies, 27*(3), 533–549.

Asad, T. (1990). Multiculturalism and British identity in the wake of the Rushdie affair. *Politics and Society, 18*(4), 455–480.

Asari, F. (1989). Iran in the British media. *Index on Censorship, 18*(5), 9–13.

Bennett, C. (1992). *Victorian images of Islam*. Grey Seal.

Bowen, J. R. (2007). *Why the French don't like headscarves: Islam, the state and the public space*. Princeton University Press.

Bulmer, M., & Solomos, J. (2004). *Researching race and racism* (p. 7). Routledge.

Caldwell, C. (2009). *Reflections on the revolution in Europe: Immigration, Islam, and the West*. Doubleday.

Castles, S. (2000). *Ethnicity and globalization: From migrant worker to transnational citizen*. Sage.

Cesari, J. (2005). Mosque conflicts in European cities: Introduction. *Journal of Ethnic and Migration Studies, 31*(6), 1015–1024.

Connolly, K., & Shenker, J. (2009, July 7). The headscarf martyr: Murder in German court sparks Egyptian fury. *The Guardian*.

Dalrymple, W. (2003). *White Mughals: Love and Betrayal in Eighteenth-century India*. London: Harper-Perennial.

Dalrymple, W. (2003). *The last mughal: The fall of a dynasty*. Bloomsbury.

Federation of Student Islamic Societies (Fosis). 2005 study.

Fryer, P. (1984). *Staying power: The history of black people in Britain: Black people in Britain since 1504*. London: Pluto; Institute of Race Relations (1985) *How Racism came to Britain*. IRR.

Furedi, F. (2009). *Culture of fear* [revisited]. Continuum.

Gilliat-Ray, S. (2010). *Muslims in Britain: An introduction*. Cambridge University Press.

Gilroy, P. (2000). *Between camps: Nations, cultures and the allure of race* (p. 100). Penguin.

Halliday, F. (2003). *Islam and the myth of confrontation: Religion and politics in the middle East*. I.B. Tauris.

Hillenbrand, C. (1999). *The crusades: Islamic perspectives.* Edinburgh University Press.

Idriss, M. M. & Abbas, T. (Eds.). (2010). *Honour, violence, women and Islam.* Routledge.

Klausen, J. (2005). *The Islamic challenge: Politics and religion in Western Europe.* Oxford University Press.

Layton-Henry, Z. (1984). *The politics of race in Britain.* George Allen & Unwin.

Mac an Ghaill, M. (1999) *Contemporary racisms and ethnicities: Social and cultural transformations* (p. 70). Open University Press.

Malik, K. (2005, February). The Islamophobia myth. *Prospect, 107.*

Marranci, G. (2004). Multiculturalism, Islam and the clash of civilisations theory: Rethinking Islamophobia. *Culture and Religion, 5*(1), 105–117.

Matar, N. (1998). *Islam in Britain, 1558–1685.* Cambridge University Press.

Meer, N., & Modood, T. (2009). The multicultural state we're in: Muslims, 'Multiculture' and the 'Civic Re-balancing' of British multiculturalism. *Political Studies, 57*(3), 473–497.

Meer, N., Dwyer, C., & Modood, T. (2010). Embodying nationhood? Conceptions of British national identity, citizenship, and Gender in the 'Veil Affair'. *The Sociological Review, 58*(1), 84–111.

Modood, T. (1998). Anti-Essentialism, Multiculturalism and the 'Recognition' of Religious Groups. *Journal of Political Philosophy, 6*(4), 378–399.

Nielsen, J. S. (1997). Muslims in Europe: History revisited or a way forward? *Islam and Christian–Muslim Relations, 8*(2), 135–143.

Abbas, T. (2010). *Islamic radicalism and multicultural politics: The British experience.* Routledge.

Parekh Report. (2000). *The future of multi-ethnic Britain.* Profile Books.

Phillips, D. (2006). Parallel lives? Challenging discourses of British Muslim self-segregation. *Environment and Planning D: Society and Space, 24*(1), 25–40.

Rampton, S., & Stauber, J. (2003). *Weapons of mass deception: The uses of propaganda in Bush's war on Iraq.* Penguin.

Semati, M. (2010). Islamophobia, culture and race in the age of empire. *Cultural Studies, 24*(2), 256–275.

Shaheen, J. G. (2009). *Reel bad Arabs: How hollywood vilifies a people.* Interlink Books.

Song, M. (2003). *Choosing ethnic identity* (pp. 16–21). Cambridge: Polity.

Van Dijk, T. (2000). New(s) racism: A discourse analytical approach. In S. Cottle (Ed.), *Ethnic minorities and the media: Changing cultural boundaries* (pp. 33–49). Buckingham: Open University Press.

Vertovec, S., & Peach, C. (1997). Introduction: Islam in Europe and the politics of religion and community. In S. Vertovec & C. Peach (Eds.), *Islam in Europe: The politics of religion and community.* Basingstoke: Macmillan.

Vertovec, S. (2001). *Transnational challenges to the "New" multiculturalism'.* Paper presented to the Association of Social Anthropologists conference, held at the University of Sussex, 30 March–2 April.

Vertovec, S. (2002). Islamophobia and Muslim recognition in Britain. In Y. Haddad (Ed.), *Muslims in the West: From sojourners to citizens.* Oxford University Press.

Weller, P. (2009). *A mirror for our times: The Rushdie affair and the future of multiculturalism.* Continuum.

Wiktorowicz, Q. (2004). *Islamic activism: A social movement theory approach.* Indiana University Press.

YOUTH WORK THEORY

JULIE GRIFFITHS

5. WORKING WITH MUSLIM YOUTH – A QUESTION OF DISTINCTIVENESS

Julie Griffiths taught in an inner London all-boys comprehensive school for 9 years, the population being mainly Muslim from all over the globe. She is the secretary of The Cal Aaj Education Partnership – a community organization that aims to raise the educational achievement of Muslim young people. She is also a senior education consultant.

What is distinctive about working with Muslim youth?

If there were nothing distinctive about working with Muslim youth then arguably there would be no need for what follows. However you may pose the question – Why do we need to think about this? Do we believe it necessary to discuss the distinctiveness of working with Christian youth or Sikh youth? Why do generic programmes seem applicable to other faith groups but somehow there is a feeling that some young Muslim will need a distinctive type of engagement? Do non-Muslims just need to 'understand' Muslims a little better in order to provide for their needs? Is there is a need for 21st Century Britain, to provide a genuine service that encompasses a section of our youth that seem to be becoming more and more disenfranchised.

It is hoped that the following material will challenge some of the assumptions about young Muslims and provide you with some questions about yourselves as well as about the client group; whether you are a Muslim or not. In my experience many of us have difficulty discussing issues of Race. However Islam is not a race – The House of Lords only accepts two faith groups as 'races' Judaism and Sikhism – the 1976 Race Relations Act defines a 'racial group', as a group of persons defined by reference to colour, race, nationality or ethnic or national origins; this is taken to mean a long shared history and a cultural tradition. This definition is shared by Muslims themselves for whom it is a matter of pride that all races are encompassed within it.

O mankind! We have created you from a male and a female, and made you into nations and tribes, that you may know one another. Verily, the most honourable of you with Allâh is that (believer) who has At-Taqwa (God consciousness). Verily, Allâh is All-Knowing, All-Aware. The Holy Qu'ran Sura 49 ayat 13

It is worth noting in the above Qu'ranic verse that 'mankind' is being addressed and not Muslims or believers.

B. Belton and S. Hamid (eds), Youth Work and Islam:
A leao of faith for young people, 75–81.

As some people have difficulty discussing race, so there is resistance to discussing faith. It gives rise to questions that sometimes are hard to grapple with, looking at our own attitudes to faith, spirituality, race, stereotypes, assumptions and prejudices and colonial attitudes. But this may be a good thing. People who work with young people need to explore themselves in this way because they are required to work alongside young people who are navigating their own way through their experiences and thoughts around these sometimes thorny issues.

HIERARCHY OF MULTIPLE IDENTITIES

What do we mean by identity? Does it mean individuality? Does it define who we are? If so is it singular Or can it be pluralistic in nature? Are there a variety of ingredients that go into making a single identity or are these ingredients actually separate identities within an individual that each and every one of us struggles to reconcile? Do these identities contend within us for supremacy or do we shuffle them with ease depending on the situation we find ourselves in.

In 1997 Runnymede established the Commission on the Future of Multi-Ethnic Britain. This was chaired by Lord Parekh, who produced a report in 2000 with six themes. One of those themes related to understanding that all identities are in a process of transition. Parekh postulated that identities need an ordering principle and cannot be equally important. Is it different to be a British Muslim than to be a Muslim in Britain? British in a Muslim way rather than Muslim in a British way. ? This leads to wider discussions about loyalty and belonging.

It is likely that each of us rate aspects of ourselves differently and this rating can change at different points in our lives. For many Muslims – being a Muslim will invariably be preeminent, be they young or old and whatever their level of observance might be.

That is not necessarily true for all faiths; nevertheless it is not exclusively a Muslim phenomenon but it has to be borne in mind when planning any provision that aims to include Muslim youth within its clientele.

How much has Islamic civilisation shaped British culture, thought, philosophy, sciences etc. over the centuries and is this acknowledged by British historians?

ASSUMPTIONS ABOUT BEING A MUSLIM AND ISLAM - WHAT TO BELIEVE?

It is often said in the media, and politicians claim that in the 21st Century that we in Britain live in a secular society. Although, at time of writing, the House of Lords includes 26 bishops as of right, and, as a life Peer, the Chief Rabbai, Jonathan Sacks there is a sceptical and agnostic outlook, which is implicit, and often explicit in the way we have things reported to us by the media. It is not unusual for individuals and sections of society that openly express a faith to portrayed and thus perceived to be a little backward or infantile in their reasoning and logic.

This leads society as a whole and individuals in particular to look for hypocrisy in people and groups who profess a faith. It is as though 'secular' society can make up its own 'moral compass' and is therefore forgiven mistake, error or misdemeanour, whereas people who profess to adhere to a faith system must be pious and error free, or else hypocrites, fanatics or extremists.

What do we really know about Islam and more to the point what do we expect from Muslim youth with regard to attitude, behaviour and lifestyle?

Do we expect Muslims to have different levels of knowledge about their religion, different levels of commitment to carrying out their beliefs, do we expect them to be influenced by their cultural surroundings and vary in the practice of their faith?

What is certain is that there is pluralism of practice within Islam and ideological debates amongst differing sects. Within Islam, Wahabism is virulently opposed to Sufism because Sufism does not recognise the duality between self or man, and God.

> *I am not a learned scholar, neither a mufti (Islamic scholar who is an interpreter or expounder of Islamic law), nor a qazi (a judge ruling in accordance with the sharia). Hell I do not desire, Heaven has no appeal to me. The thirty fasts I do not keep, neither do I say my prayers. Communion with God is all I seek, the rest is but a false game. Sultan Bahu*

Sultan Bahu (1628-1691) was a Muslim Sufi and saint. In his poems he shows a special disaffection for the functionaries of institutionalised religion. He lived during the period of Mughal Emperor Aurangzeb, known in history as the enemy of the Sufis. Aurangzeb patronized the orthodox Muslim ulema, the learned clerics and posted them to influential positions in the state bureaucracy as qazi, judges and prosecutors, muftis, the arbiters of Islamic law, and so on. Bahu dissociated himself from these men of learning and influence, rejecting the rewards and punishments they adhered to for ritual conformity that for Bahu took the place of real spiritual experience.

This is just one historical of example that demonstrates that far from being a homogeneous mass of collective consciousness, Muslims are individuals and Islam is a multi-dimensional pluralistic faith. So if we want to tailor provision to meet the needs of Muslims we will need to engage with their wants and needs and promote open dialogue whereby these needs can be expressed and understood.

THE MEDIA AND HOW IT FORMS OUR VIEWS ON ISLAM AND MUSLIMS

Many people (66 percent according to the 2002 YouGov opinion poll finding) draw most if not all their information about Islam and Muslim communities from the media. However, much of what is reported in media seems to be premised on an 'us and them' dynamic. As such, many Muslims in British society can be left feeling besieged, surrounded by a majority that sees them as 'other' – how do you meet that head on when trying to plan provision? Think about the experience of young Black males or Gypsy, Roma or Traveller groups from the 1960s to the present day, there are some similarities – Was anything done for groups like these that we can learn from?

However, the word 'Islamophobia' is one of the most common used in connection with Muslims. Contradictorily another well used word is 'extremist'. This seems to reflect something of the general confusion about Islam in Britain; Muslims portrayed as both a threatening presence and victims. However many dislike the term Islamophobia – as it implies a 'mental' sickness or aberration. However, it is a type of xenophobia, prejudice, intolerance and discrimination targeted specifically at Muslims, both overtly and covertly, which has the same corrosive effect as racism.

ETHNICITY VERSUS FAITH – THE UMMAH VERSUS TURF WAR

There are around two million Muslims living in the UK today. Just under a quarter of the world population are Muslims – it is considered to be the fastest growing religion. The Middle East and North, Central and West Africa have the highest population density of Muslims on earth.

If one were looking for bad press in Britain one might be hard pressed to decide which would be worse, to be Muslim, an asylum seeker or a refugee! Many Muslims have hit the jackpot of negative media coverage and public hostility twice over.

In the British context we have established Muslim communities who came in large numbers in the 1960s from British Commonwealth countries such as India, Pakistan, Bangladesh, Nigeria, Gambia and Sierra Leone. More recent communities have origins in Eastern Europe and countries such as Somalia, Turkey, Iran, Iraq amongst others – many of these newer communities include refugees and asylum seekers. However, growing numbers of British Muslims are converts to Islam from within the White and Black British populations.

Looking at the wide spread of nationalities and ethnicities represented in the short list provided it is obvious that British Islam is a mixture many different linguistic and cultural traditions. The one thing that brings these communities together is the Ummah – the brotherhood/sisterhood of Islam, the history, knowledge and traditions of the Muslim communities – in everything else they can be very different.

Some of the most recent Muslim immigrants have fled from countries beset by internecine war. Therefore it cannot be said that two Iraqis in a room will necessarily be kindred or two Turks or two Somalis (or even to each other – Iraq, as a nation, is made up of people from diverse cultural, religious and ethnic backgrounds). This is an important point to bear in mind when you are working with Muslim youth – the differences may outweigh the bond of the unmah.

There is also 'gang' or 'turf' war on the streets of many of Britain's cities between Somalis and Bangladeshis and Pakistanis and Turks etc. Some of these conflicts are based around organised crime such as drug trafficking – but they can be driven by straightforward 'postcode' allegiances - so causes are often more complex or superficial than conflict along ethnic lines, and may be amongst gangs of youth sharing ethnic backgrounds e.g. two opposing gangs of Pakistani heritage youth.

There are also class, caste and ethnic differences within communities that also cause conflict and differences.

YOUNG MUSLIM WOMEN IN BRITAIN

One of the things almost synonymous with British Muslim women is the hijab. This is an Arabic term meaning 'cover' derived from the meaning 'to veil, cover, screen or shelter'. In some Arabic-speaking countries and Western countries, the word hijab primarily refers to women's head and body covering, but in Islamic scholarship the word sometimes has a wider meaning of modesty, privacy or morality. The word used in the Qur'an for a headscarf or veil is *khimār*.

Dress has become central to ideas about Muslim women. I spoke to a leader of the council of churches near to where I work a while ago and he said 'I can't remember 20 years ago seeing a woman in a burkah walking on any of the streets in this area – now look at the change!'

A colleague of mine, a Muslim male, commented on the fact that neither his mother (a Pakistani woman who came to the UK in the 1960s) nor his wife (a Pakistani woman who came to the UK in the 1990s) wear burkah or niqab – only a modest veiling of the hair. However they both wear traditional clothing but neither cover their heads in daily life, strictly. However his daughters do – by choice.

I know at least two white reverts to Islam, married to Pakistani Muslims, who wear the nikab (face cover). A colleague of mine, a Bengali Muslim female in her 30s, has just started wearing hijab at the request of her 10-year-old daughter. My admin assistant at work is a British Pakistani woman in her early twenties, she had an arranged marriage (arranged marriages are not forced marriages - there are as many young Muslim men who object to them or welcome them as there are women with a similar point of view) has a young daughter, does not wear hijab, wears Western clothes to work and traditional Pakistani clothing out of work, she is juggling a full time job, a family and a part time degree course, has her daughter in private school and high aspirations for herself and her family.

As such there feels like there's a discrepancy with how Muslim women are viewed and how they perceive themselves. To what extent this exists or is felt will depend on the community they come from, where they live, their families, their ethnic heritage, their educational attainment, their aqida (denomination within Islam), their socio-economic status and themselves. However, to view all women who wear hijab or nikab as downtrodden wives, daughters, or sisters of dictatorial, misogynistic men is ludicrous but sadly prevalent in the European mind-set.

However it is important to note that many Muslim women in Britain today would like some single sex provision for them within the leisure industry. I frequently hear women (Muslim and not) bemoaning the lack of single-sex swimming provision or single sex Karate, football or Kick Boxing!

In 2007 the Muslim Council of Britain (MCB) published *Towards Greater Understanding − Meeting the needs of Muslim pupils in state schools*. This gives sound guidance on sport provision; educational visits etc. for school leaders. However there is no substitute for asking people what they want.

RESIDENTIALS

It seems questions consistently arise about the provision for Muslim young people on day trips/residential visits. Many establishments that deal with Muslim young people bemoan the fact that 'they' never go on field trips, residential trips or outings. Amongst things to consider are;
− Food − halal
− Accommodation and bathrooms − single sex
− Content of the activities − appropriate
Often it is parental concern that needs dispelling − they are not being awkward − they just take their duty towards providing for the holistic welfare of their young people very seriously. You can avoid some anxiety:
− If you explain the trip
− If you have some Muslim staff
− If you ensure the food and accommodation is appropriate
− If you invite older siblings to accompany them
− If you invite them to visit first
− If you can put them in contact with other Muslim parents who have allowed their young people to attend
− If you show photos and testimonials from other parents who have visited or sent their Muslim young people to the same excursion in the past then they may be more inclined to accede.

MUSLIM YOUTH AND THE CRIMINAL JUSTICE SYSTEM

Muslims make up around 3 percent of the British population but about 10 percent of the population of prisoners. Pakistanis and Bangladeshis, who make up in the region of 60 percent of Muslims in the Britain, are more likely than other ethnic groups to be victims of crime, including racially motivated crime.

An understanding of Muslims and the criminal justice system cannot ignore the impact of anti-terrorism legislation and policing on Muslim communities. The gap between the number of stops and searches and the number of actual arrests that lead to charges and convictions is fuelling a sense within Muslim communities that they are being unfairly policed. At the same time the incarceration without trial of detainees at HMP Belmarsh, under anti-terrorism legislation, further undermines Muslim's confidence in the criminal justice system.

The above is drawn from the 2005 paper *British Muslims and the Criminal Justice System – Open Society Institute.* It suggests that if Muslim Youth are not engaged with positively and their needs are not met, then there is a possibility, as with other 'disenfranchised' youth, that they may be disproportionably susceptible to being the suspects, victims or perpetrators of crime.

This leads us back to the beginning of our search into why there needs to be greater understanding of Muslim youth, and provision for their needs must be taken seriously. The government over the past decade or so woke up to the reality that some British subjects do not feel included in the mainstream (although over the last year to 18 months things seem to be taking a backward step). It is perhaps not the case that young Muslims do not consider themselves British enough, it is perhaps because they do not think others consider them British enough.

The above has been written to with the hope of opening up thinking about a section of British youth from whom one day you may be making policy decisions – do so wisely. You may wish to enhance your understanding by accessing more literature about Women in Islam, the contribution of Islam to Britain over the centuries.

FURTHER READING

Muir, H. (2004). *Islamophobia issues, challenges and action – A report by the Commission on British Muslims and Islamophobia.* Trentham Books.

Richardson, R., & Wood, A. (2004). *The achievement of British Pakistani learners – Work in progress.* Trentham Books.

Lingord, J. (2003). *Citizenship and Muslim perspectives.* Birmingham: DEC.

Muslim Council of Britain. (2007). *Towards greater understanding – Meeting the needs of Muslim pupils in state schools.* http://www.mcb.org.uk/downloads/Schoolinfoguidance.pdf

Runnymede Trust. (2007). *Not enough understanding? – Student experiences of diversity in UK Universities.*

Coles, M. I., Chilvers, P., & Buntin, R. (2008). *Every Muslim child matters: Practical guidance for schools and children's services.* Trentham Books.

Open Society Institute. (2005). *British Muslims and the criminal justice system.* http://www.fairuk.org/docs/OSI2004%209_Justice1.pdf

www.muslimheritage.com Discover a thousand years of missing history and explore the fascinating Muslim contribution to present day Science, Technology, Arts and Civilisation.

SADEK HAMID

6. MAPPING YOUTH WORK WITH MUSLIMS IN BRITAIN

Sadek Hamid has worked professionally in youth and community development in both the statutory and third sectors for over 11 years and has engaged with the Islamic voluntary sector for 24 years. He has a MA in Islamic Studies and his PhD focused on young British Muslims and religious activism. He was Programme Leader and Lecturer in Muslim Youth Work at the University of Chester and a Visiting Lecturer at the Cambridge Muslim College. He writes and speaks on matters related to Muslim youth and Islam in Britain, nationally and internationally and has appeared in various news media including the BBC, Channel 4 and the Islam Channel. His work has been published in numerous books, journals and newspapers such as Youth & Policy, ISIM Review, Religion, State & Society, The Guardian and The Muslim News.

In recent times the 'identity', loyalty and affiliations of young British Muslims have come under relentless scrutiny, whereby as a group they have been inadvertently homogenised and pathologised for the very real challenges and problems they deal with. As young individuals, many young British Muslims report a sense that mainstream civic and community engagement with them only occurs in the context of their being viewed as a problem, demanding unprecedented remedial measures and interventions, or as a 'high risk' group that requires constant management – not as respected individual stakeholders who have much to contribute and offer to wider society.

Akeela Ahmed, Chief Executive, Muslim Youth Helpline (2010)

INTRODUCTION

Currently, young people from the British Muslim communities are subjected to an array of corrosive stereotypes. Young males are often demonised as being either sociopaths, engaged in criminality or ripe for religious extremism, while young women are frequently portrayed as victims of religious patriarchy. These well rehearsed tropes, given episodic currency among certain media outlets, mask the more complex lived realities of British Muslim communities at the receiving end of grinding social disadvantage. The excessive focus on issue of violent radicalisation obscures the more mundane challenges Muslim youth share with their non-Muslim peers. In addition to struggling against social exclusion and

B. Belton and S. Hamid (eds), Youth Work and Islam:
A leao of faith for young people, 83–97.

religious discrimination, most Muslim youth are actually preoccupied with very adolescent concerns about 'fitting in', relationships (Younis, 2010), identity exploration and generally trying to succeed in life. This is made more difficult by the ongoing attacks on multiculturalism, a proxy for the rejection of the visible Muslim presence (Fekete, 2009) stigmatised for their alleged inability to integrate into secular British life. This chapter provides an overview of the types of youth work carried out with Muslim youth in the midst of these challenges. It begins by contextualising youth religiosity, then proceeds to map some of the main approaches to engaging young people in their communities over the last thirty years and evaluates the conceptual frameworks and methodologies used. It goes on to argue the need for faith sensitive youth work, provides a delineation of the contours of a professional Muslim youth work model and concludes with a summary of the anticipated challenges ahead for this nascent field.

YOUNG PEOPLE AND RELIGIOUS REFORMISM

From the end of the 1980s to the early 21st Century, British Muslims have become much more of a visible minority, most notably in the aftermath of international crises such as the Rushdie Affair, aftermath of the Gulf War, conflict in Bosnia, terrorist attacks in New York, London and the ongoing rise in Islamophobic sentiment in Western societies. Changing demographics, social marginalisation and the work of religious revivalist groups have all contributed to increasing religiosity among British Muslim youth (Samad, 2004, Mondal, 2009, Gilliant-Ray, 2010). However, it is important to note the vast majority remain 'cultural Muslims,' that is to say people who describe themselves as not practising their faith in a regular, committed way. This group represents between 75 to 80 percent of Muslim communities in Western societies (Ramadan, 2010). The remaining 20 percent or so maybe involved in some form of structured religious activism and within that a smaller percentage, dedicated to religious activism. This diversity of Muslims attitudes towards their faith cannot be overstated as it is possible to observe the emergence of various Muslim youth subcultural trends in the 'non-practising Muslim' segments of communities. Youth who identify themselves as 'Rude Boys' members of the 'Asian Gang', 'Gay Muslims' (http://gaymuslims.org/, fashion conscious 'Muhajababes' (Allegra, 2006), 'Heavy Metal Muslims' (Levine, 2007) and even ex-Muslims (http://www.ex-muslim.org.uk/indexEvents.html), negotiate their identities in creative ways.

Preceding these developments, most Muslim children, acquire their religious identities in their formative years when,

...the teachings of Islam are narrated, remembered and practised...consciously and consciously learn traditions and observances, thereby developing a Muslim 'moral habitus (Winchester, 2008).

Religious identities are inculcated with varying degrees of success at an early age through familial space, peer group contact and by attendance of after school mosques classes. It is an unfortunate fact that the majority of younger Muslims struggle to receive meaningful religious education in mosque provision, and that generally mosques management committees are indifferent or hostile to the suggestion that young people should be involved in any decision making capacity. Another fundamental problem lies in the teaching methods used; learning takes place by rote, most often in mother tongue languages, which young people may not always understand. The Qur'an is taught to be read rather then to be understood and the failure to do so can result in humiliation and sometimes corporal punishment. These negative experiences in part contribute to young people not wanting to practice their faith in adult life. This is an unfortunate irony as historically, mosques served as a multi-function space, catering for both the sacred and secular. They were places of prayer as well education, socialising, spiritual retreat, and importantly a place where all as sections of the community where welcomed. Young people seeking religious guidance or practical support are increasingly accessing the internet or the services of Islamic organisations. My own experience and research would lead me to suggest that presently in the UK, there are broadly three types of youth work with Muslims – Islamist reformism, secular and service based approaches.

The Islamist reformist approach to individual and social change is rooted in revivalist movements, which originated in Muslim lands in the late nineteenth and early twentieth centuries. These pan-Islamic groups combined anti-colonialist rhetoric, religious revivalism, and opposition to secular governments. The most influential of these in the Middle East is the Muslim Brotherhood (MB) and The Jamaati-Islami (JI) in the Indian sub continent. They established representative organisations among the first generation of settlers in the 1960s, such as the JI inspired UK Islamic Mission (UKIM). The UKIM influenced the work of the Young Muslims UK (YM), the Young Muslim Organisation (YMO) and the youth wing of the Muslim Association of Britain (MAB). Reformist styles of youth work were primarily about reconnecting young people to their religious heritage and were predicated on the assumption that they required a moral compass and alternative development. The UKIM pioneered youth reformism by working with children who attended their after-school religious education classes. This expanded into local schools, wherein individuals were encouraged to form the Islamic Youth Movement (IYM). The IYM held regular weekly meetings and organised other activities, including camping trips and created a magazine called *The Movement*. Declining in the late 1970s, its remnants were repackaged and launched as YM UK in 1984 (www.ymuk.net/) to create of dynamic elite that would lead Muslim youth in Britain. It caters for the 13 to 21 age bracket and has a 'sisters' section in many British cities and towns. It attempts to engage Muslim children and youth by hosting religious study circles, seminars, sporting competitions and camps. They look to provide a counter-culture for Muslim youth by producing a range of activities, media and alternatives to popular secular youth pastimes. YM has produced its own magazine as well as leaflets, audio-video materials explaining aspects of Islam. In the past, members have run 'Radio Ramadan' in cities where they have a significant membership, such as Glasgow, Bradford and London. It also has a Muslim Scouts Group, which is intended as a feeder into YM, after the age of 25. Older YM members are expected to join the adult counterpart the Islamic Society of Britain (ISB).

Another significant proponent of 'Islamic youth work' in Britain is the Islamist Young Muslim Organisation (YMO) (www.ymouk.com). Established in 1979, it caters for and is run by young people of Bangladeshi origin and offers similar activities to its competitor YM. The differences between them are minimal, although the YMO has a more conservative interpretation of Islamic law. They also have a parallel young women's organisation, Muslimat. While having branches across the UK, YMO are strongest in East London. They have paid more attention to youth work and have qualified youth workers within their movement. The YMO youth work approach includes religious education, recreation and the tackling of specific social problems within their communities. In Tower Hamlets, their highly disciplined workers have made significant inroads into raising educational attainment and religious consciousness by working with high schools, colleges and universities and have rewarded academic excellence through its School and College Link Projects.

The MAB Youth (www.mabonline.info/youth) wing is modelled on MB pedagogies and has similar ideological and methodological objectives to YM and YMO. It was created in 1997, as a response to what it says was a failure in 'youth mobilisation' in the other Islamic youth movements. Its activities again lay emphasis on reforming youngsters and providing education and recreational opportunities. Like YM and YMO, it has systematic procedures for training and channelling young people into its adult section of MAB. All of the three above are closely connected, well organised organisations. There are also similar active reformist organisations such as the Dawatul-Islam youth group (www.dawatul-islam.org.uk). Also based in East London, they run a successful school, magazines and run regular seminars and conferences.

To this inventory could be added Salafi, organisations like JIMAS, the MIT youth project created by the Brixton Mosque and the youth engagement work inspired by a form of neo-Sufism. The term 'Salafi' refers to the Muslim theological tendencies that look towards the *Salaf-us Salih* - the first pious three generations of early Muslim history. Though a strict, textual based trend, in recent years they have adopted a more tolerant approach to working with other Muslim and non-Muslim organisations. Ipswich based JIMAS, is now a registered third sector charity, holding regular youth activities, seminars, camps and liaises with local authority youth services and large annual conferences (www.jimas.org). The MIT project (www.brixtonmasjid.co.uk) works with 14 to 21 year olds and utilises a range outdoor activities such as indoor skiing, abseiling and sporting tournaments to attract Muslim young people. Work with Muslim youth has also been inspired by a form of Sufism, better known as the 'Traditional Islam' network. This trend emerged in the mid 1990s after being popularised by charismatic American convert scholars Hamza Yusuf, Nuh Keller and the British academic Abdal Hakim Murad. Rather than being contained in a single organisational entity, it is a system of networks, which encompasses learning institutions, publishing houses, websites, magazines and regular events which share the same scholars and speakers. Among the most influential of these are the website and discussion group Deenport.com, Masud Khan's site (http://www.masud.co.uk/) and the Radical Middle Way (http://www.radicalmiddleway.co.uk/). They have been at the forefront of supporting a number of artistic, cultural and educational projects that promote an 'Islamic Cool' among Muslim young people (Boubekeur, 2005, Tarlo, 2010).

The Right Start Foundation, (RSF - www.rightstart.org.uk) is also another significant project. Based in Birmingham and created by the popular Egyptian Televangelist Amer Khaled, this organisation represents a shift in traditional reformist stance, Khaled having chosen to tackle socially destabilising issues in Muslim societies. In Britain he focuses his work predominantly on drugs awareness and substance abuse prevention, sports, and supporting families with children, using a multidisciplinary team of youth workers, sociologist, scientists, and religious scholars. This method integrates work with Muslim youth into a wider strategy of 'renewing' Muslim families and communities. A subtle approach is adopted and there is no reference to religion on RSF's website. RSF have won recognition for its partnership work with non-Muslim agencies.

Another category within Islamic youth work is individual reformist inspired organisations that are city based. Often set up as youth centres, their mission and methods mirror Islamic movement methodology. Examples include the Muslim Youth Foundation (http://myf.org.uk/welcome-to-muslim-youth-foundation.html) and Al-Islah Youth Centre in Manchester. They offer support with schoolwork and provide alternative 'halal' spaces for young people to play sports, relax and where they are encouraged to attend religious study circles and events.

Reformist Islamic youth organisations form the largest number of voluntary organisations that work with young people in Muslim communities. These organisations possess a number of commendable features, which have helped many young people to learn about and practise their faith. But they also have counter productive features; principal among them is young people's needs becoming an appendage to achieving the aims of these various organisations, some of which display political vanguard movement characteristics and are quite often out of touch with the day-to-day problems of the young people they wish to attract. There is also a tendency towards elitism as they tend to recruit young people from middle class backgrounds and are reluctant to work with Muslim young people with more challenging behaviour. They usually promote themselves by distributing publicity about their work at public events, mosques and colleges. If individuals show interest they are encouraged to attend activities where they are observed. The screening process continues as experienced members get to know the young person and find out about their background, level of education, future aspirations and any skills they have. If the person demonstrates enough potential they then become targets that are seen as possible future members. At this point a person will be assigned to socialise with them and over a period of time. This individual will try to persuade the young person of the benefits of working with the organisation. Throughout this process-the interests of the group override the needs of the young person.

Another problematic feature of this type of missionary instrumentalism is the ideological indoctrination carried out which attempts to shape the young person's worldview into the outlook of the organisation. This mindset encourages the perception of other Muslim youth groups/organisations as competitors who are in some way inadequate or simply wrong. This intolerance frequently has prevented youth organisations with similar goals from co-operating and as such produces an insular mentality. It is also a huge waste of resources as rival youth organisations sometimes host events simultaneously, in the same area, for the same target group, while refusing to co-ordinate work together. In addition most reformist youth groups appear to often be oblivious to wider social trends and changes taking place in mainstream youth culture, British society and government. Their youth leaders seem to be generally ignorant of the scale of the challenges facing British Muslim youth today. Furthermore, few of the members of the reformist youth organisations have any tangible youth work skills beyond the general organising of events. Rather than being able to build broadly developmental relationships with young people, a heavy emphasis is placed upon socialisation into particular interpretations of Islamic norms and behaviour through participation in sports and recreation like football, table tennis, pool and martial arts. They also often tend not to have the ability to use constructive criticism, lacking accountability beyond their own organisational hierarchy. Ultimately this means that young people miss out as these organisations put their own advancement before the well being of those they recruit to their ranks. People associated with these organisations may protest that my description is a crude simplification of their modes of operation, however many ex-members and people who have interacted with the type of agencies referred to above, across the UK, would beg to differ; some even claim to have been harmed by this type of Islamic youth work.

On a positive note some reformist organisations are belatedly recognising the importance of social welfare work and some of their members have gone on to train as youth workers, drug and social workers. However, the challenge for them remains one of relevance and being able to serve young people without hoping that they will become workers in a movement. Islamic youth organisations need to engage the broadest possible constituency of young Muslims and move beyond the narrow ideological and methodological approaches they currently deploy. They can no longer ignore the totality of young peoples' lives. As such they need to start offering this group relevant knowledge, skills and experiences in order to meet the intellectual and social challenges that face young Muslims now and future.

To do this there needs to be a serious cultural shift within Muslim communities in terms of recognising the importance and potential of professional youth work.

WHEN FAITH MEETS PROFESSIONAL PRACTICE

Young British Muslims experience most of the common, ups and downs that charactise adolescence generally. What distinguishes them is the fact of their 'Muslimness'; the range of religious and cultural differences that inform their outlooks and values. Feedback from young people in a number of recent reports (Malik et. Al., 2007, Forward Thinking, 2008, NCVYS, 2008) suggest that most Muslim young people are not acessing mainstream services due, in part, to the fact that statutory services are not equipped to understand the religion, culture and norms that many young Muslims carry with them. This can potentially result in them experiencing a double social exclusion; they are marginalised from the delivery of mainstream services and, partly as a consequence, are excluded from adequate support structures within their communities.

A common grievance voiced is that most youth centres and youth work staff are unaware or ill equipped to understand these religious and cultural dimensions. In connection with this conclusion every so often I am asked questions such as;
– 'Why have Muslim youth work?'
– 'Isn't this promoting separatism?'
– 'Doesn't it miss the point about community cohesion?'
These are reasonable questions, reflecting anxieties behind the emergence of distinct Muslim faith perspectives in youth work in the last few years. However, given that established professional Christian and Jewish youth work practices recognise the spiritual dimension of young people, the question to be asked is; 'Why not have Muslim youth work?' We already have Muslim Mediation services, 'Islamic Counselling' and Islamic Social Work models (Crabree, 2008: 65). Similarly Muslim faith based approaches to youth work are based upon the need for specialisation, being a recognition of cultural competence skills that come from insider knowledge and training. This not seperatism, but fullfilling the duty to promote equality of opportunity in the same way that distinct, focused work is necessary with young women or young black people. The importance of exploring young people's religious beliefs and values is embedded in the professional good practice criteria with the National Occupation Standards for youth work, section 1.1.4, (http://www.lluk.org/documents/whole_suite_of_Professional_and_National_Occu pational_Standards_for_Youth_Work.pdf) which encourages the spiritual development of young people. This is understood to ensure that young people's ethical, moral and cultural values and beliefs are discussed as well as the differences between spirituality, religion and faith. It goes as far to recommend that youth workers should,

...assist young people to develop a sense of their own spiritual beliefs, values, ethics and morals by which they live (NCVYS, 2008)

and importantly

...encourage young people to explore their beliefs in relation to those of other faiths, religions and cultures, and the prevailing social norms (Ahmed, 2009: 27).

Most young people from faith backgrounds, as well as those with no particular faith experience, are likely at some points in their lives to ask themselves and/or others the perennial questions about the meaning and purpose of life, perhaps deciding to commit to a religious tradition is of course a matter of personal choice. In relation to these types of issues, Khan (2005) lists why he believes Muslim youth work approaches are important:

- Muslim youth work can enable young people to have a sense of self worth that takes on board the faith dimension of their identity.
- Young men and women need to be taken seriously in the Muslim community; the youth work process can enable this. This is particularly so in the current policy agenda where young people need to be seen to be taking an active part in the projects and initiatives put forward for funding. Muslim organisations can be seen as being put in a situation of disadvantage by policy due to the state of youth work in this community. There is a mismatch between what is required and what exists.
- Youth participation can contribute to addressing the gendered nature of the representational sphere.
- It can provide interventions in a crucial influencing space outside home, mosque and school.
- It can bring into play existing curricula in culturally appropriate ways but also develop new positive curricula that can inform identity and belonging.
- It can introduce new models of understanding work with young people and the purposes that influence it.
- Muslim youth workers can form relationships with young people that are accepting and well informed about the faith dimension of their lives.
- It can assist young Muslims constantly faced with negative images of their faith to challenge this in a constructive way. For example, the arts, creating spaces for their voices to be heard.
- It can develop new relationships with the Muslim world and influence agendas on issues of justice and minorities as members of the European community.
- Youth workers from a Muslim faith perspective in senior positions with local authorities are few and far between and are often stretched and ghettoised. The conference and any emerging organisational entity provide an opportunity to be heard outside the constraints of organisational hierarchies and community representational discourses.

- A Muslim youth work response can critique investment in the 'relationships' being invested in and cultivated with, for example, family, training, environment etc.
- Developments of theoretical frameworks are needed that authenticate a Muslim perspective/approach in work with young people.
- A national response can be more effective in pump priming local action. This is especially so in investing in new voices, ways of working etc. where existing funding is committed.

Though still at an early stage, over the last six years, these ideas have started to permeate work with Muslim youth across the UK and partnerships are now being made across faith communities. Muslim youth work practitioners could also learn much from both the successes and failures of Christian youth work. A large amount of youth work with Muslim youngsters has historically taken place within secular, voluntary youth organisations or local authority youth services. Here the youth work can be delivered in two ways:

1) By workers who are 'non-practising' Muslims, so their faith does not inform their youth work practice and is derived entirely from secular frameworks.
2) Influenced by the passion individual youth workers have for their racial/cultural heritages. This can alternate between hybrid identities or ones that privilege their ethnic/cultural/national heritages.

In both cases religion is deemed irrelevant to youth work practice. The other possibility are situations where 'practising Muslims' work in secular services, which in some cases can be difficult if these agencies have aggressively secular work cultures that effectively disallow a role for faith in the delivery of youth services.

Change is slowly but determinedly taking place through the work of the Muslim Youth Work Foundation (www.mywf.org.uk), the undergraduate degree in Muslim Youth Work that was piloted a the University of Chester, Muslim Youth Skills (www.muslimyouthskills.co.uk), and the work of the YMCA College, East London. Given the marginalisation of religious perspectives within secular youth organisations, some Muslim professionals have also started to develop faith sensitive approaches across a range of services. This has led to the development of service-based organisations whose ethoi are shaped by Islam, but who provide intervention instead of proselytisation. These agencies have pioneered faith sensitive approaches to mental health, counselling and drug work. Leading the way are organisations such as The Muslim Youth Helpline (www.myh.org.uk), and NAFAS drugs project (www.nafas.org). The Muslim Youth Help Line, developed in 2002, has pioneered valuable counselling services to thousands of young people in desperate need of advice and guidance. Its success led to the launching of a website (www.muslimyouth.net/) in October 2004. In a lively and interactive manner its magazine format addresses contemporary issues like citizenship and identity, discrimination, bullying, mental health, relationships and sexuality.

It has also initiated groundbreaking campaigns relating homelessness and supporting young Muslim prisoners. The website also includes a wide variety of articles and referral points. The only organisation of its kind, NAFAS, in East London has been operational from 2000. It targets the growing drug problem among Bangladeshi young people in Tower Hamlets. Its atmosphere is discreetly Islamic and it offers mainstream drug services in addition to specialist features that are adapted for work within Muslim communities. NAFAS also provide training packages for parents and Mosques and deliver therapies and abstinence treatment plans from within Islamic frames of reference.

PROFESSIONAL MUSLIM YOUTH WORK: TOWARD A SYNTHESIS

At the risk of being accused of semantic quibbling, it is useful to make a distinction between a 'Muslim' and 'Islamic youth work'. There is difference between the aims, methods and outcomes produced by each approach. Islamic youth work takes a largely confessional orientation, being motivated by the basic goal looking to help young people learn the values and rituals of Islam. However, emerging Muslim youth work approaches tend to be person centred and start where the young person is at in his or her life. A dialectical method is central as is the focus on facilitating self-discovery and personal development. This approach is undertaken in the awareness that young people are likely to have pressing needs that require immediate attention; ethos, style and delivery of work is informed by the values of Islam. It is insufficient logically (it is irrational/it makes little sense) to define work with young people who happen to be Muslim as 'Muslim Youth Work' if there is no role for religion in the conceptualisation or delivery of its practice. If that were the case, then youth work delivered by non-Muslim youth workers with young Muslims could be called 'Muslim youth work'. Prefixing 'Muslim' before a practice at least raises expectations of (but more probably clearly implies) a faith element. This cannot just be a cosmetic 'add on' if theoretical and actual frameworks are rooted outside of a religious value base. The following might be usefully understood as a basic starting point for the process of developing a professional Muslim youth work approach:

In reality the integration of faith values, youth work principles and individual worker expertise is likely to be organic. The diagram below only sketches the linearity that would need to occur to arrive at a meaningful synthesis that is loyal to both generic youth work values and the ideals of Islam. Put another way, it might be helpful to define the framework of what a Muslim youth work approach should and should not be:

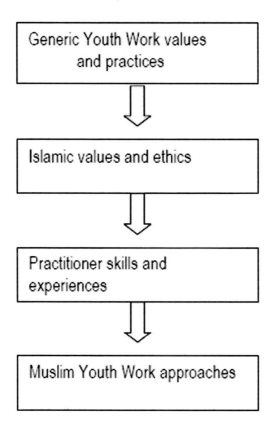

These characteristics and strategies represent the broad parameters of what professional Muslim youth work might look like but it is in many ways a work in progress. As British Muslim young people are incredibly diverse in terms of their religiosity, ethnicity, cultures and social backgrounds, an effective Muslim youth worker should be able to adapt to these facts as well as be able to work effectively with young people who are not committed to their faith as those who are not Muslim.

What Muslim Youth Work is	What it is not
Conceptually: •Faith sensitive •Values based •Recognises spiritual dimension of peoples lives •Promotes the holistic support and development of Muslim youth •Non-judgemental •Specialist	**Conceptually:** • Overly focussed with religious teaching and identity maintenance • Rules based i.e. only concerned with the what is religiously lawful & unlawful • Limits Islam to ritual performances and visual markers • Value neutral • De-inks faith from identity
Methodologically: •Youth focused-starts with young peoples needs •Strategic •Systematic and evidence based •Solution orientated •Creative •Taps into the length and breadth of Islamic tradition •Reflective	**Methodologically:** • Excludes the positive potential of faith • Selective • Pre-occupied with recreational activities • Adhoc • Mistakes means for ends • Rigid
In delivery will: •Empower and educate young people Able to work with all young people •Provides equal opportunity •Promotes social justice •Encourages integration and social cohesion •Make positive difference in young peoples lives •Provide role models	**In delivery will:** • Empty youth centres-excluded young people-irrelevant services • Denies the opportunity to utilise their faith heritage positively • Result in psychological/cultural dissonance • Reinforces alienation and prejudice

CONCLUSION

The British Muslim population is in many places disadvantaged, facing challenges both externally and internally. They are facing many critical issues, ranging from their communities being unwilling or unable to deal with the increase in social problems facing their young, to social disadvantage, marginalisation and Islamophobia. Those concerned with the welfare of young Muslims have a major task in dealing with these internal and external challenges. Unfortunately the leadership in Muslim communities is often out of touch with the daily realities of the lives of young people, while the youth work being carried out is dominated by reformist youth movements, who commonly indoctrinate them into their own particular organisational ideologies and priorities. Aside from the notable exceptions mentioned here, reformist approaches have been ambivalent at best in addressing the multiple challenges facing Muslim youth today. Muslim service based organisations are doing what the reformist organisations should have done a long time ago. Perhaps the greatest challenges facing service-based organisations are to secure sustainable long-term funding and increase their representation nationally. Given that over half of the Britain's Muslim population are under the age of 25 and growing in number, Islamic youth organisations, service based agencies and mainstream services need to work together to meet this anticipated need. Professional Muslim youth workers can work with young people to develop understanding of these issues; they can act as mentors, but also be prepared to learn about young people from young people (be mentored). A professional, faith sensitive approach that is grounded in the principles and practices of generic youth work can assist mainstream service providers to recognise the importance of understanding the faith and cultures of different young people and can act as bridge between the home, school, mosques and the street.

HOW MUSLIM YOUTH WORK APPROACHES CAN BE SUPPORTED

I would suggest the following to help consolidate Muslim youth work practice:
- Encourage the professionalisation of youth work with Muslim young people, synthesising the different aspects of youth work i.e. social education, recreation, personal development and practical support in a cohesive manner
- Develop theoretical frameworks and curricula with the co-operation of practitioners, educators and Muslim scholars
- Develop intervention strategies that integrate work with parents, schools, youth workers and general community capacity building
- Catalogue and share good practice and resources
- Development of national and international practitioner networks
- Increase the number of professionally accredited Muslim Youth Work courses such as the one that ran at the University of Chester

- Increase co-operation between secular and faith sensitive approaches of working with young Muslims
- Increase inter-faith youth work collaboration

While Muslim youth work may have much to offer there still remains a number of practical challenges in communities where there is still little understanding of the value of youth work as a profession and a preference towards encouraging children into prestigious careers such as medicine, law and science. The recognition of youth work as a valuable and viable career is perhaps one is the biggest challenge facing the long term establishment of professional Muslim Youth work practice. Among parents, there still seems to be a deal of ignorance about what youth work is as a career or anxieties around the availability of employment opportunities. This is understandable given the parental generation within those communities came from countries with no history of professional youth work. For advocates, widening awareness of the potential of youth in Muslim communities and persuading sceptical secular practitioners, remain an ongoing struggle.

BIBLIOGRAPHY

Abbas, T. (Ed.). (2005). *Muslims in Britain: Communities under pressure*. Zed Books.

Ahmed, A. (2010). (Forward) *Young British Muslims and relationships*. Muslim Youth Helpline.

Ahmed, S. (2009). *Seen and not heard: Voices of young British Muslims*. Policy Research Centre. Islamic Foundation.

Alexander, E. C. (2000). *The Asian gang, ethnicity, masculinity and identity*. Berg.

Boubekeur, A. (2005, Autumn). *Cool and competitive: Muslim culture in the West*. ISIM Review, No. 16.

Crabtree, S. A., Hussain, F., & Spalek (Eds.). (2008). *Islam and social work: Debating values, transforming*. Practice: Policy Press.

National Council for Voluntary Youth Services (NCVYS). (2008). *Faith in factor: Working towards a faith and culturally sensitive sector*.

Fekete, L. A. (2009). *Suitable enemy: Racism, migration and Islamophobia in Europe*. Pluto Press.

Forward Thinking. (2008). *Forgotten voices: Developing more effective engagement with Muslim youth & communities*.

Garbin, D. (2005). *Bangladeshi Diaspora in the UK: Some observations on socio-cultural dynamics, religious trends and transnational politics*. Paper delivered at Conference Human Rights and Bangladesh, Friday 17 June. SOAS (School of Oriental & African Studies), University of London.

Gilliant, S. (2010). *Muslims in Britain: An introduction*. Cambridge University Press.

Imtiaz, A. S.M. (2011). *Wandering lonely in the crowd: Reflections on the Muslim condition in the West*. Kube Publishing.

Levine, M. (2009). *Heavy metal Muslims*. Three Rivers Press.

Lewis, P. Y. (2007). *British and Muslim*. Continuum Publishing Ltd.

Khan, M. G. (2005). *Towards a national strategy for Muslim youth work: Report of the national conference 2005*. NYA.

Malik, R., Shaikh, A., & Suleyma, M. (2007). *Providing faith and culturally sensitive support services to young British Muslims*. National Youth Agency. http://www.ealingcvs.org.uk/documents/575.pdf

MCB. (2005, September). *Youth groups convention' Manchester town hall*. Muslim Council of Britain.

Mondal, A. A. (2008). *Young British Muslim voices*. Greenwood World Publishing.

Ramadan, T. (2010). *What I believe*. Oxford University Press.

Tarlo, E. (2010). *Visibly Muslim: Fashion, politics, faith*. Berg.

Winchester, T. J. (2008). Embodying the faith: Religious practice and the making of Muslim moral habitus. *Social Forces, 86*(4), 1753–1780 (cited in Gilliant-Ray, 2010. p. 138).

Younis, M. (2010). *Young British Muslims and relationships.* Muslim Youth Helpline.

Yunas, S. (2004, June 11). *Muslim youth in Britain: Ethnic to religious identity.* Paper presented at the International Conference Muslim Youth in Europe. Typologies of religious belonging and sociocultural dynamics, Edoardo Agnelli Centre for Comparative Religious Studies, Turin.

MAURICE IRFAN COLES

7. EVERY MUSLIM YOUTH MATTERS: THE 4 PS OF MUSLIM PARTICIPATION

Maurice Irfan Coles has been in the education service for 40 years. From childhood in Lambeth, London, he has been actively involved in issues related to education for our multicultural/multifaith society. He has been a teacher, Head of Department and an advisory teacher in challenging areas. For 18 years he held a range of senior portfolios in the City of Birmingham. He established the largest Multicultural Support Service in the country and for a period of time led one of the largest advisory teams. For 7 years he headed the School Development Support Agency in Leicester City.

He has managed countless educational and social projects, including the Cultural Understandings of Science Project (CUSP), and the How Do Ideas Travel? Most recently he has been appointed by the FSTC to head up a new curriculum enrichment company, Curriculum Enrichment for the Common Era (CE4CE). At present he is also the Director of the Islam and Citizenship in Education Project (ICE) which has developed materials for the teaching of citizenship in madrasahs and in Muslim schools all of which can be downloaded on www.theiceproject.com

He has published extensively on a large range of issues including School Improvement, Race Equality, Intercultural Education and Continuing Professional Development. He led the writing team and edited a major work on Faith, Interfaith and Cohesion: The Education Dimension. His latest book, Every Muslim Child Matters, was published by Trentham in May 2008.

INTRODUCTION

It is my contention that nature of Islam enhances and endorsees the key principles that underpin youth work provision. Although at the time of writing it looks as though the days of Every Child Matters (ECM) are likely to more of a memory than a reality, if statutory and voluntary providers of youth work took active account of the Islamic frame of reference within the ECM agenda, they would be able to better serve the needs of British Muslims, increase their participation rates and contribute to a more cohesive society.

The four Ps of Muslim participation are:

B. Belton and S. Hamid (eds), Youth Work and Islam:
A leao of faith for young people, 99–112.

Potential: This examines and applauds the enormous potential that Islam provides for Muslim youth to contribute to wider society.

Paradox: The paradoxes that exist between the ideals of the faith and the position that Muslims find themselves within British society. Helping to address these paradoxes provide some of the strategic drivers for changes in both policy and practice.

Policy: Twelve key questions that underpin Every Muslim Youth Matters.

Practice: Examples of provision that are discrete to the faith community: and some which work across groups regardless of faith background.

In what follows both Muslim and non-Muslim youth workers and policy makers are borne in mind, because the principles and the practices that underpin this chapter can be applied by all those involved in youth work practice.

Jonathan Roberts, writing in the NYA's Special edition on Muslin Youth Work in the summer of 2006 wrote:

The most significant national organisations for young Muslims at the moment may be the help lines, and web based advice. These sit alongside local examples of individual youth projects. In contrast to the presence of Christian projects in rich and poor areas, and at local and national levels, there appears to be a lack of provision and a limited range of approaches. (www.nya.org.uk)

Have things significantly changed in the intervening years? There are several examples of new and dynamic organisations and the voice of young Muslims being increasingly heard, but there is little evidence of major systemic change. But the national youth work landscape did change when all local authorities were required to provide Integrated Youth Services which included Connexions, Youth Services, Children Services and Youth Offending Teams. The hope was that this new start would involve successful engagement with Young Muslims. Government aspirations looked to create building blocks in the form of the extensive criteria underpinning the ECM agenda (DfES 2004) that had the ambition to secure improved outcomes for all young people.

ECM agenda was hard wired into the DNA of every organisation and individual connected with service provision for young people. With the coming of the ConDem coalition and the resultant massive cuts to youth provision, those of us in the field will need to accommodate a whole new practice horizon that will may not include ECM as a legislated code of conduct. However, this does not undermine its mantric five outcomes as a principled structure for practice:

- be healthy
- stay safe
- enjoy and achieve
- make a positive contribution
- achieve economic wellbeing

These considerations, or variations of the same, can continue to be relevant and provide a backbone for the improvement and of delivery of services. As such I will continue to address their importance and relevance in what follows.

Every Muslim Child Matters (Coles, 2008) was a written as a response to the ECM agenda and provides a detailed and sophisticated analysis of the issues, concerns and outcomes of and for Muslims in education. It offers a complete strategy in relation to implementing the five outcomes and thorough detail in the curriculum changes recommended. It is based upon the simple premise that faith is the key determinant in the life of any Muslim, and that any educational provision that does not take this faith into account and build upon it will struggle to achieve the five outcomes.

Although from a number of perspectives the position of young Muslims in the UK provides grounds for concern, *Every Muslim Child Matters* (EMCM) is predominantly optimistic because it evidences the enormous potential of young Muslims as individuals and groups, arguing that the government agendas have, with some modifications, suited to capitalise upon Muslim attitudes, aspirations and beliefs. I believe this will continue to be a relevant consideration even as the techniques and means of state intervention into the lives of young people is changing. In EMCM we are offered a vibrant and optimistic approach to services and as such we would be short sighted to throw this baby out with the proverbial legislative bath water.

PARADOX AND POTENTIAL

Governments (national and local) need hard facts upon which to base their interventionist policies and practices. Vast amounts of information about Muslims now exist in practically every area of life. It is upon much of this information that many arguments in EMCM are based. These facts can still be a little confusing, however, in that much, but not all, of the information is collected on a faith basis. Some, like that collected by the Department for Education (DFE), is entirely based upon ethnicity, and much of the other evidence we have is also broken down in this way.

Although the majority of Pakistanis, Bangladeshis, Turks and Somalis are Muslim, it is not good practice to assume faith according to national identity. For example nearly 15 percent of Turks and around 7 million Pakistanis are not Muslim. Data produced by the San Diego State University's International Population Center suggests that the Chinese Muslim population is 65.3 million. According to the BBC's 'Religion and Ethics' website there are up to 100 million Muslims in China; the total population of Britain is under 62 million. There are about 21 million Muslim Indians; the Russian population is over 140 million, more than 10 percent are Muslims. China, Russia and India are not majority Muslim nations, however, Indonesia is; it has the world's largest Muslim population. But 36 million Indonesians are not Muslims. The USA has up to 7 million Muslim citizens (Council on American-Islamic Relations, 2010) and Islam is Spain's second largest faith group.

Using a number of sources, including a survey of more than 250 British mosques, census data from 2001 and conversion figures in Europe, research at Swansea University has estimated that there could be as many as 100,000 converts in the UK, with white women leading the growing number of people embracing Islam. This indicates that the number of Britons choosing to become Muslims has nearly doubled in the past decade (see, Brice, 2011). Britain's approximately two million Muslims are the fastest growing faith group in the UK.

Given these figures we need to be very careful before we assume faith by way of nationality.

Muslims appear to have the most positive attitudes to school, with overall low rates of exclusion and being generally keen to help others. Paradoxically, they are also the poorest, the least well educated, the least likely to be employed, and the most likely to suffer poor health. They are now also greatly over-represented in the prison population.

At the same time there is a large and increasingly vibrant, self confident and articulate group of Muslims in the professional and managerial classes who succeed as well as any other community. The data clearly demonstrates that there are nonetheless major areas of disadvantage (See EMCM pages 6-7). This is all the more paradoxical given that Islam encourages education, sport and the promotion of good health, hard work and justice. It also espouses peace, charity, volunteering, citizenship and a wider sense of responsibility both for the Muslims and non-Muslims.

If those involved in delivering services to young people take on board the Muslim frame of reference they may be better positioned to help address some of these disadvantages, meet their statutory duties and exploit the great potential of the Muslim youth.

THE MUSLIM FRAME OF REFERENCE

For Muslims, their faith is based upon two major foundations: the Qur'an, the divine revelation given to the Prophet Muhammad over a 23-year period; and the *Sunnah*. The *Sunnah* is the tradition and practices of the Prophet and the *hadith* - the collections of the Messenger's reported sayings. In addition generations of scholars, known as the *ulama*, have sought to interpret texts and agree upon interpretation through *ijma* (consensus). You can, however, perhaps summarise this vast body of work into three key Qur'anic commandments. The first two, *attain to faith and do good works* are explicitly repeated ten times in the Holy Qur'an:

Verily, those who have attained to faith and do good works, and are constant in prayer, and dispense charity - they shall have their reward with their Sustainer, and no fear need they have, and neither shall they grieve. (2.277)

The nature of faith and of good works, of course, needs unpacking but both should lead to the third key commandment; the acquiring of 'God consciousness', of *taqwa* which is the highest quality to which a Muslim can aspire:

The most honourable among you in the sight of God is the one who is most God-conscious. (49:13)

And vie with one another to attain to your Sustainers' forgiveness and to a Paradise as vast as the heavens and the earth, which awaits the God-conscious, who spend for charity in time of plenty and in time of hardship, and restrain their anger, and pardon their fellow men, for God loves those who do good. (3:133-134)

There are some 251 references to *taqwa* in the Qur'an, but in English versions it is difficult to find them because there is no direct and easy translation. It is sometimes rendered as 'God consciousness', sometimes as 'piety' and 'good action' and sometimes as being 'God fearing'.

These three key injunctions underpin the Islamic analysis made by Imam Monawar Hussain, in his *Questions and Answers Towards A Counter Narrative*, which forms the background to his Oxford Pupils' Empowerment Programme. He cites and clearly explains the famous hadith of *Jibra-il*, where the Prophet divided Islam into three dimensions: *Islam, Imam* and *Ihsan.* (www.teachernet.gov.uk/wholeschool/):

Islam is to testify that there is no God but Allah, and that Muhammad is His Messenger (the *Shahada*). It is based on five pillars: that is the instruction to recite the *Shahada*, to pray, to give alms, to fast and to perform the Hajj. These five are the basic practices of Islam which every Muslim undertakes, but there are many other Prophetic and Qur'anic commands to submit to the will of Allah. There are those that are common to most religions, like not stealing, murdering, lying or committing immoral sexual acts. Other injunctions cover areas like inheritance, business transactions, dietary regulations, marriage rites and permissible marital relations.

In a very real sense adherence to Islam is adherence to a complete way of life, as practically every area of human activity is covered. When humans live this way of life, in harmony with the will of God, which is Islam, they are following the *din-al fitra* (the natural God-given way of life.)

For Muslims the point of life is totally clear: humans were created to worship, to remember God sincerely and devotedly (Qur'an 9.31, 51.56, 98.5). One of the greatest acts of worship is to live according to the Divine Guidance that has been sent to all humankind. Each human being in Islam is not just responsible for their own actions but for creating a just social order and looking after the whole planet as God's regent (*khalifa*) on earth.

It is perhaps this concept of God's deputy, His steward on earth that can be called upon by youth workers because it corresponds closely to the core values of respect and response, of networking of communities and cultures, and of working with young people to make a positive contribution in and to the world.

Imam might be thought of as 'faith'; faith provides Muslims with the reason why they should act in certain prescribed ways. Discussion about Imam focuses on understanding, including the understanding of the religion's basic beliefs.

Imam might also be understood as the belief in one God, His Angels, and His Messengers, His revealed books, the Day of Judgement and Divine Decree. Other religions (the monotheistic faiths) believe that there is only one God but uniquely at the core of Islam is the belief that Muhammad is God's Messenger, and the last Prophet.

For Muslims, it is the example of Muhammad that they seek to emulate, for not only was he the human vehicle through which God revealed his Qur'an, but also he put into practice in his own life all that he said and did. Aisha, the Prophet's wife, was once asked what it was like living with him; she replied that if one reads the Qur'an one knows about Muhammad, and if one sees Muhammad, one knows about the Qur'an.

The third dimension of Islam is **Ihsan.** This might be understood as 'excellence'. To quote the eloquent Hussain:

Ihsan is to bring about a synthesis of the first two dimensions... within the human being so that one's whole being is fused with beauty, kindness and excellence.

Ihsan derives from the word *husn*, which means good and beautiful; essentially ihsan is about doing well. The Qur'an states,

Do what is beautiful. God loves those who do what is beautiful (2.195)
and
Pardon them and forgive; God loves those who do what is beautiful. (5.13)

Hussain explains that the root of the word Ihsan and its various derivatives is used some 194 times in the Qur'an. Just as the other two dimensions evolved into specialist fields of knowledge, the dimension of Ihsan is known as *Tasawwuf* or Sufism:

Its vocation and discipline is the perfection of character so that the human being may truly realise his or her role as the Khalifa (vice-regent) *of God on earth.*

Ihsan is to worship Allah as though you were seeing Him because He sees you. It is generally accepted that this *ihsani* intellectual tradition has produced much of Islam's greatest arts, architecture and literature. Its ethical and spiritual dimensions seek to cultivate that excellence of character, the *Akhlaq* that all Muslims seek for their children.

These three dimensions of Islam are the most important determinants in the life of any Muslim. Religion should supersede culture, class, country and clan. The essentials of this faith unite all Muslims, regardless of sectarian affiliation or adherence to different schools of thought, but faith has to be lived to be real.

The Prophet lived his faith and taught his faith daily. He demonstrated constantly that love, bounty, generosity and justice were the true values. He repeated to his companions that they should be good to one another, respect all living beings, nature and, most importantly of all, treat with equity all Muslims or non-Muslims, men or women, young or old.

The Prophet stressed the importance of family values, of kindness and of tolerance:

No one among you attains true Faith, until he likes for his brother what he likes for himself (An-Nawawi's Forty Hadith 13)

and

He is not a true Believer who eats his fill while his neighbour is hungry (Bayhaqi.)

There are examples of the Prophet administering justice in favour of Jews and other non-Muslims over Muslims, as the faithful have to be strict defenders of justice regardless of faith background. *Behold God enjoins justice and excellence* (7:157) (sincerity).

In Islam, this goes beyond the simple implementation of overt justice and moves into remembrance and the link with God, so as to nourish the notion of justice and bring the believer closer to the love and compassion of God. This is the central message in Tariq Ramadan's, *The Messenger: The Meaning of the life of Muhammad* (2007) where he aims to make the Prophet's life a mirror through which readers facing contemporary challenges can explore their hearts and minds and achieve an understanding of questions relating to being and meaning, as well as broader ethical and social concerns. For Prof. Ramadan,

...the Prophet's life is an invitation to a spirituality that avoids no question and teaches us... that the true answers to existential questions are more often given by the heart than by intelligence. Deeply, simply: he who cannot love cannot understand. (The introduction page x11)

It is these virtues, this drive, and this desire to be a true *khalifa* which has perhaps inspired many British Muslims to become active citizens both at local and national levels. The success of the London based *Muslim Youth Helpline*, for example, is testimony to the power of young Muslims both controlling their own destiny and influencing policy. Their seminal research project funded by the NYA, *Providing Faith and Culturally Sensitive Support Services to Young British Muslim* (2007) is unequivocal in advice to providers:

It is strongly felt that mainstream service providers must begin using faith as a key identity indicator in appreciating welfare needs of young British Muslims, and there is a need to develop service models that understand the socio-cultural faith and psychological dimensions of the lives of Muslim pupils. (Page 10 www.nya.org.uk).

Similarly, Birmingham's *Hear My Voice* (www.hmyv.org.uk) in their *Identifying Patterns in Muslim Young people's voices - a West Midlands Study* (2010) provide a clear and lucid statement of young Muslim's views and recommendations. The findings of both are echoed by the Islamic Foundation's Policy Research Centre's publication, *Seen and Not heard Voices of Young British Muslims* (Sughra Ahmed. 2009). Finally at the highest government level,

The Young Muslims Advisory Group (www.ymag.opm.co.uk) have provided well argued advice to government on a range of issues effecting service provision and government policy. The potential for young Muslims both to control their own destinies and influence events at the highest levels is clear.

There are obvious resonances with the aims of youth work, as they aspire to promote young people's active involvement in decision making and the democratic processes, while encouraging them to lead action to change communities for the better. There have also been indications that the British Coalition government see faith as an important factor in British society. Baroness Warsi, Muslim cabinet member and chair of the Conservative Party, in her speech to the Anglican Bishops in September 2010, unequivocally argued that the new coalition government, 'Does God'. For Warsi,

...the challenges of the late 20th century and early 21st century have revealed a world which is more religious than ever. It is a world where faith inspires, motivates and sustains ... We need to get the relationship between state, religion and society in sync with this new reality.

For her this means recognising fully the huge contribution of believers everywhere;

...and to do that, we need first and foremost a government which understands faith, which is comfortable with faith, and which when necessary, is prepared to speak out about issues of faith. (www.sayeedawarsi.com).

These sentiments were echoed by Communities Minister Andrew Stunell who, speaking to the annual Interfaith Network in the UK in July 2010, argued that faith groups are making a vital contribution to national life, and are integral to creating the Big Society. He believed that inter faith activity and faith groups were inspiring people to contribute to public service and providing support to those in need. For him,

Faith communities make a vital contribution to national life, guiding the moral outlook of many, inspiring great numbers of people to public service, providing succour to those in need. They are helping to bind together local communities and improve relations at a time when the siren call of extremism has never been louder...Inter faith activity is more important than ever in our work towards the Big Society, so I want to push for more inter faith dialogue and action rather than individual faith groups delivering social projects...The new Government sees it as part of the solution. I want to send an important signal that we value the role of religion and faith in public life... (www.communities.gov.uk)

At the start of their tenure the ConDem government also sent very clear signals about what it saw as the future role of youth work. Baroness Ritchie, chair of the Children and Young People Board at the Local Government Association, told delegates at the Confederation of Heads of Young People's Services conference that youth work was not viewed as a "luxury add-on" by the coalition and remained of vital importance. She said:

Youth work is essential to meet the coalition government's aspirations for young people. We know the contribution that youth work makes to the lives of young people – for many it's the pivotal moment that sets them on the path to success.

She added that youth work will be 'at the heart' of enabling young people to play an active role in the Big Society,

The Big Society is about building communities that are empowered to take control of their own futures and to create solutions working with local citizens....Youth work helps them understand their role in communities and to become active and engaged citizens. (www.cypnow.co.uk/news/)

The combination of the aims of the youth work, the apparent importance the government gave to faith based approaches and the centrality of Islam in the life of young Muslims provide key drivers for youth workers to examine their policies and practices with specific reference to their own faith based provision, in the context of *Every Muslim Child Matters.*

POLICY AND PRACTICE

There are twelve basic questions that act as template for audit and upon which youth work might fashion policy:-

1) **The policy**: do you have a policy/strategy that is specifically designed to meet the needs of your Muslim clients?

2) **The audit:** do you collect faith based statistics? Do you know, for example, the number, the gender, the participation rate, the location of your Muslim clients?

3) **The monitoring and evaluation**: do you monitor and evaluate the provision that is designed directly or indirectly to serve the needs of Muslims? What actions do you take a as a result of the data you collect?

4) **The provision**: do you offer provision that is specifically based upon the needs of your Muslim client? Is it any of it gender specific?

5) **The practice**: do Islamic values such as justice, compassion and service permeate your practices?

6) **The good practice**: are you aware of any good practice that particularly relates to Muslims? If so, how have you collected it and how will you disseminate it to maximise its impact?

7) **The work force**: how many of your workforce are Muslims? How many have an empathy and understanding of Muslim issues? What positions do they hold? If Muslims are underrepresented in your work force, what action are you taking to rectify the situation?

8) **The continuing professional development**: do all your providers build Islamic perspectives into their courses, conferences, coaching and mentoring wherever applicable?

9) **The work in the community**: does your service work directly with Muslim communities? Does it have a relationship with madrasahs (places of study) and mosques/ mosques committees?

10) **The Islamic heritage**: do you use the unique contributions that Islam has made to our modern world to raise students' self-esteem?
11) **The core curriculum**: do the values underpinning youth work include:
    – a commitment to preparing young Muslims for participation?
    – the promotion of acceptance and understanding of others drawn from the Muslim frame of reference?
    – the development of appropriate values and beliefs which permit Muslims to be Muslims whilst at the same time celebrating our cultural and religious diversity?
12) **The curriculum programme**: does your programme reflect Muslim perspectives whenever possible?

There are of course a whole set of assumptions and required knowledge behind these seemingly straightforward questions. There are no easy answers or quick fixes to issues that have their roots deep in our shared histories and narratives. The keys are mutual understanding and dialogue. The development and implementation of a Muslim youth strategy and the weight given to its components will vary from institution to institution, but there are a range of materials already available that can assist in this process.

The *Islam and Citizenship Education Project* (ICE) is one example. This government funded but community led project produced a series of lessons, originally designed for students in madrasahs, but now trailing in 100 independent Muslim schools and in other mainstream settings. The product of a unique collaboration between most mainstream schools of Islam throughout both Sunni and Shia, it offered a complete programme of study for Key Stage 3 pupils.

Moves are, however, underway to adapt this to an older audience. It takes as its starting point Key Stage 3 citizenship programmes of study and Islamises them; demonstrating the basic premise that being a good Muslim means in fact that you are a good citizen, because at one and the same time, you 'attain to faith and do good works'. The whole course is dedicated to increasing participants' *taqwa*, their 'God consciousness'.

Each lesson is written to a formula which includes citizenship values and Islamic values. Extensively trialled the feedback has been overwhelmingly positive and has attracted worldwide interest. All the lessons, a training package, and the background discussion paper, 'When hope and history rhyme' are available free of charge on line under creative commons license. (see www.theiceproject.com)

The ICE project materials are ideally suited to adaptation for youth work settings as they cover familiar themes like active citizenship, volunteering and giving charity, resolving conflict, rights and responsibilities and living and working with others. They are well matched to support making the staying safe, enjoy and achieve and making a positive contribution ECM outcomes. They do not shy away from contentious issues like jihad or gender equality.

THE POSITION OF WOMEN

It is perhaps another of the great paradoxes of Islam that some later 'interpretations' of the Qur'an and the sunnah have significantly shifted the radical nature of Islam's treatment of women. Historically, pre-Islamic Arabia was a hostile place to be if you were born female, as you had no rights and female infanticide was commonplace. Islam provided the potential to radically change this situation because:

- Women were allowed to own property and dispose of it without reference to their husband. This right was not secured for British women until 1882!
- Women have the same entitlement to education as men. It is not merely an entitlement but a duty. As one authentic hadith puts it, 'Seeking knowledge is compulsory for all Muslims (male and female).' During what is known as the Golden Age of Islam there were many female scholars and scientists and Fatima al Fihri founded a university in Morocco as early as 859 CE.
- Women have the right to reject a marriage proposal.
- Women have the same entitlement to be sexually fulfilled.
- Women can engage in business or professional affairs: indeed the first person to become a Muslim was Khadija, the Prophet's first and only wife for some years she was an extremely successful business woman in her own right.
- Women should be consulted in public affairs: there are many examples of the Prophet asking the opinion of women before coming to a decision on important matters.
- Women can keep control of their own earnings (Qur'an 4.32).

Other than bearing and nursing children there are no duties that a woman must do in the house. Indeed, the Prophet himself used to mend his own clothes, wash dishes and prepare food. He was especially fond of playing with and talking to children.

Encouragingly in the UK we now have Muslim women MPs, a Muslim woman cabinet member and an increasing number of successful Muslim women in all walks of life. Unfortunately this progress has yet to be replicated in the sporting arena. Muslims girls of course undertake a range of physical activities in schools, but few appear (even with hijab) on the national stage. However, there is no reason why people in the public eye need to make their faith overt. Fatima Whitbread, Britain's 1987 Olympic Javelin Champion came from a Turkish Cypriot background, a group that is around 99 percent Muslim. Dunia Susi, Eniola Aluko, and Anita Asante are all England football internationals; Anita is of Ghanaian decent, Eniola Nigerian and Dunia is from Enfield, London. At just over 50 percent Islam is the largest faith group in Nigeria. Over 15 percent of Ghanaians are Muslims, while London has the biggest Muslim population in the UK (over a million) and (for instance) 66 per cent of Turkey-born Muslims in London live in four north London boroughs (Enfield, Hackney,

Haringey, Islington). Given this, it's hard to say anything too definitive about the involvement of female Muslims in sport. We do, however, have the Muslim Women's Sports Foundation which works to create access for Muslim women to participate in a range of sporting activities without comprising their Islamic values. (www.mwsf.org.uk).

This lack of involvement is all the more strange as the Prophet explicitly extolled the virtues of sport especially swimming, archery and horse riding and there is a touching story of the Prophet and his wife Aisha, whilst on a journey, racing each other and she outpaced him.

Youth work is ideally placed to promote single sex sporting activities to meet these sensitivities. There remain, however, many other sensitivities and youth workers will need to respond, even if this does mean providing gender specific provision as this might well be the only provision that some Muslim parents will permit for their daughters.

Young Muslim women do however attend madrasahs, as do their sons. Although there are no accurate figures, it is estimated that up to half as million young people attend after school or weekend madrasahs at least up to the age of 14. This might be seen as one of the most successful examples of youth provision in the country.

The ICE project has demonstrated that with careful planning, a process that is inclusive and a great willingness to listen and act on Muslim advice, those responsible for madrasah education can be brought more closely into the mainstream without compromising their integrity. Youth work might usefully consider how it might be able to liaise effectively with madrasahs. A good starting point would be to consult with the Mosques and Imams Advisory Board - MINAB (www.minab.org.uk). Amongst other things, discussions could well centre on issues like youth work, recreational activities, residential settings and youth workers in madrasahs. The Karimia Institute have pioneered such an approach and employ four youth workers, funded from their own sources (http://karimia.com).

It will take time and imagination to adapt ICE for youth service settings. No such issues arise with the UK Race and Europe networks /Runnymede Trust's 'Young Muslim and Citizen-identity empowerment and change'. This provides a series of activities for parents, teachers and youth workers. The comprehensive downloadable pack consists of 18 activities and practical approaches which can be delivered in a range of settings to a variety of audiences. Advised by young people, tried and tested, there is even a youth based activity entitled 'Every Muslim Child Matters'. The pack is available from the Runnymede Trust (www.runnymedetrust.org).

YOUNG MUSLIMS UNDER ATTACK

Identity is a key that permeates much of these materials and was at the heart of the ECM agenda. The rise of Islamophobia and much of the mainstream negative media treatment of Muslims has led many young Muslims to feel that they and their faith are under attack. This attack exists not merely in the present, but also in interpretations of the past, in how people perceive the Muslim contribution to the modern world. Here too enormous strides have been taken to achieve historical accuracy; to counter what Professor Salim al-Hassani calls the '…missing 1000 years of Islamic history.' His brilliant and seminal book *1001 Inventions: Muslim Heritage In Our World* (FSTC 2006) is now accompanied by a range of resources, many of which are freely downloadable. (www.1001 inventions.com and www.CE4CE.org).

Entering the 1001 website takes you on a magical journey with their Library of Secrets download staring Sir Ben Kingsley, which over the period of a few months took over one million hits. There are posters and a teaching resource 'City 1250', and 'How Do Ideas Travel?' which brings together history and science activities in a major piece of curriculum innovation. The 1001 materials are as important to non-Muslims as they are to Muslims because they address issues that are common to a better understanding of the place of Islam in our contemporary world and can help to address some of the Islamophobic negativity.

The same is true of MYX which is the 'one-stop shop' for people who want to help Christian and Muslim young people get together. Designed for youth workers, faith leaders and young people, it is designed to offer a range of practical activities like:-
- Becoming an MYX Group
- Setting aims and objectives
- Finding Young People
- Finding Leaders
- Running an Event – Practical Issues
Their hope is that through their resources they can inspire many MYX groups to set up across the country, so that Christian and Muslim youth grow up in the UK with friends of other faiths. Many of the activities they promote can be used for other groups in different circumstances for they too, at their heart, have the ECM agenda. (see www.myxencounter.org/index.php)

CONCLUSION

The EMYM agenda is daunting, especially given the demise of Youth Services nationally under the ConDem regime that, at the time or writing, seems to have betrayed much of their rhetoric before and just after the General Election of 2010. But the imperatives are pressing. The willingness to act however is still present and youth workers need to make the most of this in what is perhaps the darkest hour since the inception of a national service in the early 1960s. Unless we actively take on the Muslim frame of reference and think creatively and radically about provision for Muslims youth, and combine our ideas into an overarching strategy and implementation plan, we will continue to lament a lack of provision and a limited range of approaches, while the position of Muslims in Britain will have change little and probably for the worse.

BIBLIOGRAPHY

Ahmed, S. (2009). *Seen and not heard voices of young British Muslims.* Policy Press.

Al-Hassani, S. T. S. (2006). *1001 inventions: Muslim heritage in our World.* FSTC.

Brice, K. (2011). *A minority within a minority: A report on converts to Islam in the United Kingdom, faith matters.* Swansea University on behalf of Faith Matters.

Coles, M. (2008). *Every Muslim child matters.* Trentham.

Every Child Matters. (DfES 2004).

Hussain, M. (2008). *Oxford Muslim pupils' empowerment programme: Empowering pupils' through education.* Eton College.

Malik, R., Shaikh, A., & Suleyman, M. (2007). *Providing faith and culturally sensitive support services to young British Muslim.* NYA/Muslim Youth Helpline.

National Youth Agency. (2007). *Providing faith and culturally sensitive support services to young British Muslim.* NYA.

Ramadan, T. (2007). *The messenger: The meanings of the life of Muhammad.* Oxford University Press.

Websites:

www.communities.gov.uk

www.CE4CE.org

www.cypnow.co.uk/news/

http://karimia.com

www.theiceproject.com

www.minab.org.uk

www.mwsf.org.uk

(www.nya.org.uk)

www.myxencounter.org/index.php

www.runnymedetrust.org

www.sayeedawarsi.com

www.teachernet.gov.uk/wholeschool/

www.hmyv.org.uk)

www.1001 inventions.com

REFLECTIONS ON YOUTH WORK PRACTICE

ANON

8. LIVING ISLAM

The following is the life story of a person (who asked not to be identified for personal reasons) from a Muslim background and a description of a cultural experience in a particular manifestation of the Turkish Cypriot community, within an Islamic heritage.

The focus of the piece is not Islam as a religion, but the cultural traditions of a particular group of people in a specific social situation, one that might be recognizable to many. It reflects an Islam as practiced (or not) in a unique family context (as all families are to a greater or lesser extent).

This chapter includes reflections on the development of a youth worker coming from Muslim traditions, in Britain. It is included to provide a comparative experience and it is hoped this will be helpful in terms of reflecting on personal and social values, experience and the circumstances of those we come into contact with as part of our work.

A PERSONAL PERSPECTIVE ON ISLAM

I begin to write this piece with a definite feeling of who I am and how faith has impacted on my identity and path in life. I am a Muslim; I always have been and always will be a Muslim. In that sense it is the start and conclusion of all things in my life. But being 'of Islam' has a more expansive influence on how I see the world and my own place in it. I am aware that I do not 'practice' being a Muslim in a way that others might, but there are also many Muslims world wide that have similar outlooks to mine with regard to their faith. The human who thinks they know how all Muslims should be has, I think, lost more than what they might believe they have gained. We, as humans, are of course, each one of us, fallible. For me God knows that and as he is merciful can forgive us our failures if we are willing to identify them and, if we can, do something about them. I suppose I think that knowing that I am imperfect, that I will make mistakes, about myself and others, may be more helpful than forgetting it, which can lead one to think one knows what is right for oneself and everyone else; in short, coming to believe that one is God.

For all this, Islam, for me, is a 'way of being', which encompasses a whole range of attitudes, indeed most of the means by which one lives ones life. You might call this a 'cultural' or 'community' influence, although I'm not sure that

B. Belton and S. Hamid (eds), Youth Work and Islam:
A leao of faith for young people,115–125.

would quite capture the 'oceanic' character of what it is to come from a 'tradition of Islam'.

The 'effect' of Islam is in most of my responses to the world; it is almost instinctive now. I'm not 'being good' (when I am good – which I'm not as good at as I'd like to be) or because that is what the faith I was born into says I should be. To an extent that work has been done. At my best, I do what I do because that seems like the correct thing to do and that 'correctness' is set in the very foundations of Islam (it is who I am). I do not often consciously force myself to be a 'good' Muslim, but I would say (and hope) that overall I am a good person and I believe that is partly because I am a Muslim. That said, I also feel that as a Muslim I don't have a monopoly on goodness; I believe there are and have experience of Christians, Humanists, Hindus, Buddhists and Jews who act, react and feel much the same as I do in terms of their relationship between their day-to-day life and their belief.

Yes, I make mistakes and in my time I have been 'naughty'. If any of us think otherwise we are saying something like, 'I am better than human'. Of course, apart from being a little mad, statements like the latter are a blasphemy (the two often seem to mean the same thing); being human is to err. However, being a Muslim and being of Islam draws us into an idea that we can, and probably should, strive to err less and look towards, in simplistic terms, making the world a better place (not a worse place at least). This is something we can do, which doesn't necessarily involve making people more like some me or some abstract idea of an 'us'. This only creates dichotomies (good/bad etc.) and such cleavages, schisms and categorisations, which are really acts of violence as, in the last analysis, they involve people more or less aggressively, becoming set on dividing the world up. This practice does not really have much of a track record for making things better.

Therefore, in Islam I accept who I am but that 'I' has a purpose to become something of an instrument to 'refine experience'; how I experience others, how I experience myself, how others experience me. The experience of the precepts of the Muslim faith and being 'of Islam', I believe (have faith?) have, for me, enhanced this process. Again, this does not preclude other faiths from providing something similar, but here I am writing about me, so I'm writing about Islam (Islam and me are inseparable as I am at one with my faith).

The Christian mystic and thinker, Abbess Hildegard of Bingham once wrote 'I am a feather on the breath of God' and I think that reflects something of the notion of 'submission' that is entwined in the Muslim faith. However, what is often missed out when thinking about this is that this submission, just to be 'a feather on the breath of God', is an exacting discipline, but one that is basic to Islam as a tradition. Particularly in the contemporary period perhaps, what might be called humility or even modesty seem to contradict the ambitions and expectations that society has for any one of us. But that submission, accepting who we are and working on that, seems to me to be not a bad place to start in the context of youth work. Certainly it is where my Islam starts from and goes to, although I also accept the process has no end. But Muslim thinkers have indicated this for centuries.

At the same time God has made me more than a feather; I (like most human beings) am a very special feather. I have metaphorical sails, a rudder, a moral compass and in the Qur'an a map by which I can navigate myself through life. I (you) have been given responsibility and the means to work out the consequences of our actions.

There are many responses to Islam world wide, as will be evident from what follows, this is not without its challenges when people from different traditions come into contact or enter into relationships. There are those who will become embroiled in debates and arguments about which is 'wrong' or 'right' but I'm not sure how far this gets us or why, in general, someone wants to 'convert' another from their cultural/community perspective to another - the Qur'an counsels against such ambitions

Wilt thou compel men to become believers? No soul can believe but by the leave of God. (99-100, Qur'an 10)

But faith apart, it all feels a bit like colonialism, which historically wasn't really a successful response to any group.

Carving up our work to show we have been involved with people who share national, cultural and maybe religious backgrounds, for all sorts of reasons, sometimes has to be done, but does it always need to be done? For instance, it is not unusual to hear someone claim they are 'working with the Muslims community.' I can't help wondering which Muslim community they might be talking about; Sunni, Shi'a? Were any of the group Suffi? Would this make any difference? If it happens that the people referred to live in a prescribed area, does this make them a community anymore than a group of British (English, Scottish, Irish, Welsh) Christians (Catholics, Presbyterians, Baptists) living in New York (Bronx, Queens, Brooklyn) involved in a range of interests and employment?

Even a blanket referral to (for instance) 'Bangladeshi culture' and in particular gender relations within this grouping, seems a bit amorphous. What Bangladeshi culture is, to some extent dependant on where it is being expressed (Bangladesh/California/ Ipswich). I have found it a common practice to conflate ideas about the basis of traditions and social interaction, some of which could be national, cultural or rooted in lore related to religion/status (or any combinations of these factors and others).

I think I have learnt to listen to different perspectives and have found that asking questions takes me further than forms of categorization, patronization or condemnation, simplistically saying or implying 'this is what Islam is and all it is' or 'that's 'good' Islam' and 'that's bad Islam' (or not Islam at all). All faiths are made up of diverse communities and the person who believes they will 'unite' the faith by one form of preaching or another is hardly being modest. Perhaps at best we can grow in our understanding of Islam by holding on to its organic and expansive nature. You might be able to oblige someone to conform by brute force or guilt or fear of damnation to some particular set of precepts or practices, but is that propagating what might be called 'the spirit of Islam'? Do we want people to 'believe', 'behave' or conform? What is it to 'want' another person to 'do' something?

I became the first full time, qualified, Turkish Cypriot youth and community worker in London in 1979 and youth officer in Hackney in 1991. I have worked in the voluntary and statutory sector in both formal and informal educational settings.

I have looked back over my experiences and asked myself a few questions about my beliefs and value system and how I overcame my personal conflicts.

My parents arrived in London in 1950, as did so many others from all over the world at that time, to escape poverty, war, persecution or just to find a better quality of life. My parents were peasants who had received an elementary education until the age of twelve, and then did whatever work they could find to be fed. Following the end of World War Two, in 1945, the British economy was still weak and so food was still being rationed when my parents came to the UK.

I remember listening to my mother telling me, my four sisters and brother stories of hunger and beatings but always ending with "we were poor but we were happy, El Hamdurillah!" Although my parents were not devout Muslims, they did raise us to practice certain rituals and celebrate our religion and culture. Thanking God's will was something that was done automatically, without thinking because we were conditioned from a young age to accept that God or Allah in our house was responsible for our lot in life and nothing could change that. I watched the film *East is East* on television the other day and laughed because it depicted our household so accurately, except my parents were both Turkish, but the conflicts and identity clashes we experienced were the same.

My father was very controlling and used religion to reinforce his authority. However, it is ironic that when we were young and he wanted peace and quiet at home, we would all be sent to Christian Sunday school (it was actually more of a multi-cultural youth club) where we did Bible Studies and learnt scriptures. At other times he would refuse to sign letters from school for us to go to church for Harvest Festival or Christmas Carol Service. Although, as a Muslim, he accepted Jesus as a prophet, he did not want us to be involved in Christian acts of worship.

He tore down a picture of Father Christmas we had stuck on the wall in our lounge, telling us we did not celebrate Christmas because we were Muslims and to wait for Eid. Although his actions seemed harsh at the time to a five year old, I later understood that he was trying to retain our religion and culture while we were young and too frightened to challenge his authority. We took our lead from our mother who never questioned what her husband said or did.

In our culture boys were revered and indulged, so imagine my parents' disappointment when they produced four daughters and only one prodigal son who unfortunately had severe learning difficulties or ESN (educationally sub-normal) as he was called in those bygone ages. My brother went to the local 'backward' school as it was known and was badly bullied because he was fat and did not speak English. This became significant later on as we were growing up.

Being a Muslim girl was not a problem as long as you followed the rules. When I was young, I did not eat pork, show bare flesh or speak to boys, not even male cousins (marriage between cousins was practiced). I accepted (thought) that this was how everyone was raised because I did not know any different. We were not allowed to mix with other children in our street or in the community because my parents were afraid the English or other cultures would corrupt us. Again, we were told stories of Muslim girls who disobeyed their parents, refused to have an arranged marriage, and became prostitutes, a common theme in a lot of Muslim films I saw and one, which is still slow to change even today.

It was expected that Muslim young women were virgin brides and her family waited to be shown evidence of her chastity once the marriage had been consummated. Only then could the family celebrate that they had succeeded as Muslim parents. This was certainly the case with my eldest sister who had an arranged marriage in 1981 and is something I witnessed regularly when I was in Egypt.

My husband is Egyptian. His family have a much more 'traditional' heritage of Islam relative to my own background. The reputation of the whole extended family is at stake regarding a young woman's purity but nothing is said about a male's chastity.

There is much debate about honour killings now but there was little awareness or action to challenge this in my childhood. I recall some of my friends suddenly disappearing from school during the summer holidays and not returning, or tales of families who had decided to 'emigrate'. I sometimes wonder how they fared.

For me, as a girl growing up, everything was fine until my sisters and I went to secondary school and began to see life from a different perspective. We went to a single sex school so we would not be 'corrupted' by young men.

My father had decided that when we were sixteen he would arrange our careers and marriages, but by this point in our lives we had set our sights on getting the education our parents never had, finding a well-paid job and leaving home to lead an independent life. This caused arguments and violence as my father felt justified in meting out punishment for our ingratitude. "I give you life, I take it away," he would shout as he kicked, punched and beat us with belts and sticks. His violence did not escape my mother who was completely downtrodden and subservient to him and believed he had the right to abuse her because she was 'only a woman'. My father did not respect women and I believe he learnt this from his own father who was even more violent and abusive towards his wife and daughters.

Later, as I entered youth work, it was hard to know what to say to a young woman who told me that she is going to run away from home because her parents were arranging her marriage. The treatment this young woman was experiencing felt 'wrong' but by that time I had been part of a wider culture very different from the one my parents or this young woman's parents had grown up in.

It has become something of a cliché for those looking to critique the Muslim faith and more broadly Islam to cite experiences and reports of the abuse of women in particular cultures or communities. However, I like Nawal El Saadawi's views on such matters and her praise of an early Islam in which 'women had an active role' in community and cultural affairs.

But, the oppression of women is not something restricted to a few designated Muslim communities. There are particular instances in various faith communities and in communities with no faith traditions at all where the oppression of women is routine.

Like Saadawi I do not believe that the position of women can be addressed by the referral to one group of people or even one family. Taking a more global perspective it seems that the abuse and oppression of women is sustained by ignorance, social pressures and sometimes government policy rather than being something 'of faith'. The bottom line in most religions is to treat all people with respect and decency, and expect the same from others. Where the overt oppression of women is evidently sustained we probably need to look very closely at the situations before jumping to conclusions that they have any one source. At the same time we might consider that what one person sees as liberation might be another's idea of oppression. Some women might want the 'freedom' to go to work, others might not see this the same way; freedom hardly ever comes for free – as the influential economist and social commentator Thomas Sowell had it *Freedom has cost too much blood and agony to be relinquished at the cheap price of rhetoric.* And according to Thomas Jefferson *Freedom is the recognition that no single person, no single authority or government has a monopoly on the truth.*

However, my grandfather was a deeply religious man who read the Qur'an and regularly went to the Mosque in Finsbury Park. He was highly respected in the Turkish Cypriot community. The fact that he was so abusive was irrelevant to most of the family and friends. Women needed to know their place, to serve their husband, and their father, both of whom were considered as her master. It was a very Victorian attitude being upheld in Islington in the 1960s with women as chattels.

At school, I was encouraged to have my own opinions and listen to the point of view of others My teachers were influential in preparing me for my future career and I found that I could talk to some of them openly about my ambitions as well as my home circumstances that were becoming difficult. They were careful not to offer a personal opinion about the pressures I was under regarding my culture (there were many Muslim young women at the school). But they tried to be as supportive as possible without appearing to take sides. My teachers were good role models, but I feel they could have done more to protect the young women who were being oppressed and abused by their families. The Every Child Matters agenda arrived too late for them! You can see why I worry that it looks to be on the way out now. It seems we currently have a government who cares little, or perhaps they just don't know very much about the potential for divisions and injustice in society and how easily they can appear.

At the age of sixteen, I got my first paid job as a youth worker at a summer scheme. This was on the recommendation of the play centre supervisor at my primary school where they had an after school play centre I attended with my siblings when we were young. This was the opportunity I was waiting for; money, independence and freedom to make decisions. My summer with young children was rewarding and can be seen as my introduction into youth work.

I decided that I wanted to work with young people and started to do voluntary youth work at St. Francis Church Centre, Islington two evenings a week. The young people from the local estates were mixed ethnically and most were deprived and disadvantaged. Drugs and crime were common and the church was broken into several times with the sweets and takings from the tuck shop stolen. Reverend P...... or 'The Rev', as he was called by the young people, was forgiving and understanding. He continued to open the club as he believed that to take away the only meeting place for young people in the local area would result in major problems and drive them onto the streets. Unfortunately, many estate-based youth clubs/centres were closed over the years with predictable results. This of course got worse than we ever could have imagined possible as from 2011 the ConDem coalition cut local authority funding to the bone and so strangled voluntary services supported by funding from the local state.

The 'Rev' was a member of the local area youth committee and had a degree in youth work. The young people never took notice of the fact that he was a vicar and he never tried to indoctrinate or preach to the members of the youth club, the membership of which represented practically all faiths/religions. It amused me to think that two of my sisters, my Jamaican friend, who was a Rastafarian and the 'Rev', were running the youth club without any consideration for the fact it was in a church. However, I believe the 'Rev' certainly saw the club as saving souls, but never tried to recruit them to his congregation. He practiced community work without overtly preaching. There was a need and we felt we were making a difference to the lives of young people through the discussions and activities that we offered, in what was seen by parents and the community as a safe haven. I learnt that I could function in my Turkish Cypriot community as well as other communities without compromising myself. I was able to overcome the stereotyping I experienced as a youth worker in a similar way to the 'Rev' but it took years for others to accept the work I was doing. Why would a twenty-one year old, unmarried, young woman want to undertake 'dangerous' work outside of her own culture and give herself and her family a bad reputation?

My mother would lie to my father when he asked where we were on the youth club nights, as she knew he would disapprove, as would members of our community. She would often ask why we were doing the voluntary work and warn us not to let the 'Rev' try to convert us to Christianity, as she thought we were naïve and may be tempted to give up our values and culture. In fact, the thought had never entered our minds, but I can understand their fears, particularly remembering the difficulties with mixed marriages at the time, not the least being decisions that had to be made about the religion children would follow; this could become fraught from both perspectives when observant Muslim families found themselves suddenly linked by blood and the law to devout Catholics. Someone should write a book or a film about that one day – the dramatic potential almost matches the prospective comedic content. This 'meeting of cultures' sometimes felt more like 'the war of the worlds'! Both of my younger sisters married non-Muslims (English and Welsh).

London today is a much more diverse city than it was in the 1970s when I first started working in the Youth Service. 'Equal Opportunities' was the buzz phrase along with 'positive discrimination'. In fact there were few full time qualified Black, Muslim, Ethnic minority youth workers, and those that were, did not get senior positions. The same applied to schools and colleges where head teachers were predominantly white, middle class men.

Although I originally trained as an English teacher, I chose to go into youth and community work. My first full time youth club was in King's Cross in 1979; the membership was predominantly Black Afro Caribbean. My family wanted me to be a teacher because it was a respectable job. As such they were horrified when I told them I had found a job in King's Cross (then a notorious red light district in London). 'You prostitute!' my father would shout. My reputation amongst the Turkish community was terrible as I had chosen a career that was not understood or appreciated then and even now, many would deter their daughters from being a youth worker. I had stepped outside of the norms of my community and my father felt I was being forced into a different community where I would be more readily accepted.

Then as now, explaining youth and community work was not easy and when I gave answers such as, 'I think I can make a difference to young people lives' or 'It's about working with communities to take action to bring about positive change'. I would be ridiculed as a 'Mother Theresa' or accused of sacrificing myself and my culture as a martyr for the good of others.

Many thought I was being paid to play table tennis or snooker, but those activities were tolerated. When I took young people on residentials (at that time it was mostly camping) around the UK and to Europe, there was outrage that I was staying and sleeping away from home (I lived at home with my parents until I was twenty-six years old, which was normal in the north London Turkish Cypriot community at the time).

Rumours were rife throughout my youth work career; from sleeping with men and not being a virgin, to being a Lesbian, because I had not married (homophobia has not changed and Gay relationships are still considered sinful in a number of religions). I cannot deny that I was very hurt by the way I was being portrayed, particularly, probably mostly, as there was no truth in the rumours about my lack of decency. I was also upset because my parents and extended family were blamed for the way I had turned out. I was still determined to be a youth worker and face the challenges. The youth club members and staff initially tested me out, which was expected, as they were curious to find out why I was working with them and not my own Turkish community. They wanted to know if I was a strict Muslim or whether I was 'Europeanized'. They were curious if I would consider dating Black men, as they were unsure of how they should treat me or if they had to follow certain protocols. I had an awareness of many cultures and aimed to treat people equally and respectfully. The relationships I developed meant that I did not have to prove myself to them in the same way I felt I had to within my own community.

The focus of my practice was drug and crime prevention and involved detached and outreach work. I was quite tough and assertive and this helped me to survive relatively unscathed, although, I was attacked a few times by people who were under the influence of drugs. I saw this as a learning experience and avoided the most dangerous situations thereafter, but I never told my family what had happened to me. I did not want their fears to be confirmed that I could not handle the pressures of the job.

I spoke about my brother earlier and the fact that he had learning difficulties and as a result was treated as a waste of time by my father, who was embarrassed by the fact that his one and only heir was only capable of performing 'menial' or 'manual' work. Males were 'prized' in many communities and, as you might have gathered from what I have written above, sexism was generally perceived as normal. My father hated the fact that all his daughters were well educated and earned a good salary. He would warn people not to educate their daughters, as they were more likely to rebel and bring shame on them. Instead, for him, marriages needed to be arranged as soon as possible as this would resolve the problem.

Unfortunately, my brother left his special school without qualifications and worked in a garage repairing tyre punctures. However, in his spare time he would help children to make go-carts, fix their bikes, make kites etc. He became a well-known character in the local area as he also helped the elderly by tidying their gardens, taking them shopping and doing chores. He is still doing the same thing now.

In his own way, he was doing voluntary youth and community work and making a contribution. His actions to that extent are those of a 'good Muslim' but like me, he does these things because he does them, not to be pious or sanctimonious. The fact that he has overcome peoples' prejudices of having 'special needs' should have been a cause for celebration but he was treated as a village idiot by my family and nothing he did was taken seriously.

In some ways, in the last few decades there are more opportunities to be involved in youth work (although sadly this looks destined to change) but attitudes are slow to alter. Had I been a Muslim male would I have met the same challenges? I doubt I would have been expected to leave school, marry and have children or been the subject of gossip in the community.

I worked mainly with young offenders and people with drug issues and as a result I developed a wide network of multi-agency work. Becoming a youth officer was quite an achievement, but it was still not considered a respectable job. In addition, I was still unmarried, but by this point, nobody was interested as I was too old in the eyes of the family unless there was a divorcee or widower available.

As a youth officer I sat on management committees of many cultural youth organizations in the voluntary sector in Hackney; Chinese, Vietnamese, Jewish, Pakistani, Bangladeshi, Kurdish, Turkish, Afro-Caribbean etc. When I walked into one, the youth worker thought I was a parent collecting her child. I was told I did not look like a youth officer. At another, I was given various excuses as to why I could not attend the all male committee meetings. I knew it was sexism and stereotyping. Sadly I'm not sure those involved did; it was just the way they were and they expected the world to merely follow their way unquestioningly. The reality is the world just doesn't work that way. Culture is fine until it insists on practicing blanket injustice; at the point that culture becomes the camouflage of oppression and inequality, so effectively it has given a hand in its own demise.

Being taken seriously as a woman and a youth worker or youth officer and having to fight discrimination made me a stronger and more determined as a person. I have, as a Muslim, a woman, and a person concerns about injustice, and have consistently challenged, questioned and argued against the senseless and wasteful tyranny of the many by the few; for me it would be contradictory to Islamic principles to do otherwise.

I have always been outspoken and this has not endeared me to others, especially where there is a belief that women's roles in life are preordained. I have succeeded in my career and given an example for many women to enter a profession that is full of challenges and conflicts.

Young people deserve youth workers, teachers and social workers who represent their identity and culture, but at the same time there is a need to be cautious that we are not pigeon-holed according to our faith and cultures. 'Getting in a Muslim' to work with young Muslims can feel like a sort of disguised prejudice; 'all Muslims are the same, job done!' Amongst the basic tools of the youth worker are being able to understand, embrace and sometimes tolerate or question young people's attitudes and outlooks. An intolerant Muslim is about as good a youth worker as an intolerant atheist. But none of us are entirely tolerant. We are all tolerant to the point where we will not tolerate something any longer. The 'good' youth worker, Muslim or otherwise, has some awareness of this and what to do about it.

As a youth and a youth worker I have found that it is not approval, disapproval of or neutrality towards young people that provides the basis of a working relationship, but if a young person is convinced that a youth worker has awareness on their (the young person's) situation, or at least is in a position to learn about their situation from them (in our best incarnation, perhaps we are more often those who are educated than educators) then we can work alongside young people as they create their own world of identity and action. This might be what the great educationalist Frederick Froebel (1885) called the 'divine spark'; recognizing the divinity of humanity as the creation of God.

Finally it is fair to say that having lived in a multi-faith, multi-ethnic society has caused me to almost constantly reappraise my views and feelings about being a Muslim and my experience of my Islamic heritage. But if anything this has made me more secure in who I am and how I want to be. As a Muslim I (like all other Muslims and all other people) do have a choice in terms of the way I am understood by others. I can either leave it up to the media etc. to portray me as just a mere representation of an imagined mass or I can have an influence on how I am seen by my behaviour and example. There is not much evidence to show that complaining about how others see us will change the perception of how we are seen (whatever our faith background).

It was Muhammad Ali, a Muslim of some repute, who once said that if a person has the same views at 50 that they had when they were 20 then they have wasted 30 years of their life. For me the foundation has stayed the same; however it has been embellished and sometimes scarred by the developments that have taken place in my life.

For the renowned architect Richard Rogers, creativity arises out of constraint; we have to innovate to overcome limitations. I think being Muslim or a Christian or a Buddhist or a Hindu or a humanist or a Marxist might help one do this, but 'might' like 'if' is a big little word. In the end, as the practice of youth work has shown me, it is how we do things, our ability to take responsibility for and deal with the consequences of our actions that turn 'mights' and 'ifs' into potential and actuality. That process is something inherent in being a youth worker as well as in being a Muslim and the oceanic experience of Islam.

BIBLIOGRAPHY

Froebel, F. (1885). *The education of man.* Appleton-Century Co.
El Saadawi, N. (1980). *The hidden face of eve.* Beacon Pr.
El Saadawi, N. (1885). *God dies by the Nile.* Zed Books Ltd.

FIRZANA KHAN

9. YOUNG MUSLIMS AND MARGINALISATION

Firzana Khan has been a youth work practitioner for ten years, and is currently working as a fundraiser for a Youth Charity, Frenford Club and is a tutor at the YMCA George Williams College in London.

Firzana pent 9 years working in High Wycombe in Buckinghamshire at Green Street Youth and Community Centre, in the heart of the Black community in Central Wycombe. She also has experience of working with Muslim young women, running an Asian young women's project for 8 years.

Firzana has worked as a full time Centre based worker working across different parts of High Wycombe and Buckinghamshire, deployed on a range of projects. She has also worked intensively with housing and homelessness, benefits, welfare entitlement affecting young people and teenage pregnancy issues.

When appointed in 2004 Firzana was one of the youngest Connexions PAs ever appointed in the country.

INTRODUCTION; 'WEAK POWER'

Often the youth worker role involves targeted work with specifically defined groups, the 'disaffected', the 'excluded' etc. This might included people categorised according to their perceived culture, ethnicity or race, sexuality, age or religion. In this Chapter I will call on my knowledge and experience as a youth work practitioner. However my personal familiarity with being defined as member of marginal groups, as a woman, as Muslim and as a representative of a minority ethnic group, by society, the state and the media cannot be divorced from my analysis. At the same time I am clear that naming a group as 'marginal' is effectively labelling that group; of course this involves a process of one group being labelled and that group accepting that label (although this process is hardly ever an equal partnership between the forces that label and those that embrace, tolerate or accept the label).

I grew up in High Wycombe, Buckinghamshire and lived in the Oakridge and Castlefield ward. What follows is written from my background working with Muslim young people from this area; individuals and groups who have been labelled as marginalised.

Labelling does bring some advantages, using what Hall (1991) described as 'weak power' marginality becomes an asset. For Hall;

B. Belton and S. Hamid (eds), Youth Work and Islam:
A leao of faith for young people,127–134.

Paradoxically, marginality has become a powerful space. It is a space of weak power, but it is a space of power nonetheless.

This is 'weak power' as it confirms, endorses and extends marginality; a cost that might be thought to more than outweigh the admitted benefits. According to Hall the oppressed and relatively powerless are placed at the fringes of society and as such lack access to the conventional routes to power. As a response they can make the source of their marginality an asset by cooperating with wider social and economic forces and processes in 'categoric corralling'; that is, they take part in a trade that posits identity as a currency that can be exchanged for a level of influence over resources and/or the management or even measures of political authority

One of the implications of working exclusively with young Muslims is that the advantages of solidarity and cultural homogeneity can effectively result in a form of apartheid ('separate development') with clients identifying themselves as 'different' (accepting the label) and so identifying less with the wider sphere of social inequality.

THE PROCESS AND CONSEQUENCE OF MARGINALISATION

In the first part of the Twenty-first century, Islam in the West has been increasingly understood as the source an often vague and omnipresent anxiety, the most straightforward signification of which is visible difference. This can be as innocuous as a young woman wearing a headscarf to school. However, difference is also emphasised in most youth work with young Muslims, which tends to result in the segregation of Muslim youth. This effectively confirms the labelling of this group as being 'different', involved in mysterious (covert) activities and therefore 'dangerous'?

While particular groups of Muslims are marginalised by what might be thought of as external influences, they can also marginalise each other. We might all (Muslim and non-Muslim) be understood as both confirming and conforming to the production of culture; people create their own culture at the same time as they adopt cultural models that are socially generated. It is probably fair to say that many Muslims would perceive themselves as adhering to traditional practices which are intrinsic in them forming, sustaining and developing their own culture. However, it might be generally agreed that flexibility is limited; departures from a given practice norm could mean becoming marginalised (or even ostracised – there is a fine line between these 'treatments' in any situation) within ones own culture.

Clothing is a subject to a great deal of attention as a marker of Muslim identity and as such a means of marginalisation. Young women in particular are often labelled within their communities as being 'too westernised', or are made the subject of controversy beyond the boundaries of their community as they fail to fully comply with 'mainstream' dress conventions. But there is no real consensus amongst young Muslims, for example one young person told me;

I don't know about the scarf. There are more and more women wearing it now. Obviously that is part of being 'a good Muslim girl' but sometimes you also associate those who wear scarves with being bad as well because sometimes they wear it to cover up their own bad things that they do

Another response exposed how the idea of 'Muslim dress' is in itself something of an imagined category:

Muslim or Pakistani? .... Muslim clothes would be the long Aabayah, Jilbaab and Pakistani would be Shalwar Kameez

As a Muslim female, I feel there is a pressure to conform to avoid being marginalised within my own community. But I also feel that I do have the flexibility to design and live within my own culture, including the way I dress. However, a woman who wears a headscarf but smokes might be more at risk of marginalisation in some communities than she might be if she dressed in 'Western' style and didn't smoke openly in public places. A fear of being marginalised within a community is perhaps more powerful when that community is itself marginalised. I choose to take, what I see as, a balanced approach in terms of how I behave and dress. I see echoes of this when working with some Muslim young people who are enacting/creating their own culture while at the same time looking to respect their family's feelings.

As a youth worker I have asked myself if the promotion of conformity within a marginalised group is altogether helpful for that group as people seek out ways to escape social marginalisation (being sidelined by society) while fearing marginalisation within their own marginalised community. This complex situation is made more confused as Muslims recognise that as a marginalised group they are not being treated equally. Young Muslims of course are part of another marginalised grouping; youth, who are clearly not treated equally to adults.

The state response to marginality is often to provide funding that is ostensibly aimed at stopping/preventing marginalisation. But this in effect rewards those who take on the label of 'the marginalised'; there is an incentive to enter the 'marginalised category' - to be defined within a prescribed set of criteria (often not designed by those being defined) to obtain the benefits/funding/resources. This is 'weak power'.

HIATUS IN HIGH WYCOMBE

The National Statistics Census of 2001 showed that 3,509 Muslims lived in the Oakridge and Castlefield ward within a total population of 8,693. The area is seen as being relatively deprived (on a national level). The project I worked for was set up with the aim of 'Working with Asian Young People in High Wycombe'. It was a local authority project employing specifically Asian workers to target what was a predominantly Mirpuri[1] Pakistani community. The workers were often left to run the centre based on what we felt the needs of local Muslims were, as long as outcomes fitted into the wider curriculum and agenda set by the Local Authority.

The feeling I got from the project was that as long as the centre didn't draw too much attention to itself, the workers had a free reign in terms of direction and activities. In the first instance there was a struggle for the use of a building, half of an old school, and there had been a long-term threat of closure. There had been local pressure for a new building, which was supported by the findings of extensive consultation in the area. The new building was finally completed, but the resources to run and maintain the project were very poor and relied on the good will, dedication and the hard work of volunteers.

When the building was finished people felt they had been listened to, but in effect the provision was a smoke screen, as without having adequate resources the project could not be effective. This scenario is not an unusual outcome for marginalised groups. The providing of a particular resource makes it seem like something has been done, but in reality the provision often amounts to little more than a token. In the Castlefield area there had been long standing issues with anti-social behaviour. Every time a problematical situation arose involving young people e.g. setting fire to cars or fights, workers were tasked to organise trips and/or the district became the focus of a detached team. But the work was not sustained and generally it was carried out against background of ignorance about Muslim young people. Workers were limited to the simplistic following of policy, based on general initiatives rather than tailoring their practise, via an understanding of local needs, to inform policy and so provide the means for young people to see their situation with a little more clarity. In short the excercise of professional judgement was limited.

One common response in such circumstances is to use resources to generate focus groups to identify what work needs to be carried out. This usually includes detailing how the marginalised group should be treated differently. This activity serves to highlight difference (marginalisation) but often funding is simply not available/sufficient to meet the wants and needs identified, or responses are simply dismissed as being outside more general targets. This can lead to frustration and the feeling of not being heard, which also emphasises feelings of marginalisation. As such, these tactics represent a double edged sword that strikes twice in one blow!

Providing inadequate resources sets people up to fail and as such confirms perceptions as being part of a relatively powerlessness, marginal group. However, the situation has other dimensions. I have found that work aimed at young women has been measured through their participation while the evaluation of work with young men has been premised on their 'at risk' status. Marginality has been made a space for groups or individuals to actively identify themselves to be seen as marginalised and this is sanctioned/rewarded by funding for marginal groups. The marginal space then appears to have influence, but in fact those identified (and taking on the identity) as the marginalised have been manipulated. This exemplifies the allocation, adoption and result of weak power.

PREVENTING VIOLENCE AND EXTREMISM

We can and do work within marginalised spaces, but in the main this work exists to strengthen the barriers that create and maintain the marginal group. For example, following the 9/11 terrorist attacks, funding has become available through the government initiative of Preventing Violence and Extremism (PVE). Muslims were the specific target for this funding. Working in this context meant that I was obliged to identify the young people as potential terrorists and then work with them with the aim preventing them from actually fulfilling that potential. However, I understood PVE could be used to facilitate young people expressing what they felt about terrorism, develop their understanding about the generalisations that are being made about them and the impact of the same on Muslims in general. In practice the need to work with young Muslims overtook my personal discomfort about the nature of the funding for this work. But of course, my practice was compromised between the proverbial rock and a hard place. Arrests of Muslims and raids in the High Wycombe area made a big impact on Muslim communities but rather than allocating resources to address this situation, efforts were concentrated on the prevention of potential terrorist recruitment, despite their being no known criteria for the development of potential terrorists. Targeted work of this sort produces inequality as it involves practitioners effectively setting up segregated groups, providing activities for only specified groups. For example, the PVE initiative effectively segregated Muslims and non-Muslims. This, together with the media portrayal of any given Muslim as a potential terrorists (which is prejudice and discriminatory in itself) and the self-categorisation outlined above, works to squeeze Muslims into a tighter and tighter form of marginalisation from which it becomes hard for any individual to extract themselves from. This process is directly linked to the seduction of weak power.

SUCCUMBING TO MARGINAL CATEGORIES

Practice responses to the marginalised seem to be intrinsically contradictory. For example, I was assigned to work with a young man who punched another young man in response to being called a 'Fucking Paki' and being told to 'Go back home'. The young man who had been punched called the police and the result was that his assailant was given a court order for mentoring which was intended to help 'integrate him into society'. I was called in as a youth worker to carry out the mentoring. At the start of this process I asked why the person who had expressed racial hatred was not being worked with or charged. I received no adequate explanation. But here you can see both the young people reacting to the marginalisation process. The young man who had involved the police believed in the categorisation as much if not more than the young man who had been subjected to the court order. But there was no inherent problem between these young men; the situation arose out of social categorisation that both, in their own ways, were merely responding to, although it is clear one was expressing what might be legally understood as 'racial hatred'. But overall categorisation and marginalisation seemed to leave everybody involved, the two young people and myself as a worker, disempowered.

This mirrors the contradiction of the young centre situation looked at earlier. A marginalised group may have there own youth centre, but it is provided by the forces of marginalisation and as such reinforces the same. The centre has to get permission for every move they make and the work being carried out, being targeted on that specific group, creates a form of separate development. But this does not mean that the needs of the marginalised group are being met, although the existence of the specialist provision might cause them to believe they are 'being heard'.

INTERNAL OPPRESSION

My spirituality versus her religiosity, my militancy versus her passivity, my sophistication versus her naivety, my location outside the class system versus her middle class background, my consciousness versus her internal oppression. (Moallem 2005)

The above quote is taken from a book that includes descriptions of the lives of Muslim women in Iran. The quote portrays a very articulate level of empathy, which for me, as a Muslim woman, echoes the different forms of perception and categorisation that are imposed upon women. When working with young women, I am in a quandary as a professional; to challenge particular mindsets and attitudes or assume/hope/allow that the person will learn in their own time an at their own pace. I have worked with young people who happily remain ignorant of, or choose to ignore or deny what is going on around them, while others are become angry at institutions and/or society in general.

The quote portrays the different ends of the same view and, in their own right, each is justifiable. But this helps to highlight the tensions that exist within our work. Do we respect young people's wishes/autonomy or do we make more direct efforts to heighten their awareness about their categorisation or marginalisation so, at least if they choose not to understand they are conscious of that decision? As a worker in the field, the idea of consciousness versus continued external and internal oppression relate to the types of challenges I have to weigh up when working with young women. How much of our role as social educators is just about the young people we work with consuming the knowledge we provide them with or do we work with them in order that they might become more aware of themselves and their environment? The latter has clearly more to offer in terms of moving out of a state of personal and group oppression Conciousness seems to offer young people the chance to take authority over their lives and their situation. But the potential they have to use their influence to take authority often seems to go unrecognised by them and those of us who work with them. This feels like another form of succumbing to forms of weak power.

ANTI-OPPRESSIVE PRACTICE

As youth workers we aim to work to an ethical standard, promoting anti-oppressive practice. I carried out a workshop with a Pakistani Muslim group focusing on what this type of work entails. The young people were asked to consider a definition of anti-oppressive practice and then write down their own definition of the term. One young woman responded:

...so when my mum says to me no I can't go out' that means she's oppressing me.

The power of this perspective threw me a little because if I agreed with her conclusion I would risk upsetting her mum (whom I knew personally). But if I disagreed there seemed to be a good chance that I would discredit this young person's understanding, and she did have a point. As argued above, the label of difference which gives rise to marginality can effectively segregate people. This young person is marginalised as being young and as a Muslim. It is one or both of these labels of difference that lead her to the conclusion that she is oppressed; this is not a space of power. But as a youth worker I cannot 'free' her by way of my anti-oppressive practice. In this case Steve Biko's argument resonates; that the oppressed taking on the label of 'the oppressed' play as much of a part in their oppression as those oppressing them (Biko 1987).

There are many consequences of professionals working with marginalised communities and there needs to be an increased awareness of the impact these have not only for the marginalised but also on the practitioner. The latter is particularly vulnerable to effects that employers can transfer onto professionals that oblige them to work with the marginalised in an oppressive manner by not developing the delivery of services according the changing needs of clients but according to bland operational programmes, effectively premised on confirming marginality. However, probably the most useful response the youth worker has is the continued development of their understanding of the engines of marginality and finding the means to work with their clients to continually develop this kind of consciousness.

In the last analysis, while there might well be temporary benefits identifying those we work with as being marginal, and so due compensatory resources, based on social conscience or cries for justice, at some point this process, if those we label as marginal are ever going to move in from the margins, has to conclude. The alternative is that we all, Muslim and non-Muslim, live on the margins of each other's existence. This will be in effective purposeful abandonment of the hope of unmah and so diametrically opposed to Islamic principles, but also the best of humanitarian ethical practice.

NOTES

[1] A person or people **with orgins in** the district of Mirpur in Azad Kashmir, which lies at the foothills of the Himalayas minor

BIBLIOGRAPHY

Biko, S. (1987). *I write what I like*. Heinemann International Literature & Textbooks.
Hall, S. (1991). The local and the global. In A. D. King (Ed.), *Culture, globalization and the World system* (p. 32). London: McMillan.
Moallem, M. (2005). *Between warrior brother and veiled sister: Islamic fundamentalism and the politics of patriarchy in Iran*. University of California Press.

IRFAN SHAH

10. PREVENTING VIOLENT EXTREMISM SCHEME AND THE NEXUS OF CONTROL

Irfan Shah was born 20th June 1979 in Barking; he lived in Ilford with his parents and five brothers. He attended Cleveland Junior School and Loxford High School. As a 16 year old he left school to pursue a career in professional cricket. He received his first semi-professional contract with the London Cricket College, which lost its funding two years later and had to close. Needing to earn a living he found retail work, but after three months he received a call from the Lords MCC Ground Staff who offered him a contract as a semi professional cricketer.

He spent 3 years at Lord's and learnt the skills and aptitude needed to become a professional sportsman. In 1999 he signed a professional contract with Hampshire County Cricket Club. He toured South Africa twice and spent six months in Perth, Australia, which he found challenging, especially during Ramadan. His contract with Hampshire finished in 2002 and Irfan settled back in Ilford.

In 2004 he was offered a job as a Club Development Worker with Frenford Clubs and started a YMCA Diploma in Youth and Community Education, which he completed in 2009. He married in 2004 and now has two young girls. In 2006, he and his wife went to Hajj on pilgrimage. He continues to reside in Ilford and still works for Frenford Clubs. Irfan achieved a BA Hons in Youth and Community Education in 2011.

INTRODUCTION

This chapter will focus on the issues and boundaries that were crossed with regard to the recent history of anti-terror laws and in particular the Prevent strategy that was linked to the state sponsored Prevention of Violent Extremism scheme (PVE). It will look at how Prevent impacted on young people and ask who might have benefited from such legislation. Following the devastating, tragic and barbaric terror attacks labelled by their dates, '9/11' and '7/7', many young Muslims often felt and found themselves to be effectively made scapegoats. However the state's response was to devote over £140 million to making young people the focus of a strategy that quickly took on the mantle of 'combating violent extremism'. With Prevent now disappearing below the political horizon to make way for the National Citizenship Service, it is perhaps

B. Belton and S. Hamid (eds), Youth Work and Islam:
A leao of faith for young people,135–143.

timely to look at how such policies can be something more damaging than merely temporarily counterproductive of their own logic.

PREVENT

Following the 7/7 bombings the message from government was that Muslim communities needed to take the initiative. Prime Minister Tony Blair along with Ruth Kelly, as the Secretary of State for Communities and Local Government, accused the Muslim Council of Britain of not doing enough to fight extremism. The government resisted significant demands for a full public inquiry into the 7/7 attacks, as Tony Blair insisted that a new initiative needed to be put in place to combat the growth of violent extremism. The Government launched its Action Plan, 'Preventing violent extremism: winning hearts and minds' in April 2007 and announced the Preventing Violent Extremism Pathfinder Fund; Prevent. Prevent was one of four strands of the Government's long-term strategy to countering violent extremism and was linked to CONTEST[1], the governments international counter terrorism strategy, which was summed up in four words;
* Pursue
* Prepare
* Protect
* Prevent
The Pathfinders fund was badged as PVE or Preventing Violent Extremism programme as the Home Office moved towards the use of the term 'Prevent' to describe the area of work.

The purpose of Prevent was straightforward; to stop people becoming or supporting terrorists and violent extremism. It was a response to the belief that such an aim could not be achieved solely by the work of the police or the Security Service.

The Prevent programme was summarised as follows:
Four key aims;
1) promoting shared values
2) supporting local solutions
3) building civic capacity and leadership
4) strengthening the role of faith institutions and leaders
Five key objectives;
1) challenging violent extremist ideology and supporting mainstream voices
2) disrupting those who promote violent extremism and institutions where they might be active
3) supporting individuals who are being targeted and recruited
4) increasing the resilience of communities
5) addressing grievances

There were two strategic enabling functions;
1) developing understanding, analysis and information
2) improving strategic communications.
Local authorities receiving Prevent funding would be measured against the indicator, NI 35 which concentrated on the following four areas:
a) Understanding of and engagement with Muslim communities
b) Knowledge and understanding of the Preventing Violent Extremism agenda
c) Effective development of an action plan to build the resilience of communities and support vulnerable individuals
d) Effective oversight, delivery and evaluations of projects and action.

MUSLIM FOCUS

Youth groups and Local Authorities applied for funding under the Prevent banner but found so called radicalised young people difficult to identify. In my area of practice, the London Borough of Redbridge, on the borders of East London and West Essex, the Local Authority established a Preventing Violent Extremism program (PVEP). Initially Muslim youth were targeted with the aim of identifying any who would admit to holding extremist views and/or violent intentions. However, unsurprisingly it proved difficult to find young people willing to sign up to the program. So a new appellation, the Muslim Inclusion Program (MIP), was adopted. At a stroke this excluded everyone except Muslims as, in practice, only Muslims were overtly targeted, but the PVEP could in theory have been used as a means of prevention of any type of extremism (for example racist/Fascist extremism). However, the change of title also worked to deceive young people as the MIP had the same aims as the PVEP, focusing on religion and the possibility of radicalisation. But, at the same time this approach was intrinsically unfair and discriminatory, in that just one section of the community was to receive resources. While there are other examples of state, local authority and private funding being focused on particular groups, over short and long terms, for instance young parents, young people at risk etc., in this situation it was *all* young Muslims who were being targeted, as it was they that were seen to be the most likely group to be exposed to radicalisation. JUST (the Standing Committee on Justice and Human Rights) spoke out against the PVE strategy in an open memorandum whilst giving evidence to the Communities and Local Government Committee inquiry in 2010, stating;

The government's PVE project has led to the abandonment of funding traditional community development, capacity building and empowerment work with BME (Black and Minority Ethnic) communities, replacing instead with community cohesion, anti-extremism and anti-terrorism approaches which have put Muslim communities under the intense spotlight of the far right and the press and media. It is vital that all young people can access youth clubs, activities and projects and by only allowing the Muslim community to benefit from this program, the government has created resentment and hatred amongst young people outside of the Muslim faith.

According to a document produced by the Reading Muslim Crisis Group[2], in one London borough, those working with young people, under the auspices of PVE were told to add information to databases they held to highlight which youths were Muslim. They were also asked to provide information, to be shared with the police, about which streets and areas Muslim youngsters could be found on. Given this, it is too easy to conclude that Muslim communities were effectively being subjected to surveillance to a degree that was hard to justify (spying). This would seem to be potentially damaging any relations or possible partnership opportunities that could happen by handling funding in this way.

The Prevent funding was mainly accessed by local authorities but was also available to small organisations and groups working with Muslims. So it is not surprising that organisations and local authorities reacted to this in a similar way as they might other funding streams; to facilitate projects and salaries to run the same. The funding came under close scrutiny from Muslim groups, non Muslims and MPs. The An-Nisa Society in a document, entitled 'A Response from the Muslim Community' by Khalida Khan (March 2009) responded to the steps taken by the government through the introduction of Prevent strategy. In short she concluded that the Muslim community was being treated as potential terrorists and the Prevent strategy looked to Muslims to act as a surveillance mechanism of themselves. Khan made the point that there was no consultation with Muslims about the introduction of Prevent scheme, that did not have the backing of MPs and some local authorities, such as Bradford Council.[3]

A manager of a project in London said:

I think part of the point of the [Prevent] *programme is to spy and intelligence gather. I won't do that.*[4]

In another London borough wardens on council estates were told to inform on people not because they were suspected of crimes, but because they were supposed to be susceptible to radicalisation. According to a Guardian source, who had been involved in Whitehall discussions on counter-terrorism:

There is no doubt Prevent is in part about gathering intelligence on people's thoughts and beliefs. No doubt.

He added that the authorities feared "...they'd be lynched" if they admitted Prevent included spying.[13]

MONEY WELL SPENT?

Millions of pounds were spent on the Prevent scheme. It is hard not to agree, given the cost of terrorist activity in terms of human life and suffering, that as a society we need to look at the way we live, the way in which we interact with each other and the decisions we take. We also need to think about the implications that our actions have on others. As I interact with the young people that come to the youth club where I work, which includes young people of all faiths, I ask myself, 'Would the money allocated to Prevent have been beneficial to the young people I work with?' I refrained from applying to the scheme as I saw it as alienating the non-Muslim young people we worked with. On 17 June 2009 the Guardian reported that 230,000 young people aged between 16 and 18 were not in employment, education or training. Nearly 15,000 anti social behaviour orders had been issued between April 1999 and December 2008 according to the Home Office Crime Reduction Statistics reported in 2009. At the same time the teenage pregnancy rate was higher than any other country in the European Union. Of course, in 2011 youth unemployment and crime rates amongst the young are far worse than two years ago, and even if young people were in danger of being radicalised there is no apparent evidence that this is more or less the case because of PVE strategy. So perhaps this demonstrates that the resources devoted to Prevent might have been put to better use supporting young people back in to education, funding youth services and positive activities, such as training and short courses to increase skills. The UK Youth Parliament told the House of Commons Committee in March 2010[5] that overwhelmingly, young people did not approve of tokenistic youth organisations. They asked, 'Why is there a Young Muslim Advisory Group but not a Young Christian Advisory Group? Why is there not a Young Hindu Advisory Group?' It was stated that it seems, 'that it is all tied to the one community when the problem is not exactly with that community'. The Youth Parliament also criticised the government for not providing democratic engagement for young people,

I see that as a criticism of you guys [MPs] *because there are not any opportunities for young people from those backgrounds to get involved in events like, Project Safe Space. We did one conference in Slough and the opinions we got there from the young people were very different from the opinions we got in the North East and the North West of England. They are not given the same opportunities as us because we are going into those communities but we are not getting the funding to continue doing that work, giving those young people youth leadership opportunities and stuff like that.*[6]

Young people are giving a clear message of wanting more support. This being the case it seems something worse than a waste to throw millions of pounds on a relatively few young people just because they happen come from a Muslim background. It appears obvious that radicalisation (a phenomenon that has never been clearly articulated, identified or quantified) is not the source of youth disaffection or dissatisfaction. However, the resources devoted to Prevent were seductive. Redbridge, like other beneficiaries, drew down hundreds of thousands of pounds from the government, although even after the re-development of the programme only around 20 members got involved by way of incentives (bribes) such as free pizza, trips and a residential. For all this, radicalisation was not a central focus as issues ranging from family breakdowns to belonging to street gangs took precedence. However, are these not the same issues that all young people potentially face from all backgrounds?

A NEXUS OF CONTROL

The above demonstrates that Prevent was ineffective by any measure and chronically ill-conceived. It was effectively set of inappropriate ideas and aims to be serviced by agencies that effectively attempted to use the resources for other means, probably, as seemed to be the case in Redbridge; the intended use was something of a practice cul-de-sac. However, it is perhaps too straightforward to understand Prevent as a stand-alone failure in policy. Section 45 (Exercise of power) of the Terrorism Act (2000) was designed to give the police powers to stop and search any vehicle or person and seize 'articles of a kind which could be used in connection with terrorism', in a specific area over a period of time. Unlike other stop and search powers that the police could deploy, this did not require the police to have 'reasonable suspicion' that an offence had been committed, to search an individual. In January 2010 the stop-and-search powers were ruled illegal by the European Court of Human Rights. This judgement was vindicated by subsequent findings. In March 2011, Corinna Ferguson, a lawyer for human rights group Liberty, said:

A threefold increase in anti-terror stop and search is the clearest signal that these powers are being misused.

At the same time it was reported that Asians are more than twice as likely to be stopped than whites.[7] However other facets of the 2000 Act continued to be used. Section 41 of the Act provides the police with the power to arrest and detain a person without a warrant for up to 48 hours if they were suspected of being a terrorist. This period of detention could be extended to up to seven days if the police could convince a judge that it was necessary for further questioning. This section marked a break from ordinary criminal law where suspects need to be charged within 24 hours of detention or be released. This period was later extended to 14 days by the Criminal Justice Act 2003 and to 28 days by the Terrorism Act 2006. Section 58 (Collection of information) created the offence, liable to a prison term of up to ten years, to collect or possesses, 'information of a kind likely to be useful to a person committing or preparing an act of terrorism'.

While much of this legislation might be portrayed as necessary given a declared 'war on terrorism', the impact on the freedom young people and the focus on young Muslims (the groups that are apparently most associated with potential acts of terrorism) has yet to be fully felt. However, the consequences of socially mediated and legislated mistrust and suspicion are probably predictable; a group who are not trusted by society will not trust society – too quickly mistrust gives birth to contempt, just as the progeny of continued suspicion is alienation of those continually under suspicion.

CONCLUSION

The Prevent scheme isolated a minority community while subjecting the majority to discrimination (they did not have access to the funding). The Prevent scheme had initially started as way of combating potential radicalisation of young Muslims. However as many Muslims and non Muslims have stated, this is not the way to deal with a global situation. Perhaps some of the actual and supposed resentment from Muslims towards the West is an indirect result of foreign policy and the treatment of Muslim people at an international level? I am confident if the government wants to eradicate the potential for the radicalisation of young people, then it must look at the education and welfare system as they affect young Muslims. As a youth worker of some experience I see that Muslims are often left behind in education and social integration. This barrier must be addressed if young people are not to become targets of the hardliners. I am extremely disappointed that the resources used to fund the Prevent scheme were primarily focused on young Muslims alone as this seemed to do little more that fuel the resentment felt towards the Muslim community.

On 16 October 2009, in the Guardian, the Director of Liberty, Shami Chakrabarti branded Prevent as the biggest spying program in Britain in modern times and an affront to civil liberties. But this apart, the program was extremely flawed as the cases below, some of the many reported by the Reading Muslim PVE Crisis Group, demonstrate:

- *In the Midlands, funding for a mental health project to help Muslims was linked to information about individuals being passed to the authorities.*
- *In a college in northern England, a student who attended a meeting about Gaza was reported by one lecturer as a potential extremist. He was found not to be.*
- *A nine-year-old schoolboy in East London, was referred to the authorities after allegedly showing signs of extremism – the youngest case known in Britain. He was "deprogrammed" according to a source with knowledge of the case.*
- *Within the last month, one new youth project in London alleged it was being pressured by the Metropolitan police to provide names and details of Muslim youngsters, as a condition of funding. None of the young Muslims have any known terrorist history.*
- *In Birmingham the programme manager for Prevent is in fact a senior counter-terrorism police officer. Paul Marriott has been seconded to work in the equalities division of Britain's biggest council.*
- *In Blackburn, at least 80 people were reported to the authorities for showing signs of extremism. They were referred to the Channel project, part of Prevent.*
- *A youth project manager alleges his refusal to provide intelligence led to the police spreading false rumours and trying to smear him and his organisation.*[8]

Prevent needs to be understood as just one facet of a whole control nexus that, despite Prevent's demise, still surrounds young Muslims. While its seeming

SHAH

replacement, the National Citizenship Service (NCS), does not seem to have the same overt capacity for surveillance, many young Muslims that might take part, given legislation of the recent past and other social legislative control that seems to apply more specifically to them than other groups, will (or perhaps should) enter into this unguarded. Article 2 the Universal Declaration of Human Rights states that,

Everyone is entitled to all the rights and freedoms set forth in this Declaration, without distinction of any kind, such as race, colour, sex, language, religion, political or other opinion.

Prevent did not reach Muslim youth in a way designed to redirect them from the possibilities of radicalisation. The government could do more to combat violent extremism by addressing the very issues that young Muslims are facing, such as education and the high rate of unemployment, but these are not issues that the NCS has the capacity to deal with in any meaningful way. There is also a need to address foreign policy, which gives the impression that Britain is against the Muslim states and only wants to follow the example of the USA; for many young Muslims (and non-Muslims) we are not living in an independent nation at all, but a sort of client/servant relationship with a monolithic, but increasingly cumbersome international bully state. Is it surprising if anyone might be alienated from such a marriage of inconvenience?

I have had discussions with non Muslims who feel that Muslims need to stop using foreign policy as an excuse and look within their own communities. I would tend to agree and disagree, as I also feel that the Muslim community, and all communities, need to unite and stand against oppression. Unfortunately with former leaders such as Hosnei Mubarak of Egypt and the Saudi Princes, there has been little chance of this. Although the events of the first part of 2011 might signal hope in this direction, these two countries have been true examples of yielding to the worst of modern Western colonialism and as such remain colonial states. This is an example of the frustration that young Muslims face; the West will talk to dictators but will not talk to the democratically elected Hamas in Gaza. There are two potential consequences of this as Fanon (1965 and 1967) observed; the outcome of colonial relations for the colonised are disaffection and/or apathy.

Young people in general often find themselves subjected to discrimination on many fronts but discrimination is generated socially and as such something that needs to be degenerated, not on only an individual and legislative basis, but on a social scale. If we are not to create groups of people who feel outside society, who are made to feel like permanent 'suspects' by implication, with no stake or interest in society, our social activity needs to be of an inclusive nature. It seems society, schools, local authorities, professionals and the policy makers are far too quick to make rules and policy without consulting young people. Of course, some decisions need to be made based on facts and long term development and sometimes young people have not reached that specific time in their life where they can make certain decisions. However the restrictions and pressures that are placed on them are not entirely fair.

Terrorism laws are used effectively to terrorise while legislation aimed at combating drugs, knife and gun crime, which in reality are applicable only to a small section of young people, impact on the majority and do more to alienate them from the adult world than anything else. How is it fair to treat all young people as if they all, and not just a minority, are potentially criminal? Is this the shameful result of us not really knowing our young people? They walk the streets (and will do even more so following the massive cut backs in the youth service from 2011) largely as an anonymous threatening presence, rather than the vibrant hope they could be. Prevent and the consequences of the poorly conceived and clumsily delivered terrorist laws provide examples of how we socially and negatively categorise young people. If we are to harness the hope of young people, all our young people, we need to stop this and begin to know them personally, as people, not religious, age or racial categories, who are understood as more or less threatening or dangerous according to the category they are placed in. This depersonalisation has a huge cost for them and the whole of our society, perhaps the world.

NOTES

1 The official name of the United Kingdom's Counter-Terrorism Strategy
2 Reading Muslim PVE Crisis Group - http://pvecrisisgroup.com
3 Khalida Khan (2009) An-Nisa Society *Preventing Violent Extremism (PVE) & Prevent.*
4 *Britain: Government anti-terrorism strategy 'spies' on innocent.* Data on politics, sexual activity and religion gathered by UK government by Vikram Dodd http://www.globalresearch.ca/index.php?context=va&aid=15722 and http://www.guardian.co.uk/uk/2009/oct/16/anti-terrorism-strategy-spies-innocents
5 http://www.publications.parliament.uk/pa/cm200910/cmselect/cmcomloc/65/6506.htm
6 *91. The Youth Parliament witnesses criticised the lack of opportunities for truly 'democratic' engagement for young people* http://www.publications.parliament.uk/pa/cm200910/cmselect/cmcomloc/65/6506.htm
7 http://www.telegraph.co.uk/news/uknews/law-and-order/5251053/Police-accused-of-abusing-powers-as-anti-terrorism-stop-and-searches-treble.html
8 http://pvecrisisgroup.com/2009/10/17/government-anti-terrorism-strategy-spies-on-innocent/

REFERENCES

Fanon, F. (1967). *Black skin, white masks.* Grove Press.
Fanon, F. (1965). *The wretched of the Earth.* MacGibbon & Kee.

MARK ROBERTS

11. UMMAH AND YOUTH WORK

Mark Roberts has practised youth work for over two decades. Currently practicing in Epsom, Surrey, he was also based in Wandsworth, South London for three years. Mark established a new youth centre in one of the poorest areas of Surrey, and has had experience of home education with his own children and other families from the area and managing a youth justice project. Mark has close links with Gypsy and Traveller communities in Surry. He has worked with young people in Sri Lanka, Zambia, Denmark, and Switzerland. Since gaining his BA Honours degree in Informal and Community Education with the YMCA George Williams College in East London, his writing has featured in two publications by the college.

The underlying themes of this chapter are closely connected with the following chapter and it is advised that they should be read is sequence.

In this chapter Mark looks at some of the most ubiquitous terms/guiding precepts used in youth work and compares and contrasts the same with aspects of Islamic thought, principally the concept of 'Ummah'. As part of this he broaches what have often described as major aspects of the youth work role; the notion of community and informal and community education.

In the past few years there has been a growing concern amongst youth workers about the purpose and character of informal education as interpreted and delivered in the youth work arena, in particular its apparent contradiction to some of the central principles of youth work practice, including the promotion of fairness, democracy, transparency and honesty. These ethical anxieties are connected to some of the precepts of informal education as often promoted and enacted in the youth work sphere, it being largely delivered under the guise of leisure activities or projects (the educational content is effectively camouflaged) mostly without the knowledge or request of those being targeted. The level to which this equates to covert activity, the more it inherently contradicts Articles 12 and 13 of the UN Convention of the Rights of the Child and the 'Main Principles' of Children's Act 1989.[1]

This does not relate to the straightforward participation of young people in event/activity planning that most youth workers promote. The concerns are with practice that involves policy aims/ambitions to 'educate' targeted groups without telling them that this is the primary aim of the work and/or informing them about the purpose or rational of the same. Such practice, which embraces clandestine

B. Belton and S. Hamid (eds), Youth Work and Islam:
A leao of faith for young people, 145–154.

activity/agenda, principally promoted and planned by professionals, outside of the social environment of those focused on, brings into question if what is going on can be education, if those potentially being educated are purposely kept unaware of the process. As Mark demonstrates covert education might be taken to be indoctrination and/or propaganda, however his attention to Ummah provides the reader with something of an alternative response.

INTRODUCTION

In this chapter I will demonstrate how education confirms Western notions of community, which have been shaped by a long history of capitalism and colonialism and how the Islamic notion of 'Ummah', which developed independently of Western influence, can both inform and develop a more humane approach in the contemporary realm of youth and community work practice.

UMMAH

The Qur'an uses the term Ummah, to refer to all those united under Islam (Yunus, Chapter 10, and Verse 47). However, in its widest sense, the term can be understood to potentially encompass all humanity. As such the usual interpretation of this Arabic word as 'community' or 'nation' does not really express its all embracing possibilities as an expression of all-inclusiveness. According to a fellow youth worker and Muslim scholar Tahir Alam, an individual might connect with the worldwide community through the 'traditions' (the handing down and on of statements, beliefs, legends, customs, information, etc., from generation to generation, by word of mouth, writing or by practice) of Islam. In Tahir's words;

You know, I'll go to Japan and they will have their own traditions and people might feel out of place, but the thing is, as Muslims we already know what they are going to do, they are going to pray, read the Qur'an in Arabic... and if we eat it will be Halal meat.

Another understanding of Ummah can encompass everyone (including non-Muslims) who is part of a land where Muslims reside; for example 'Al-Umam' or 'Al-Muttahida' can be understood as the United Nations. However, other than the traditions and the land, Tahir explained how Muslims treat each other, which offers the potential for further exploration:

Within Islamic teaching there is no such thing as racism. The concept of racism is quite alien. In the last sermon the prophet Mohammed made, he said 'No Arab is above another man, and no man is above an Arab'.

This perspective enlivens a sense of humanity unlike Western definitions of community that, in the main, is a means by which people are identified, categorized or isolated and labelled. Gilchrist uses an example from practice where she distinguishes between the disabled, the religious, Lesbians, young mums and pensioners;

This juxtaposition of very different lifestyles and moral values was deliberate, but not without its risks and tensions...Through sensitive and strategic networking we managed to create a positive atmosphere (Gilchrist, 2001:113)

The undertaking this labelling creates problems, risks and tensions. Youth and community workers deploying this strategy of categorisation are assuming that they are equipped to fix relational cleavages that exist between people. But a rational analysis of this situation demonstrates that they are in fact making themselves the answer to the situation they had a part in creating, via the faith in the notion and prospect of community differences.

THE GRAFFITI PAINT HEIST

The notion of community education in bolstered by the idea that reflection is a necessary aspect of 'education and learning' (Doyle, 2001:8). This has become something of a tradition of informal education. However, education, if seen from a different standpoint, not only has the potential for politicising but can also be something which is part of you and us (ummah).

My practice is situated in an area where graffiti is a concern of residents, councillors, police, and housing associations. It was reported at a residents meeting that the housing association spent £14,500 on removing graffiti over the course of a single year. Perhaps surprisingly it has been on the state agenda at least since the Blair government:

Councils spend millions of pounds cleaning up after graffiti vandals and Tony Blair has lumped graffiti with drugs and mindless violence as "bad symptoms" of modern society.(http://news.bbc.co.uk/1/hi/uk/2383725.stm)

For all this, the local young people like creating graffiti, and as such asked to paint walls outside the youth centre. They gained funding from the government (via Youth Opportunity Fund) for the paint. This became known as a 'Graffiti Project'. It was justified as a means to teach young people that there are consequences arising from being involved in graffiti illegally and that there is a place for graffiti (usually supervised by the adult/professional) in a space decided by the youth worker at a time that suits him/her (generally called an intervention - although it is a moot point if graffiti remains graffiti if it is not illegal).

At the start of the project I was involved in a residential. However, I had arranged cover for my work at the youth centre. It was during a 'drop in' session that the boys who were taking part in the Graffiti Project took an opportunity to acquire the paint for their own Graffiti Project; a sort of informal, spontaneous, autonomous, self empowered offshoot of the 'official' Project. They asked one of the workers to bring out some badminton equipment and when his back was turned one of their number unlatched one of the double doors of the cupboard where the paint was stored. The worker had locked the cupboard but had not realised that the door could still be opened. The young people proceeded to remove the spray cans and exited the building having seized the means of graffiti production. All this occurred without the worker realising what had happened. The following day I came in to find approximately hundred cans of graffiti spray paint missing following the 'liberation' of the same.

This is a story; it is what happened from my perspective - it could be called 'reflection-on-action'. Reflection is said to be an opportunity to go back over events and deal with how you feel and 'make sense of what happened in light of our present position' (Doyle, 2001:11). However, the likes of Doyle (2001) do not seem to recognise the distortions that occur in any reflection on what has happened. In other words what are we trying to make sense of? For example, in my account of what would generally be taken to be the theft of paint I am trying to make sense of something that happened when I wasn't there. It therefore seems more appropriate to think of what I can learn about society and community than about me, us and our experience of what happened. For Belton, reflection is:

As such it [reflection] *has two levels of explanatory power. It tells us a version of what was and something about the type of society that shaped understanding of what was. This being the case, our knowledge of the past is not an untarnished reflection of what was. It is a way of telling something given the confines of a given social milieu. It is a narrative construction.* (Belton, 2005:119)

Belton goes on to suggest that unless 'each aspect could be conveyed immediately' what we are left with is an 'impression' (Belton, 2005:126). Therefore, reflection-on-action, as a theory of education, might be thought of as a method of learning that is flawed. Perhaps it could be seen more as a tradition of informal education? Calling what I had to report an impression of what happened and recognising this impression is shaped by society (in this case as theft) is as such more accurate and therefore probably more constructive.

My impression of what happened with the spray cans is that the young people had their own ideas about how to use the paint and did it without our knowledge or consent. This seems to me to mirror some of the ideas that surround youth work in terms of our ideas about informally educating young people. The education that we offer so often is delivered to them as something we as professionals want to do, without their knowledge or consent; they did not make a request to be informally educated.

Listening to the Imam teaching at the East London Mosque gave me an impression of a different outworking of community education. He was referring the conflict in Palestine and the role the media have in not presenting an accurate view of events. Tahir explained:

If Palestine is going through some kind of conflict you should be feeling it, because he (the Palestinian) is your brother, this is your community.

The traditions of Islam can be traced back to the life of Muhammad, and here there is a foundation or substance to what Muslims call Ummah. For Tahir one of the important sayings of Muhammad was, 'all you Muslims are one community'. Tahir went on to say,

You are like a body of a person... if your hand hurts your whole body feels the pain. Your brain feels the pain.

Theories attached to the notion of youth work can become traditional if left unquestioned/unscrutinised. When we share and to some extent believe in our distorted experiences/traditions of practice, these could become 'myths' (an idea that is widely held but untrue or unproven). However, the stance Tahir is taking appears more humane and ethical. It is more about the enhancement of positive feelings than acting on bald impressions. Within Ummah the sharp distinctions that exist in Western traditions between, 'them and us', 'professional and clients', 'youth and adult', 'thief or victim' are not as certain or stable; we are all one body.

REPRESENTATIVE CRIMINALS

If we take a step back from what society might understand as the theft of paint it can be seen to have caused consequences for us and the young people:
- What happened? - We got robbed
- What would we do differently? - More control - deal with feelings (thankless job being a youth worker).
- What more can we learn about the type of society we work in?

Here the issue can be seen to be one of control. The 'paint robbers' seized the opportunity to control and we, the workers, tend to feel inclined to make provision to maintain control (of paint and what is done with the paint) in our hands. However, young people could be seen to be one of the oppressed groups in society (in terms of what they are not allowed access to, laws to control behaviour etc). So wouldn't they seek to take more control over their lives?

Schools are the great control centres of youth. For Chomsky:

Far from creating independent thinkers, schools have always throughout history, played an institutional role in a system of control and coercion. And once you have been socialized in ways that support the power structure, which, in turn, rewards you immensely (Chomsky, 2000:16)

Chomsky goes on to argue that the less democratic schools are, the more they have to teach about democracy. In much the same way we find ourselves working in situations promoting a notion of community. However, if we consider using the concept of 'Ummah', a human community, based on the notion of equality and inclusion, then perhaps community wouldn't need to be taught, imposed or sign posted. Indeed, that community needs to be promoted or taught indicates there is nothing natural about it.

For example, in one school setting I noticed a sign instructing the students on what was expected of them. It was entitled 'community behaviour' (walk to the left, no running, eating, etc). This understanding of community seems to be attuned to everyone behaving in exactly the same way, prescribed by someone else (not those being instructed); it is not generated by the people that need to follow the instruction - it is generated for them. Rather than seeing people as able to think for themselves, take responsibility etc. (wanting them to be independent thinkers) this sees people as being in need of instruction in order to behave reasonably although the non-conformist would need to use their reason in order not to conform.

This is a model of an understanding of people as being creatures without reason. Those who won't or can't conform are seen as rebelling; rejecting the regulated forms of behaviour. This often results them being 'excluded', 'referred', or 'targeted'. In other words they have become labelled and categorized. As Belton points out, this is part of the experience of colonisation:

I followed the path laid down for me by those who had nothing but contempt for my humanity, those who had labelled and categorized me. To that extent I was colonized (Belton, 2005:138)

In the colonial situation one either conforms or is labelled. This opens the way to resources being deployed to help or make one conform. The colonial society cannot remain colonial if it tolerates non-conformity. The Graffiti Project was framed as an attempt to 'educate' (control/indoctrinate) young people into believing that what they are doing is not only wrong (illegal) but they need reforming (through the Graffiti Project). This is not to say that on an individual basis people's lives and homes need or should be subject to abuse by way of graffiti and other forms of what is usually understood as vandalism or anti-social activity, such as playing loud music, littering etc. However, there are other dimensions to this. Angela Davis talks about 'representative criminals' (Davis, 1997) an example of this would be young people taking drugs, getting involved in graffiti etc. But, as she points out, there other types of crime:

We can talk about corporate crime as well. We can talk about crime against the environment that will effect generations to come....these people generally only pay fines if they do that. They are not considered criminal. (Davis, 1997)

An 'infamous' graffiti artist named 'Banksy' supports this:

The people who run our cities don't understand graffiti because they think nothing has the right to exist unless it makes a profit, which makes their opinion worthless (Banksy, 2006:8)

Almost everything published in books, newspapers, magazines etc. and nearly every second broadcast, is in some way mediated and/or controlled by commercial interests. As such we are told what these interests want us to be told. But graffiti undermines this commercial/capitalist structure and the notion of community that arises out of the same. It is this that creates the need for the state and its agencies to send youth workers out to 'educate' communities. As no one as asked for this, and for the most part people are not told that the point of what is happening is to educate them, the process is hardly democratic or transparent (central tenets of youth work practice). As such what is going on is more a form indoctrination, delivered by way of informal education, a generally covert activity which confirms itself as a means of indoctrination (that, like propaganda, is what covert education is).

As such graffiti has something in common with Islam (that is not to say Islam *is* graffiti!). The latter is a set of principles, ideas is separate from the state institutions (the structure of Islam is not shaped by state finance or government policy) and therefore might necessarily be regarded, because it is one of the minority of structures independent of the state, as having the potential to undermine or threaten the 'dominant segment' (Chomsky, 2000:17). Of course, there are some states that are seen to be Islamic, to have co-opted Islam for state ends. But even a cursory knowledge of Islam indicates the Islamic state is a contradiction in terms; states cannot use or adopt Islam, Islam is not limited to or restricted by man-made borders or rules. Ummah is a borderless concept in that it has the capacity to embrace all humanity. It is not bounded in the way community is. As such, the notion of an Islamic state demonstrates a Western misunderstanding of the nature of Islam.

A DIVIDED WORLD

Ideas that influenced Western thinking and the notion of the state can be traced back to ancient Greece, in particular the work of Plato. In a number of professional youth work training courses his work is thought to guide informal education practice as it places emphasis on dialogue. However in Plato one can see what some have thought of as the beginnings of the divisions and dichotomies that litter our perception and ideas of community:

We have bred you both for your own sake and that of the whole community to act as leaders as king bees in a hive; you are better more fully educated than the rest and better qualified to combine the practice of philosophy and politics. You must therefore descend in turn and live with your fellows in the cave and get used to seeing in the dark (Plato, 1974:32).

If you can get past the thick layer of pomposity, assumptions, discrimination, prejudice and snobbery entailed in the above, one can determine Plato's belief in his story 'The Cave' as an example of the role of the professional educator. Socrates describes how most people see reality as only shadows on the wall of the cave in which they are chained. It is the job of the philosopher, or the educator, to turn their eyes to the light outside the cave, and help see things as they really are.

This perhaps shows how theory is interpreted and supports/creates a new theory (the job of the educator). However it could also be argued that it supports Western ideological models of education and/or the colonial environment. Taking this into account the cave situation is a distortion - we help people see the light - passed off as theory. But this can be understood to support the myth, in this case the myth of the community educator. People can see light without help and they choose not to even with help; light seeing is often a choice rather than the result of the work of a blessed enlightener/saviour figure. So I can say this Bond film is not as good as opera and I can show you opera, but that doesn't mean you will find opera 'better' than Bond; in fact there is nothing to say that opera is better than Bond.

As such, what Plato is touting as light, might not even be light; isn't that the premise or trick of commercial advertising, taking what one is told to be light?

However, this story also presents the idea that things are separate, for example the cave's shadows (illusion) and the upper world (reality).

It was Plato's plan to destabilise our lives by dividing them. He did it with a definite agenda in mind. You have probably heard about situations where a person creates a problem and then presents himself as the solution to it.

This ploy worked to make people think that they needed someone wise and powerful, some person or institution, to get them from here to there. (Thwaites, 2001:46)

As such, Platonic thought suggests the educator is the 'expert' or the enlightened one; it is everyone else who is fooled. Ummah might be contrasted to this as it represents something more about equality (e.g. brother/sisterhood - a belief that people should act with warmth and equality toward one another, regardless of differences in race, creed, nationality, etc.) unity and inclusiveness. In this teacher and learner are mutual and interchanging roles as the people performing them are encompassed in the organic spiritual unity of Ummah.

Jewish theology shares this notion and Thwaites points out the distinction between this and the basis of Western thought about our relatedness:

Remember Plato's world vision was marked by the world divided. In contrast to this, the Hebrew worldview is unified: it's one (Thwaites, 2001:50).

HIDE YOUR HOOD!

An understanding of Ummah can facilitate our work with people, perhaps helping us to move beyond the habit of labelling others (youth, young people, adolescence, teenagers) that often seems to support our existence as professionals. It can offer an approach to people, as opposed to effectively making them objects in an objectified category. For example I was working at Chicago Rock Café when a young person was asked to 'step outside' by the Police because he had been seen on surveillance cameras tucking something (thought to be a weapon) into the hood of his jacket. The young person informed them that he was trying to comply with the widely publicised ban on young people wearing hoods in certain public places. The reaction to him was dictated not so much by what he did but by the categories he was consigned to, principally his youth, but his gender, complexion, dress, demeanour or his ipod could all be used as markers of categorisation. You can perhaps see the violence (violation) in this; just like informal education, the starting assumption of which is the people one targets are relatively ignorant (else why would they be taken to be in need of education?) all sorts of suppositions were made about this person based on superficial (prejudicial/discriminatory) indicators.

CONCLUSION

What I have argued is that much of what we are told about informal and community education could be aligned with tradition. In stark terms we could call these the myths of youth work. It is also apparent that these traditions are passed on via notions and ideas dominated by division, colonial systems and commercial/capitalist interests. Ummah offers a different model; something that can include all, as it has within it the means to see people's common humanity as something sacred beyond man-made categories.

Referring to prisons Angela Davis has proposed an idea about creating 'new institutions' (Davis, 1997). Prisons might be necessary, but some of the walls need tearing down and new environments need creating where people can come together e.g. into educational environments, where the prisoners can be teachers. What would a new institution look like in the youth work field? Davis also talks about losing the 'missionary posture – we need to save these poor souls' (Davis, 1997). In a small-scale survey I asked young people why they come to the youth centre. The answers were based around 'cotching' (sitting), eating food, and playing pool. We can make youth work into something else, but let's hear the people who we work for, let them teach us. This must bring us closer to a Ummah sensibility.

NOTES

[1] 1. Article 12 looks to assure that young people have the right to express their *views freely in all matters affecting* them. The child cannot freely express their views about matters affecting them if these are purposely kept from them. In the youth work field the policy agenda connect to the aim to informally educate young people is not, in terms of custom and practice, shared with the young people it is aimed at. Within the regime of informal practice they are rarely told that what is being delivered to them is an educational programme; activities and projects are largely labelled and delivered under the premise of leisure/recreational facilities. This means (as Article 12 continues) that the young people involved have not been *provided the opportunity to be heard in... administrative proceedings affecting* them.

Article 13 states; *The child shall have the right to freedom of expression; this right shall include freedom to seek, receive and impart information and ideas of all kinds,* in *media of the child's choice.* But again, how can one be free to express and impart ideas about matters that one has not been informed about?

Further, the 'Main Principles' of the Children's Act 1989 state that: *Children should be kept informed about what happens to them, and should participate when decisions are made about their future.*

BIBLIOGRAPHY

Banksy. (2006). *Wall and piece*. Century.

Belton, B. A. (2005). *Questioning gypsy identity*. Rowman & Littlefield Publishers, Inc.

Chomsky, N. (2000). *Chomsky on MisEducation*. Rowman & Littlefield Publishers, Inc.

Davis, A. (1997). *The prison industrial complex*. Alternative Radio.

Doyle, M. E. (2001). On being an educator. In L. D. Richardson & M. Wolf (Eds.), *Principles and practice of informal education*. RoutledgeFalmer.

Gilchrist, A. (2001). Working with networks and organisations in the community. In L. D. Richardson & M. Wolf (Eds.), *Principles and practice of informal education*. RoutledgeFalmer.

Oliver, D., & Thwaites, J. (2001). *Church that works*. Word Publishing.

Plato. (1974). The Republic, Book VII. In *Education thinkers reader, Part 1* (pp. 317–325). London: YMCA George Williams College.

Richardson, L. D. (2005). *Education thinkers reader, Part 1*. London: YMCA George Williams College.

ZOEY WILLIAMS

12. ISLAM AND EDUCATION IN THE COMMUNITY CONTEXT

Zoey Williams is Muslim youth worker. An experienced practitioner with both Muslim and non-Muslim young people, she gained professional qualification and BA Hons degree at the YMCA George Williams College in London.

The underlying themes of this chapter are closely connected with the chapter above and it is advised that they should be read is sequence.

It has become part of youth work tradition to understand the practice as being underpinned by an educational ethos; youth workers, while having a primary concern for the welfare and care of those they work with, look to outcomes that might be understood to be related to social education; the intellectual and personal means to interact and develop in the social context or as Davies and Gibson (1967, p.12) had it, *any individual's increased consciousness* themselves, their *values, aptitudes and untapped resources and of the relevance of these to others.* For them, social education *enhances the individual's understanding of how to form mutually satisfying relationships.* This involves a search for the means to discover *how to contribute to, as well as take from* associations with others

However, in recent decades the aim to socially educate has become largely supplanted by the drive to enact informal and community education. The site of this educational practice is taken to the community, as youth workers are not bound to the parameters of the class room or even the youth centre in terms of delivering and extending their practice.

In this chapter I will explore the nature of informal and community education, in the first instance by developing a critical analysis of both education and community. I will look at East London Mosque's New Muslims Sisters Circle as a test and contrast to some of the precepts of community education. I will go on to discuss media as a means of community 'mis-education' and finally look at ways forward for workers across contexts but essentially in the spirit of Islam.

WHAT IS COMMUNITY?

'An ideal community' might be understood as a group of people who share and/or are working towards common interests/goals; it would be a close knit and supportive, offering unity, safety and support, a sense of belonging and identity.

B. Belton and S. Hamid (eds), Youth Work and Islam:
A leao of faith for young people,155–166.

It might also provide opportunities for people to learn and share ideas, opinions, views, experiences and form relationships. However, the term community is very broad and it has to be questionable if the ideal community does or could exist anywhere outside the professional imagination. In reality, all too often labelling a group as a community leads to 'us and them' divisions. The denser a community is (the more tightly its connections are) the harder it is to get into or out of it. Logically, given this situation, outside influences are minimised while, at the same time, the outside sees those 'inside' as relatively remote and essentially different. Hence the less permeable a community is, the more it becomes comparatively isolated and a site of segregation. Conversely the more porous the boundaries of community are, with people moving in and out, the more imprecise the label of community becomes. In this sort of situation, with people having a plethora of connections with a range of groups or subgroups, more or less interrelated, the notion of community becomes problematic as it is difficult to see individuals as representative of a single community. Perhaps this is why there is no agreed clear definition of what a community actually is.

WHAT IS EDUCATION?

Education might be understood as facilitating the recognition of one's personal potential, talents, skills and abilities. Generally speaking the education practice of youth workers is formulated via the exploration the possibilities of a given environment, using a range of methods and mediums.

However the concept of education and how the notion is used in our society are somewhat contradictory. For the influential educational thinker Friedrich Froebel (1885), the purpose of education is to encourage and guide humans as conscious, thinking and perceiving, ethical beings by personal preference. Froebel argues that without education we are lost souls; we need someone or something to steer us in the right direction, in order for us to be able to think, understand make decisions and achieve. The idea that we can enable ourselves, via education, to choose to move towards a more enlightened state, suggests our development is not essentially about turning ourselves into a particular political or institutional model citizen, who follows dictated rules or who merely obeys the instructions of a ruling group or social class, although this is what a great deal of current youth work practice seem to be implicitly and explicably about in terms of state policy and legislation.

Throughout schooling we are taught to follow directions and regulations and are rewarded for being good students (conforming). The alternative is to be punished for failing to conform (this has come to be called 'rebelling'). This suggests that the purpose of education, as most of us encounter it as young people, is to instil structure, control, discipline and instruct about consequences, rather than to think about and question in order that we might work towards realising our potential, allowing space to explore ideas, promote individuality or freedom of choice. However if everybody stuck to the rules and followed the same paths and lines of thought without questioning and/or trying things out, it is hard to see how scientific advances in medicine and technology (for example) would have been possible.

In the UK educational institutions appear to be more geared to passing exams than promoting an explorative, critical or questioning state of mind. It is clear that this is not suitable for all, as so many fail or drop out of education[1]. Or, looked at another way, what we call education, for a huge number of young people (perhaps the majority) is a process that fails or rejects them. Despite this, society or the state, places a high premium on the attainment of qualifications and continuing education and training into adulthood. With training programmes like 'Skill me Up' and 'Entry to Employment' and their successors, it has been apparent that there is a strong connection between education and employment in the Britain, although this might not apply as directly to young people from more wealthy sectors of society. While education may help individuals progress into better paid jobs and gain status, it is in fact geared to making people more useful in terms of advancing commercial enterprise and keep the UK competitive (with the likes of China and India) as a site for the maintenance of capitalism. The overriding rationale of education in Britain is to produce a comparatively cheap, comparatively flexible/amenable workforce, to supply the means to generate profit for an economic elite investment cadre. As such, education is not about socialising knowledge, or working for the greater good for all, it is an integral part of a greater economic system, tied to rules, structure, order and control. It is manipulative as it encourages collusion with ideas, opinions and values and conformity, while largely maintaining a guise of a benign process of betterment, being linked to employment it is a mechanism to make money (see Chomsky, 2000, 2002). Gilchrist argues that:

Informal educators can help people to develop and value their social networks, thereby making a contribution to the development of 'community'. This enhances individual well-being, social cohesions (not conformity) and creates a collective capacity to organise and manage shared resources. (Deer Richardson. L and Wolfe. M, 2001:116)

This seems to be arguing that without informal educators (the educators that work in and through the community – informal educator also being an appellation sometimes taken on by youth workers) people will not recognise the opportunities and organisations or contribute to wider society. This being the case their development and well-being will be hindered as they are lacking in some way. I feel that this assumes that the role of youth workers is similar to that of a broker; they are seen to have the knowledge and networks and communities rely on them to direct them as they do not have the capability to do this of themselves. It seems that these professionals are also there to help people to become well-rounded and redress the inabilities of communities thus 'empowering' (giving power to) them. Gilchrist goes on to reiterate this assumption;

As individuals their lack of understanding, lack of influence and lack of resources may leave them feeling powerless. Informal educators can help people to overcome this sense of apparent apathy. (ibid: 111)

Another assumption tacitly expressed here is that communities need to be educated (they are relatively ignorant) as they are in need and are not equal to others (those outside the community and of course the professionals). The professionals are called in to solve their problems and educate them as they have the answers:

The professional commitment of informal educators to promoting equality and empowerment for disadvantaged groups means that we need to find ways of combating inequalities and prejudice and restoring an equitable flow of information and resources. (Gilchrist 2001:110)

On the surface professional intervention (incursion) is geared to enhance communities and aid them in development. But Gilchrist (typical of much of the literature surrounding informal and community education) demonstrates the underlining assumptions behind such ambitions.

WHAT IS COMMUNITY EDUCATION?

It has become popular in some of the literature to refer to youth workers as 'community educators'/Community Learning and Development. However, community education in England is funded (at present) by the Skills Funding Agency (SFA – formally the Learning and Skills Council – LSC). There are particual funding streams:
- Employer responsive (skills for work)
- Learner responsive (qualifications/certification)
- Adult safeguarded learning (non-accredited learning – often leisure learning, e.g. wine tasting, flower arranging, craft pursuits and other community based activities classed as 'first steps learning' - also known as PCDL – Personal and Community Development and Learning.)[2]

This work is specifically aimed at adult learners. The Young People's Learning Agency (YPLA) funds young people's learning, such as apprenticeships and advanced apprenticeships and learner responsive provision for young people. While some youth workers, some of the time, might be involved in schemes drawing on this funding, it does not overtly or specifically provide for voluntary, generic or issue based youth work or informal education provision (although Adult Safeguarded Learning is also known as Adult Informal Education). While the Scottish model of community education is more closely related to a youth worker role in England, community education outside Scotland in the British context is usually recognised as being class based, structured and formal learning (although classes, where appropriate, can be based in sports halls, dance studios etc.). This begs the question how can those of us not obliged to follow Scottish policy/legislation (the vast majority of youth workers in the UK) understand ourselves to be community educators?

According to The White Paper on Adult Education published by the DES in 2000 there are two forms of community education. Firstly it is understood 'as an extension of the service provided by second and third-level education institutions into the wider community (section 5.1, p.110)'. This view could be seen to incorporate almost all adult learning opportunities provided by the formal education sector at community level - it is education in the community but not of the community. The other perspective has it that community education, in an ideological sense is;

...a process of communal education towards empowerment, both at an individual and a collective level...it is as an interactive, challenging process, not only in terms of its content but also in terms of its methodologies and decision making processes (DES 2000 section 5.2, p.110)

So, on one hand community education is bringing the educational system out into the community, but not educating about the community or the whole community. There seems to be a focus on adult learning, but what about programmes like the Summer University, which provides tutor lead accredited courses for young people during the summer holidays? Isn't this also formally educating the community to some extent? On the other hand it is argued that community education is for 'empowerment', which seems to assume that there was a lack of power within the community to begin with. No evidence for this supposition is given or implied. Community education is apparently delivered less formally, both on an individual and group basis, and is interactive and challenging, which suggests dialogue and opportunities to explore possibilities. These are two very different ideas about one topic from one document, but this is indicative of the confusion and uncertainty surrounding community education. It appears that there is no overall agreement or appreciable, consensual certainty, as to what it actually is, certainly one that might readily encompass the role of the youth worker/informal educator. This being the case how then can youth workers claim to be doing it (in a definite way)?

IMPACTS OF THE TERM 'COMMUNITY EDUCATION'

While there is no one clear or agreed definition of what community education might be throughout the UK, or consensus what it might do, the term community education exists and a number of people and organisations claim to be carrying out community education and calling themselves 'Community Educators'. So what is role of these 'community educators' and how does this impact on the community? A community education officer works to promote and facilitate access to a wide range of voluntary educational activities by all members of the community, regardless of age ' ...The aim is to enable individuals and communities to take control of their learning and to help break down barriers; the role is, therefore, closely linked to current widening participation and lifelong learning initiatives'. (Teaching and Related Professions Task Group (2007) *Education - Alternatives to Teaching* p.8)

However, it appears that the notions and assumptions of community education undermine the intelligence of the social collectives that are labelled as particular 'communities', as the underlying aims of the proposal of community education presumes that its target group (the community) has a power deficit, and in some cases is deprived of the privileges of other (unspecified) communities. There is also the point that the will to extend 'education' must be based on the postulation that those who are the target of education are in some (unspecified) respect, ignorant. Like aid extended by Western nations to non-industrialised regions, community education can also be used as a tool or weapon to keep control of, or divide a group of people. Aid is promised, given, or withdrawn as a reward, punishment, or encouragement to pursue specific policy courses. It also creates an environment that shapes the norms, outlook, and expectations of the actors in the relationship (Rugumamu 1997. p 11). At the same time, the 'community educator' is often sent into a community in order to change it, so it might comply with standards (extended in policy) set by groups and interests external to that community, such as national or local government. This strategy may involve little or no knowledge or consideration of the needs or culture of the targeted community (indeed some communities are not considered to have any specific culture). At the same time 'change' is used like a battle cry. However, it seems this 'change' is more about altering particular behaviours to correspond to a sort of 'ideologically correct community' that is apparently more like some (unspecified) desired model. The tactics to bring about 'change' are set in place by the setting of 'common targets' in community education. It seems that the aim is to undermine the potential for the generation and maintenance of unique collective social identities in favour of the imposition of a template of the 'right kind' of community.

For all this, outside influences may not be necessarily beneficial to targeted areas, as external interests can underestimate the needs and, in some cases, a population can become worse off as a result of outside intervention. The history of colonisation is the most powerful testament to this perhaps. Over decades African countries have experimented with various development policies, strategies and ideologies that were developed outside the continent with little success (Rugumamu 1997 p. xi). Despite huge amounts of aid from industrialised states, the economic, social and environmental condition of most of non-industrialised nations, and particularly in Sub-Saharan Africa, are in many cases no better and in some worse than they were in the 1980s (ibid. 1997 p.2). In place of a robust economy and improved standards of living, foreign aid has resulted in unprecedented economic stagnation and waste, a crippling debt crisis, human rights abuse, and has encouraged extensive foreign interventions in the national economic policy management. (ibid. 1997 p.1) What appears to be happening is that one model is being applied to several areas, which fails take into account the fact that what works for one area or social setting may not be suitable for another. This sort of strategy seems too replicated in terms of educational and youth work resources in the UK.

This raises a number of questions for youth workers in the British context. For instance:

- If we value difference and identity why then do we go into particular areas that are in many ways unique, organic social spaces with the view of changing them and making them more like others?
- Should we not look to learn from the various cultural structures that arise within our society rather than attempt to crassly change them to conform to some 'grand pattern'?
- If we are setting up professional intervention for the greater good of a particular district or distinctive group, shouldn't we be starting with what the individuals, groups and families want or need rather than seeking to apply what often are generic policy agendas?

Carl Rogers (1979 and 2004) like many others, has noted that if we value independence and as such are concerned with the increasing conformity of knowledge, values and attitudes, prevalent in the contemporary period, we may need to create conditions of learning which encourage uniqueness, self-directedness, and self-initiated learning. When working with others over a period of time in a professional/client relationship, patterns of behaviour tend to form. In some cases the client becomes dependant on the professional. Slowly but inexorably, like foreign aid, this can became a habit-forming drug which erodes self-confidence and the general sense of persona (national) dignity (Rugumamu 1997, p.6). In the youth sphere hard questions need to be asked; what happens when the contract ends, funding runs out or the professional is placed somewhere else? How then can those professionally and/or officially counted within the 'community' (those that have been 'treated') respond? The collective has been 'cordoned off' and has learnt to some extent to rely on its label, the 'entity' that is allocated resources, but the labelling force (the conduit of categorisation) has abandoned them.

COMMUNITY EDUCATION AND THE NEW MUSLIMS SISTERS CIRCLE

Given its vague character together with its apparent purpose and impact, community education, like informal education, is hard to measure. This said, there is a plethora of anecdotal evidence for its success; however most of this has been orchestrated by those with a vested interest in developing a positive picture, those who claim to be community educators and/or academics involved in writing about informal education or the qualification of community educators or related disciplines. As such, the case for community education can hardly be secure and as such must be questioned as a destination for resources and scarce funding.

During my research with the East London Mosque's New Muslims Sisters Circle. The group met once a week. The women only circles listened to lectures, took part in discussions, question and answer sessions lead by an Imam. Members of the group also attended and took part in open days, events and gatherings for Eid etc. They used a crèche facility run by volunteers, as many of the members had young children who also attended the group. In terms of the ethnicity the members identified themselves as being White, Mixed, Asian, Black, British, Bangladeshi etc. The majority of this group were in employment, however some were unemployed or caring for their family. There was also one member who was unable to work as she is disabled. The members travelled to the group from across the London Boroughs such as Tower Hamlets, Newham, Barking and Dagenham, Hackney, Camden and Hammersmith and Fulham, although the majority lived in Tower Hamlets. When I met with them many had joined within the previous 12 months, although others had been involved for up to 12 years. The majority of the members found out about the group through other members, while others found out about it via the internet, friends or through attending open days at the Mosque.

When asked why they attended the group there was a range of responses which included to learn about my religion, to become closer to God, friendship/sisterhood, to have contact with other Muslims, as they do not live near to their family or their family are non-Muslims, to share and gain knowledge (as this is part of their duty as a Muslim) to socialise and to get out of the house.

While there is a socialising theme to the above, there is a strong seam relating to gaining knowledge and education. To seek knowledge is a sacred duty; it is obligatory for every Muslim. The first word revealed of the Qur'an was 'Iqra' – 'READ!' This is about seeking knowledge; an urge to educate oneself, as an autonomous individual, in the case of these women, this was happening within a supportive group. This is very different from the deficit/colonial models that seem to accompany ideas and policy relating to professionally delivered and mediated community and informal education.

The members of the Sisters Circle tended to view the Mosque as a resource for advice and a community centre, as well as a place of worship. This of course is historically what a Mosque has been. However, the Mosque was not the only place where members of the Circle accessed education. The group lead separate lives and had a range of experiences; they come from different places and had encountered various people they may have learnt from. They were, influenced by the mass media (television, the internet, newspapers). They read the Qur'an and complementary books, attended seminars, met with friends and family or were part of secular educational institutions.

One is struck by the both the communal nature of the Sisters Circle but also the independence of its members. From a religious perspective it could be argued that community education started with a divine message giving guidance from God through the prophets and that they were the first religious community educators or community leaders. Their main tasks were to relay the message, confirm the messages from the Prophets that came before them and spread the words of God (laws, morals and manners, ways to worship etc.) and to be role models by practising what they preached. They also shared their knowledge and wisdom and gave guidance and advice thus educating people. Their messages and teachings are still evident today with many remembering the examples of the Prophets and turning to the holy books for guidance. From an Islamic point of view it is believed that all the Prophets were sent with the same underling message to worship and serve one God and to live by His laws, rather than laws made by humanity and that without seeking knowledge and understanding of Islam it is impossible to class oneself as a Muslim.

But to call the Prophets community educators is like claiming what was is the same as what is, which is rarely the case. A penny-farthing or a camel is not a motor bike, even though all three things might be about getting from A to B. Community and informal education are roles produced by a certain type of society while the Prophets, for the most part, were a product of a very different type of social and faith realm. In the present day one could argue that the role of community education in terms of the Sisters Circle is not only to educate those in the community, but to branch outside of the community to spread the messages and breakdown barriers and prejudice through raising awareness of Islam. This might be further justifiable as in the contemporary period there are clear indications of misunderstanding, myth and distortion surrounding the faith and traditions of Islam.

DISTORTED COMMUNITY MIS-EDUCATION

Much of this misapprehension about Islam comes from people who are not representative of Muslims, or by way of politicians or the media representations that are often harmfully distorted. Research into one week's news coverage showed that 91 percent of articles in national newspapers about Muslims were negative (*Jihad Watch*, May 27, 2009)[3]. The authority given to the media is a potent tool to influence society in general. It might be argued that it can educate, but it is sometimes hard not to see much of what is produced as 'news' being more than clumsy propaganda. It is not unusual for depictions of what is sometimes called 'Islamist activity' to be anything but a warped and partial reflection of what is really going on. Exaggeration and bias proliferate, propagating what collectively is an outlandish mythology about the nature of Islam and Muslim populations. This insensitive manipulation of the public mind can and does cause chaos and confusion, while at the same time spreading the seeds of prejudice and division within society. This is really an effort to promote fear to generate sensationalism that is used as a foreground for the main purpose of much of the media; to incline people to think that they need things that they don't, in order that they go out and spend money to bolster the profits of commercial enterprise (which sometimes have direct financial links with the very sections of the media that generate emotive and barely rational 'news'). In this sense the media is perhaps the most prevalent and intrusive source of community education. It has the means to reach out to people all over the world and persuade them to think and act certain ways and as such it does much to determine how we see each other. This great force of mis-education (or propaganda) divides local, national and global society and because of the way it interprets events many now view Islam as a threat and Muslims as extremists or terrorists. This is a problem particularly when there are some whose only knowledge of Islam is based on the negative stereotypes in the media.

It is the west's obsession with Islam, and the tendency to look at Islam through the lens of terror or security....That creates alarm, resistance and further distortion. (Anthea Lipsett, *Education Guardian*, Thursday 28 June 2007)

CONCLUSION

With this in mind, perhaps a major task for those of us working within Muslim social contexts is to become more conscious of developing role models that are able to demonstrate that the negative views are largely unjust and unfair fabrications. A means to this seems to increase our faith and so our urge to seek to understand education as a two way phenomenon that can work to enlighten wider society, portraying the truth to redress the imbalance created by media distortion within society. As Muslims what does this mean? Well, we can have no purposeful part in dividing the society by way of majorities and minorities. Dividing people up into distinct categories or groups on the basis of creed, colour, sect or language risk coming close to racism and sectarianism, such as Islam disallows. Islam encourages unity and aims towards achieving the spirit and fact of Ummah, wherein everyone can be understood as needing to live under one sky in order to flourish rather than perish. This provides us with both a starting point and an aim.

It seems that we need to aband on the less humans aspects of informal and community education and begin to resuscitate the aim to socially educated and use this as a means to question differences and as such become a force that unites people in their potential for solidarity: we all share the same basic needs. For this to happen those of us working in the field need to have a sound knowledge and understanding of the social context of our practice, but also a lasting commitment to its development and growth. But at the same time, by necessity we probably need to be prepared to learn from those we work with, allowing our role to move and follow the gravity of awareness. This will, with the help and collaboration of those we work with and amongst, minimise the risk of misrepresentation and mis-education. The notion of and assumptions that appear inherent in informal and community education seem to insult the intelligence of the people labelled as community members, viewing them as lacking or being deprived. While groups like the Sisters Circle disprove this, far from empowering a given population defined as community these limiting views of the purpose and trajectory of education would appear to be more disempowering than anything else. But this makes it clear that the label of community is a means of categorising, separating and targeting particular groups. In the professional sphere the whole notion of informal and community education is based on a deficit model which suggests that the role of the educator is to be or act like as a saviour (latter day missionaries reminiscent of colonial times). The literature surrounding the notion of informal education often appears to suggest that the professional has a monopoly on awareness, knowledge and power (without anything close to an awareness of what constitutes 'power' in the informal social setting). 'Community' seems to be shorthand for 'a group of victims' or 'non-conformists' which needs 'educators' in order to function or 'reform'. This is not a healthy perception; it cannot promote sustainable or beneficial relationships as firstly it creates dependency, which can lead to communities becoming manipulated and controlled, and secondly it robs local populations of a sense of their own influence, (the type of potential Sisters Circle used) which is the means to taking authority over their context and lives. For professionals to set themselves up as the controllers of people's destiny is close to a blasphemy in any religion, but it is equally an affront to any humanitarian response to those with which we share our being.

In informal and community education practice there is usually a set agenda, it includes targeting and labelling people as 'community members'. This is carried out in order to make some form of desired change in line with policy objectives (it would be hard for any community educator to counter organisational objectives, generally drawn from state policies and corporate aims, for any length of time). This pre-set agenda, although ostensibly produced alongside the 'community' is always delimited by outside influences (it results in a choice of similar alternatives rather than a reflection of a purely locally generated schema) and by necessity (of funding and legislation) a means to meet aims and/or targets arising out of organisational objectives that themselves are the progeny of policy engendered at a national and sometimes international level. Yes, consultations are invariably part of the preamble to provision. But is it usual that needs or wants expressed in these consultations that even have a chance of contradicting the wider political motives of local or national government will be addressed? Professionals and their employers (the bodies that pay them) have their own agendas and need to meet objectives and targets. This might involve (as in the African and Asian contexts) that 'aid' is provided but (as in the African and Asian contexts) this does not automatically mean that those getting the aid will ultimately benefit.

With no clear explanation of what community education actually means or does, together with the inherent problems measuring whether a community has been educated, how can we persist, with any confidence, pursuing the notion of community education? If we are asked to just believe in it without any solid evidence of its applicability or credibility can it be anymore than a somewhat

WILLIAMS

shallow faith (a myth)?. If it is not something between a superstition and a legend it is merely a transparent tool of the state which is committed first and foremost to the growth of commercialism.

If community education can be salvaged it might be as a definitely locally based practice that is formulated and lead by people that inhabit that area, using their knowledge and understanding of it. Formal education, set in schools and colleges, needs to follow national curricular. This is hardly ever hidden; what a school is speaks for itself for the most part, and part of that is to make sure, as far as possible, that children from every background have a chance of getting a similar level of education. For any informal practice to be authentically educative the current clandestine operation of the same will need to be abandoned; it needs not to be controlled by state funded (directly or indirectly) organisations, nor can it be controlled by professionals that in reality are no more than largely covert agents set to achieve policy targets under the guise of benign actors on a stage that they, their employers or the academics who trained them define as 'community'. If we can reinvent community education as a shared social pursuit in something like this spirit it will unavoidably be better equipped to address issues both from within and about the local social realm. However, in the last analysis it might be we need to revive interest in and direct our practice much more towards an overt and honestly mediated social educative trajectory.

NOTES

[1] For example see http://readingroom.lsc.gov.uk/lsc/2006/externalrelations/press/nat-gcsedropoutsunemployable-pr-aug2006.pdf
[2] See Skills Funding Agency Policy Summaries 2010/11
http://readingroom.skillsfundingagency.bis.gov.uk/sfa/skillsfundingagencypolicysummaries-201011.pdf
[3] http://www.jihadwatch.org/2009/05/saudi-gazette-negative-coverage-of-islam-and-muslims-in-the-media-is-no-secret-and-its-making-people.

BIBLIOGRAPHY

Chomsky, N. (2000). Chomsky on miseducation (D. Macedo, Ed.). Rowman & Littlefield.
Chomsky, N. (2002). Chomsky on democracy and education (C. P. Otero, Ed.). Routledge.
Davies, B., & Gibson, A. (1967). The social education of the adolescent. University of London Press.
Deer Richardson, L., & Wolfe, M. (2001). Principles and practice of informal education- learning through life. Routledge.
Froebel, F. (1885). The education of man. Appleton-Century Co.
Rogers, C. (1979). Freedom to learn: A view of what education might become. Merrill Pub Co.
Rogers, C. (2004). On becoming a person. Constable; New ed edition.
Rugumamu, S. M. (1997). Lethal aid: Illusion of socialism and self-reliance in Tanzania. Africa Research & Publications.

BRIAN BELTON

13. MERCY – CROSSING THE BOUNDARIES

In this short chapter I want to show how a central facet of belief in God can demonstrate how we share our humanity. As believers in God we rely on His mercy in our everyday existence. However, God's mercy is necessarily reflected in our actions towards each other if our existence is to mean anything or be of any worth. The opportunities for this occur throughout every day of our life, although we might miss them in our hurry to get our life lived.

As youth workers we are constantly presented with decisions that might involve mercy (either the giving or the getting of it). Mercy of course is central to Islam as a faith and so as a way of life. The allusions to mercy in Islamic teaching are too numerous to catalogue here, but a few examples are provided below to illustrate the range and nature of mercy within Islamic thought and belief:

...This [revelation] *is a means of insight from your Lord, and to provide guidance and, mercy unto people who will believe.* (Qu'ran 7:203)

Affliction has befallen me: but You are the most merciful of the merciful! (Qu'ran 21:83)

My Mercy overspreads everything (Qu'ran 7:156-157)

If an unbeliever were to know the abounding mercy of God, not a single one will despair to make it to Paradise. (Saheeh Al-Bukhari, Saheeh Muslim, Al-Tirmidhi)

Indeed, My mercy supersedes my punishment (Saheeh Al-Bukhari, Saheeh Muslim)

Even one percent of divine mercy fills our mortal existence;

God created a hundred portions of mercy. He placed one portion between His creation due to which they have compassion on each other. (Saheeh Al-Bukhari, Saheeh Muslim, Al-Tirmidhi, and others.)

Islam also recognises the place of mercy in other faiths. For instance in the Torah of Moses:

...In the writing whereof there was guidance and mercy for all who stood in awe of their Lord. (Qu'ran 7:154)

Mercy is premised or founded on listening; the Qu'ran itself was written to be read but also listened to in recital;

Hence, when the Quran is recited, listen to it, and listen in silence, so that you might be graced with [God's] *mercy.* (Qu'ran 7:204)

B. Belton and S. Hamid (eds), *Youth Work and Islam:*
A leap of faith for young people,167–171.

However, while youth work theory values listening it very rarely outlines what listening actually entails. At the same time notions of 'justice', 'democracy' and 'freedom not only supersede mercy, they take up the moral space, although it is hard to understand how without mercy we can see ourselves as fully human let alone experience spiritual well being.

Mercy is of course a central tenet of Christianity. This is beautifully expressed by the Christian mystic Julian of Norwich in her *Revelations of Divine Love*, written in 1393.

Julian was born towards the end of 1342 and was concerned centrally with, *The constancy of God's love.* For her, no power in heaven or on earth can stop God loving us. God's love, which is pure compassion, will search us out to the end, in whatever state we may be. But, in our everyday lives, the hours that will make up the rest of this day and all our tomorrows, how do we express this 'pure compassion', this 'constant love'?

To be compassionate means 'to share in suffering' and that often means to share in love. The opportunity for this sharing arises in our relationships with others and might be exemplified in the silence of the listener.

The true listener is the person that, in active quietude and benign stillness attends to what the other is saying. This is distinctly different from the technical performance of the counsellor or the mechanical response of the therapist. They who *listen* offer open humaneness, a path of concentrated tranquillity.

Frequently, what we think of listening is a pastiche of this. As James Joyce depicted in *Ulysses* (1922) what looks like listening can be merely a queue for the opportunity to talk. In such exchanges little is absorbed of what the other person is saying and whole evenings are taken up by a kind of blank and cold form of verbal table tennis. Each person occupied by the point they want to make or the tale they want to tell, to entrance, entertain or impress. The result of this is often frustration; the feeling that nothing has actually been communicated, and that is perhaps because nothing has been really heard.

This kind of dissatisfaction might be related to what Julian, in her *Revelations of Divine Love* described as wrath, that which opposes peace and love.

Julian argues that in the spiritual love of God there can be no wrath. According to her wrath is in us, not in God. It arises out of a fear of God's love and the possibilities this offers. Maybe it is the fear of such intimacy that stops us from truly listening. For it is in relation to others that we come closest to God. 'When two or more of you are gathered in my name there is love' (Matthew 18:20)

Wrath arises because we have not felt God's all compassionate love that has the power to free us from the frustration of being made mute through the lack of listening, the opportunity of silence. This profound expression of calm serenity can be a mid-wife of compassion, the very soul of love and mercy.

Julian's God is gentle, forbearing, patient, understanding and…quiet. For her, our love for one another must necessarily follow the same pattern as God's love for us.

One place to express this is in the dynamic silence of really, really, really listening; a merciful listening.

Julian is the apostle of reconciliation. When we diminish others we diminish ourselves. This is the result of a lack of mercy. We undermine our capacity to express our spirituality and in the process, put ourselves in hell. So, as the speaker remains unheard and undernourished, so the listener, having gained no sustenance from the encounter, also experiences similar hunger pains.

Julian tells us not be fearful, she asks us to live fully and this must include the expression of our spirit. For this to happen we need to be able to hear each other, above the din of the world. In quietness we can listen and in return be heard. Mercy is a mutually enforcing emotional phenomenon.

To conclude I want to leave you with one last compelling idea from Julian. Love is not exemplified in equality or in its progenitor justice as we usually think of it. According to Pope John Paul II: *True mercy is the most profound form of justice.* In Julian, justice is swallowed up in mercy. Isaac of Syria, Bishop of Ninave in the 7th century, is acknowledged as one of the greatest writers of the Christian East. He told us, *Do not speak of God as just, for his justice is not in evidence in his actions towards you* (Patton, K.P. and Stratton Hawley, 2005 p.263)

As such, to enhance our spiritual selves, we need to move beyond seeing conversation, the active being with another, as a 'just' form of exchange, a 'my turn now' encounter. Conversation is not an expression of equality. 'Fairness' is not an issue. When we are in conversation we are involved in a mutual process of giving and receiving. Within this we accept each other; we embrace one another's feelings, ideas and passions. As such, we are involved in a reciprocal act of mercy. Listening becomes a form of symbiotic mercy; a commensal, amenable situation, wherein we express and experience expression.

In youth work, justice is a word that seems to be used every working day. But I have rarely heard a youth worker refer to mercy. However, can justice, without mercy, be justice? Justice without mercy precludes expressions like 'everyone deserves a second chance'; the carrying out of justice means no one gets any breaks, as codes of practice, rules and regulations are preeminent – 'he deserved to score a goal' but the laws of the game disallowed it. The law might be an ass, but the law is the law and rules are made to be obeyed. Justice weighs up the facts; in English common law you have the likelihood of guilt given all the facts, in criminal law one is innocent until proven guilty beyond reasonable doubt; there is leniency but not real mercy – in a court of law, where justice is metered out, you can't, once guilt is pronounced, be 'let off' as such – even a Royal pardon needs a reason set in the process of justice.

In the prologue to his autobiography, *A Sparrow's Flight,* a figure with quite a high profile in relation to justice, Lord Hailsham[1], quotes a passage from the Venerable Bede's 'Ecclesiastical History'. At an assembly near York in the year 627 (five years after Muhammad migrated to Medina, then known as 'Yathrib') before Edwine, the pagan king of Northumbria, an unknown member had spoken;

Such, oh king, seems to me the present life on earth, as if, on a Winter's night a sparrow should swiftly fly into the hall and coming in one door, instantly fly out through another, somewhat like disappears the life of man, but of what follows or what went before, we are utterly ignorant.

Taking up that pagans theme, Lord Hailsham offers a poem in his epilogue, the *Sparrow's Prayer*. Perhaps it can help us focus on the place of mercy in our practice; mercy for those we work with and amongst and ourselves;

Father, before this sparrow's earthly flight
Ends in the darkness of a winter's night
Father, without whose word no sparrow falls
Hear this, thy weary sparrow, when he calls.

Mercy, not justice is his contrite prayer,
Cancel his guilt and drive away despair,
Speak but the word and make his spirit whole,
Cleanse the dark places of his heart and soul

Speak but the word, and set his spirit free,
Mercy, not justice, still his constant plea,
So shall thy sparrow, crumpled wings restored
Soar like a lark and glorify his Lord.
Thanks be to God!.

Mercy, in our modern world, feels unfashionable. What it means to those we work with is hard to say, perhaps you might find out. But it is implicit and explicit in every faith; it is something which crosses the boundaries of faith as it is so fundamental to our human needs and the means of faith. As I started with an Islamic theme I will conclude with the carnicht of Anchoress Julian of Norwich:

Most holy Lord,
The ground of our beseeching,
Who through your servant Julian,
Revealed the wonder of your love,
Grant, that as we are created in your nature,
and are restored by your grace,
Our wills may be so made one with yours,
That we may come to see you face-to-face,
and gaze on you forever.
Through Christ our Lord. Amen.

NOTES

[1] Between 1970 and 1974 Hailsham was Lord Chancellor, a role in that era, which made him by law, responsible for the efficient functioning and independence of the courts and the head of the judiciary in England and Wales.

BIBLIOGRAPHY

Hailsham. (1990). *A sparrow's flight.* Collins.
Joyce, J. (1922). *Ulysses: A novel.* Sylvia Beach.
Julian of Norwich. (2003). *Revelations of divine love* (A. C. Spearing & E. Spearing, Eds.). Penguin Classics.
Patton, C. P., & Stratton Hawley, J. (Eds.). (2005). *Holy tears: Weeping in the religious imagination.* Princeton University Press.

ANDREW SMITH

14. PROMOTING CHRISTIAN/MUSLIM DIALOGUE BETWEEN YOUNG PEOPLE OF FAITH

Dr Andrew Smith grew up in East Sussex and has lived in Birmingham since 1988. He has worked for the Christian charity Scripture Union since 1994. In the year 2000 he pioneered the Faith and Young People programme which ran Christian-Muslim dialogue for teenagers. He is currently the Director of Youth Encounter at Scripture Union which seeks to further this work.

He is the Christian youth specialist on the national Christian-Muslim Forum and is the founder and chair of 'The Feast' a Birmingham based charity that promotes work with Muslim and Christian teenagers. His doctoral thesis looked at how churches can help Christian young people build confident friendships with Muslims. Dr Smith has written for a variety of publications on Christian Muslim relations. He regularly speaks and lecturers on these issues particularly focussing on the involvement of young people in dialogue. He is married to Sarah, a primary head teacher, and they have two sons. They are members of a local Anglican Church where both Andrew and Sarah are involved in leadership

INTRODUCTION

I recently asked two young women, both 15 years old, to explain to a group of Muslim and Christian young people how their faith helped them live in a secular society, which many see as often contradicting the teachings of their religion. The young Christian woman spoke passionately about the time when, at a meeting, she really committed her life to being a follower of Jesus and felt God touch her in a real and powerful way. She talked about how that felt and what it meant to her. When I asked what difference, if any, it made on a day to day basis she paused and said; 'Well I swear less!' I then asked the same questions of the young Muslim woman. She expressed herself with equal passion about a trip to Mecca for the Umrah. She talked about how she felt close to Allah and how he had touched her life. I concluded that interview with the same question as I had asked the young Christian. She too paused before saying (to much laughter) 'I also swear less than I used to!'

For me, this experience summed up the potential that bringing Muslim and Christian teenagers together has:

B. Belton and S. Hamid (eds), Youth Work and Islam:
A leao of faith for young people,173–186.

- *It offers a situation wherein their faith can be taken seriously*
- *It can provide the space to demonstrate and develop the skills to discuss this with people of another faith*
- *It gives an opportunity to deal with their world, not just the world of adult interfaith specialists*
- *It can highlight the similarities and clear differences between their faiths*
- *It might also be fun.*

However, the event at which the young people spoke also epitomised the challenges of this work. It was a small event (18 young people) with groups who had met before, but it needed practitioners to encourage and persuade the young people to attend. We also needed to convince parents that this was a good and/or useful activity for their children to be involved with.

The event had been postponed once because one group of young people had too many other things on, but after some hard work, it turned out to be one of the most inspiring and creative events my agency has organised for many years.

I'm a Christian who has been involved in Christian based youth work since 1988. I have worked in a variety of contexts in Birmingham. For over 10 years I worked in schools in that city. I was employed by a Christian charity as a schools worker and would be invited by schools to lead Collective Worship and to teach Christianity in RE lessons. As I undertook this work I often asked myself, 'How can I, as a Christian, discuss faith with the Muslim young people I work with, who are very keen to discuss religious issues?' Wrestling with this led me to re-evaluate my attitude towards the Muslim young people I met and worked with. Eventually this led me to develop a programme of dialogue events based on constructive faith discussion.

The comments and observations that follow are my reflections as a Christian who has worked amongst Muslim young people for over 15 years. This work has led me to read widely both Christian and Muslim texts on youth work and attitudes towards young people. It has involved me meeting regularly with and working alongside Muslim youth workers. What follows is a reflection of this journey and the lessons I've learnt. Where I make observations about attitudes I've seen, read or encountered within the Muslim community I trust that these will be taken in the spirit in which they are given, that of a colleague who has been asked to work with Muslim youth practitioners, thinking through issues of inter-faith encounters between young Muslims and Christians.

THE HISTORY

When I was working in schools, quite often some pupils would want to carry on discussing some of the topics outside the classroom. I had many fascinating conversations with them over lunch or during break times. But there nearly always came to a point where the conversation got stuck, usually because we got bogged down in discussions about whose faith was the most reliable or true. At such points we would bring out the latest 'proof' that we had read or heard. As I reflected on the nature of these conversations it occurred to me that all of us were struggling to find a way to authentically speak of our faith to someone else who also had deeply held convictions about their faith. In a country with large numbers of people of different faiths (and secularists, some passionately committed to their world view) finding a the means to live out and speak about our beliefs, in ways that lead to positive engagement rather than dismissive rejection or conflict, feels both useful and developmental.

HOW TO ENGAGE

The conversations I had with the young people in schools sometimes ran into difficulties for a variety of reasons. These included:
1) The ways we had been 'taught' (and perhaps sometimes habituated) to engage with each other's faith.
2) The emotional and spiritual development of those involved
3) Explorations of truth

TEACHING

A while ago I undertook some research into the role of young people in Christian/Muslim dialogue. As part of this I looked into what Muslims and Christians in the UK are teaching their young people about other faiths and how to relate to them (Smith, A. 2004). If one spends time looking into the variety of printed and web based resources for young Muslims and Christians it often becomes apparent that the writers from both faiths have similar attitudes towards one another.

Not unusually, in terms of the issues discussed (identity, sexuality, prejudice etc) attempts to understand other faiths are absent. Young people are often encouraged to discuss a wide variety of topics, but it is rare for such material to ask how they might understand or relate to people of other faiths. Given this it is hard to avoid the implicit assumption that the young people accessing this material live in mono-cultural communities. Consequently relating to other faiths can be made to seem irrelevant. However, when other faiths were mentioned explanations and analysis can be very simplistic, occasionally bordering on straightforward stereotyping; 'all white people are Christians', 'all Asians are Muslims' etc. This sort of material might also advise young people to stay away from the influence of other faiths, to avoid confusion, offering a fairly simplistic theology of 'them and us'; 'we're right, good and going to paradise; they are wrong, bad and going to hell'.

This seems to lead to the rather hopeless credo that it was better to only have friends from the same faith, or if you do have friends from another faith, the friendship should be maintained only whilst there is a chance that they will convert to your faith (for a Muslim perspective see, for example, Burney, S 1999 and Maqsood, R 1994: 57).

This approach to speaking of other faiths can easily lead to a competitive or confrontational attitude. The challenges I had in speaking effectively to Muslim young people came about, partly, because we had each gown up with the ideas that suggested that looking to understand other faiths was something harmful, while the only point mixing with people from other faiths being proselytising. Whilst I would, as a Christian, affirm my belief and the truth I find in the Bible, I am happy for Muslims to tell me of the truth they draw from the Qur'an. However, often the challenge is to find ways to tell of these truths, while developing appropriate attitudes towards the 'other', which allow perspectives to be both spoken and heard.

The kind of defensive approach highlighted above risks putting people in a position where they are dismissive of or deaf to the beliefs of others and as such insensitive in the way they speak the truths they hold so dear.

THE EMOTIONAL AND SPIRITUAL DEVELOPMENT OF YOUNG PEOPLE

James Fowler pioneered research into Faith Development. He devised a systematic method for analysing and understanding faith development, regardless of faith background (Fowler, J 1981). Within his model, although he doesn't tie it directly to age, and is cautious of broad generalisations, he suggests that many teenagers go through a stage which he refers to as *'synthetic-conventional faith'*. This is a conformist stage, wherein the opinions of significant others are paramount, and where beliefs are tacitly held. Any ideology adhered to at this point will often be a fairly consistent cluster of beliefs, but won't have been objectified. As a consequence when their perspectives are challenged young people can feel that all their belief structures (along with those of the significant others with whom they agree) are being called into question. In my experience, the reaction of many young people when they feel their beliefs are being questioned is to become defensive. This can be expressed as anger, frustration or disengagement.

TRUTH

Unfortunately, quite predictably, encounters between Muslims and Christians can result in significant emphasis being placed on determining which scripture is true and therefore most reliable. The unavoidable implication of this is that the debate centres on defining one or the other scripture as false and consequently unreliable.

Many Christians and Muslims might want to assert the exclusive truth claims contained within their faiths. The problem with this approach is that it is all too easy to get stuck at the level of trying to 'prove' which is 'most true' while failing actually discuss the usefulness or meaning of the ideas contained within the scripture one is effectively defending against.

Many of the young people I have spoken to have some loose grasp on the arguments used by polemicists to prove the validity of their faith, but with little understanding of the wider issues our discussions rarely got beyond quite crude assertions that texts had been altered. What transformed our conversation was when I just asked these young people to tell me what was the best thing about being a Muslim. I then told them what I thought the best thing was about being a Christian. Suddenly we were discussing our faith as a lived reality, not a defensive theoretical discussion borrowed from vaguely understood scholars.

Given the issues highlighted above it seems to me that if we are to work with young people to engage with others from different faiths, we need to take these issues seriously. We need to develop credible, legitimate theological reasons for engagement that can be communicated to young people and their 'gatekeepers'. As youth workers we can, by example and intentionally, seek out opportunities to meet with people different to ourselves. Along with this we need to work with young people develop a confidence in their own faith that is not predicated on the dismissing of others. This might equip them to listen effectively to questions, avoiding the resort to defensive aggression.

This being the case, we are obliged to find ways of speaking about faith that works to spark the imagination of young people in order that they might engage with the content of the faith of people they meet and its meaning for them, rather than constantly reworking the rather isolationist arguments of others.

MUSLIM AND CHRISTIAN YOUTH WORK

Working to bring Muslim and Christian young people to come together a number of similarities and differences might be highlighted, in theology, practice and attitudes towards youth work. While the theological differences between Christianity and Islam have been well documented by Muslims and Christians (see for example al-Faruqi, I 1998), there has been less attention paid to the differences between youth work in the two faiths. At one level the differences are obvious and the result of history and scale. Churches have been running youth work programmes in the UK for several decades and have been involved with specialist work with young people for centuries. Within Christian youth work there are a wide range of approaches, methods and activities for young people and practitioners, including holidays, music festivals, training weekends, degree courses and many published and on-line resources (you can read about the development of this in 'Growing up Evangelical' Ward, P 1996).

The Muslim community in Britain is both smaller and newer (although it has been present for much longer than most people think – see Ansari 2004) than the Christian community, consequently the resources for youth work in the Muslim community are overall fewer, although they are growing and diversifying rapidly, perhaps more so than any other sector at the time of writing. Both faith communities have challenges caring for and nurturing the belief perspective of the young people in they work with and amongst, as well as finding and training suitable practitioners to forward an appropriate faith vision alongside effective practice, so finding the time, resources and enthusiasm to promote and engage in inter-faith work often comes low down the list of priorities. Not only that but both run to different timetables and schedules. Much Christian youth work during the summer tends to revolve around holidays and music festivals, so many youth workers from the sector are not available for local initiatives. This isn't always the same with Muslim youth workers who, if they are available for interfaith activities, it is during the summer school holidays.

Another difference hinges simply on the term 'youth work'. For many churches this means the 13-23 age bracket, with most emphasis on the under 18's. In the Muslim context I work with it refers to the 18-30 age group. Consequently one group might be working with the young people with the issues arising out of puberty and GCSE's, while the other is dealing with work and marriage considerations. If one is looking to bring the two groups together being clear about the age group concerned is important but easily overlooked (until a group of 13 year olds arrive to find themselves spending a day with a bunch of people in their late 20's!).

However, if one delves beneath the surface there is another difference which can say something important about the differences between the work Christians and Muslims undertake with young people. Christian youth work usually places strong emphasis on 'relational youth work'. This involves the passing on and nurturing of faith and is seen as being passed from one life to another. Faith is modelled and lived as well as taught; knowledge of the faith matters but it is communicated through what is understood as appropriate, genuine relationships (for a more detailed description see Bishop Graham Cray in 'Mission Shaped Youth' Sudworth, T 2007). The underlying reasoning for this is the belief that Christians have a relationship with God. The Bible says that Christians are adopted as God's children and so call God 'Father'. The consequence of this is that churches invest a lot of time and energy in employing, training and resourcing youth workers who then recruit and train groups of volunteers to assist in the task.

While there are exceptions and things are changing all the time, my observations of Muslim youth work is that it is much more based on the passing on of knowledge. There are many resources both on-line and in print for Muslim young people that give a lot of knowledge about the faith. There are numerous websites offering the chance to 'Ask the Imam' where young people send in their questions and concerns. Whilst there is a growing number of Muslim youth workers and volunteers, it has been more usual for Mosques to provide activities that are based around the passing on of knowledge. When I've talked to Muslim friends about these differences they point to the Islamic idea of submitting to the will of Allah and the subsequent desire to understand his will. The youth workers do get to know and build relationships with young people but this seems (to me as an observer) to be rooted in the desire to pass on knowledge to the young people.

These differences are sometimes articulated by young people themselves. When I speak to young Muslims about their faith they commonly refer to growing in knowledge; Christians tend talk of growing in their relationship to God. At the same time each community have their own expectations of the events and activities they organise for young people. Many Muslim's I've spoken to want young people to learn and such to be taught about their faith as a first priority. Generally speaking, Christians want to facilitate the development of relationships with and between the young people and as such tend to favour a more informal practice atmosphere. Of course Christian young people are more used to this model; they don't expect youth work to replicate school. It is not unusual for Muslim young people (and more certainly their parents) to feel more comfortable with a more structured and formal programme.

What I hope the reader will understand from this very brief and necessarily (given the space I have) generalised overview of youth work within the Christian and Muslim faith communities, is both have similar concerns that exist alongside with some significant and some more subtle differences in terms of their approach to and their experience/understanding of youth work is or might be. It should also be noted that there is also diversity within the faiths' expectations of youth work, while there are also differences of emphasis within faiths; particular examples of Catholic youth work might have quite different emphasises to incarnations of Baptist or Methodist youth work (all have their own traditions and organisations).

I hope to show that bringing the two groups together is both possible and productive and that while there are distinctions and dissimilarities, there are also a range of commonalities; if we were to number both sides of the issue it is likely that the latter might outweigh the former (we are all human). For all this, the considerations that might prevent engagement and/or cause friction or confusion, need to be thought about when planning and running events for young people.

GETTING TOGETHER

Over the past decade I have run a number of events for young people and have carried out some research as to what motivates them to attend. Overwhelmingly their main reasons for getting involved are to:
– *Meet people*
– *Make friends*
– *Understand one another*
        and
– *Work for the good of society.*
I have found that young people approach inter-faith encounters from a pragmatic and relational perspective; 'It's a good thing to do and we'll make some new friends'.

179

Very few young people I have spoken to have a clearly worked out theology as to why they should engage, although often the command to 'love your neighbour' will be cited. While it is not uncommon for Christian young people to quote this as it is a direct command from Jesus (see Mark, Chapter 12 verses 28-24), I hear this being used more frequently by Muslim young people as well. As I understand, the importance of caring for neighbours is taught in Sura 4: 36 and the concept of loving our neighbour formed a central part of the letter 'A Common Word Between Us and You' sent from Muslim to Christian leaders in 2006 (www.acommonword.com).

The idea of engagement being motivated by relationships has also been explored by writers such as Talal, who argues that now that Muslims and Christians are living in close proximity to one another they need to concern themselves with the well being of each other (Talal, H 2000: 166).

As well as being motivated by friendship, young people are inspired to get involved if the discussions are going to be relevant to them. This often involves practical considerations rather than theological ones; addressing issues that matter to them. I've found that the young people are much more interested in talking about life as a teenager, the media or fashion than analysing faith related questions like who Jesus is, or in what way are our sacred texts revealed or inspired (topics that seem to exercise a number of academics involved in dialogue, and not a few youth workers, which have their importance but in the appropriate context).

I've asked young people about two other issues that are often cited as important as important in dialogue events:
* *Conflicts between Christians and Muslims*
   and
* *The place of Da'wah or evangelism*
It is informative that, in my experience, no teenagers have ever raised the issue of Christian-Muslim conflict as a significant issue for dialogue with other teenagers. Clearly there have been, and sadly continue to be, significant conflicts between people of different faiths and there are important issues about the way minorities are treated when any faith group are the majority population in any situation. However, I have found that such considerations have not been significant in terms of young people to getting involved in interfaith discussions. When I have asked whether we should discuss such areas there has been reluctance. When it has happened there is a desire to learn from the mistakes and to do what can be done to see that such discord is avoided.

A much more complicated issue is Da'wah or evangelism. Is there any place for this is dialogue? Can we meet without in some way bearing witness to our faith?

Recently I accompanied some Muslim and Christian young men on an outdoor activity weekend. Between the mountain biking, canoeing, low ropes course and football we discussed the types of risky behaviour that young people might get involved in and possible motivations for the same. This led us to think about whether there are good risks as well as bad risks (e.g. sticking up for someone being bullied might risk our credibility but be a good thing to do). Within this we asked if our faiths might inspire us to take good risks. The question was asked whether going away with people of another faith was in any way risky. After one or two people had talked about the physical risks of mountain biking (one lad had gone over the handlebars and ended up at A and E!) a young man quietly said, 'there's the risk of conversion'.

For many people (especially adults – and I write this as a parent of two young men who regularly mix with friends of a variety of faiths and none) this is the big fear. Will they come back the same faith as they went? But also, for some, there is the concern that their calling to engage in Da'wah or evangelism is being denied them in dialogue encounter, so that by participating they are already compromising a deep and important part of their faith.

Some, in their concern to protect young people use the language of 'no compromise', suggesting that we can meet with people from a different faith and come away unchanged in any way. I firmly believe that when we meet anyone, and particularly those that might at first seem very different to ourselves, we are almost certainly likely to be changed in some way, even if only slightly or in quite a subtle way. The challenge for those of us involved with young people is to work with them so that they might be able to decide and agree on appropriate boundaries; what do they think of the 'no compromise' stance? Are their issues on which on consensus is possible or desirable?

When I've asked Christian young people if their Muslim friends have influenced them a number have been able to highlight ways in which they had been influenced and changed through their encounters and friendships with Muslims. I'm pleased to say that most (although sadly not all) of the encounters were positive and they could identify ways in which they had changed for the better as a result of meeting Muslims (Smith, A 2009). These young people remained firmly Christian and many had a deep desire to share their faith with their friends (Muslim or otherwise) yet they were open to the positive influence of these 'other faith' friends. Interestingly they received very little direct guidance on this from Christian workers. This contradicts the often mooted idea that non-Christians might, through the influence of peer pressure, lead young Christians away from faith. As has already been stated one can find a similar attitude amongst Muslim writers such as Burney.

Bringing young people together can provide a place and a means wherein each bears witness to their faith and at the same time generate a space to do this sensitively. We can make ourselves equipped to listen to others without feeling intimidated or threatened. While such situations are not appropriate for the language and ambition of conversion, they can be places of authentic witness (Board for Mission and Unity 2984).

How we can accomplish this will be looked at later in the chapter, but I just want to conclude this section by confirming that young people and particularly teenagers have a specific role to play in Christian/Muslim relations.

INVOLVING YOUNG PEOPLE

There are, at least, four reasons why I would suggest it is vital that young people are encouraged to meet people of other faiths and should be equal participants with adults, not just people practicing for the future.

1. Many of young people are already mixing with people of other faiths in daily life, perhaps more than the majority of adults. In schools, colleges, shopping centres, universities or on-line, young people are often socialising and building friendships/relationships more regularly than their parents or faith leaders. Yet as I have tried to show, this often happens with very little good guidance as to how they can be faithful to their beliefs and yet open to others in their routine interactions and friendships with individuals and groups from other faiths.

    Even if young people are not mixing now, the chances are that as they move on to university or out to work they will find themselves rubbing shoulders with people who have a deep commitment to other faiths, and as the writers of the 'A Common Word Between Us and You' argued, how Muslims and Christians get on will affect the whole world.

2. Young people meeting with folk from other faiths is important for the future direction of our faith communities. Logically young people are not just the future of our faiths but are a full and active part now (they do not exist as population separate from the wider faith). However, there are young people in our Mosques and Churches now who in the future will become significant local, national and international leaders.

    If we look at the history of Christian/Muslim encounters one can argue that people's attitudes towards each other have been influenced both by their sacred texts and the contact they have had with people of the other faith. How sacred texts are used or interpreted is often deeply influenced by the context in which they are read. If they are read in the context of secure friendship with others this can lead to a very inclusive and positive reading, which can remain faithful, yet allow space for others to consider ideas and ask questions. If we accept this premise then we need to ask what we can do to prepare those who might go on to be the leaders and influencers in the future.

    Imagine what the relationship between Christianity and Islam in the UK might look like if all the leaders of various denominations, traditions and organisations had grown up having friends of the other faiths and having learnt how to speak of their faith sensitively, knowing how to listen, ask constructive question and give informative answers; being open to the positive influence of others.

3. Young people can play a key role in Christian/Muslim relations because they often have far fewer hang ups or concerns about discussing issues or asking questions than adults, who can become embarrassed or overly self-conscious about their position.

    It is not common for young people to bring a list of grievances or historical concerns to such events. It is rare for them not to come ready to build friendships and have a good time. They also ask questions with a refreshing honesty and are not (as sometimes some adults might, consciously or unconsciously) looking for offence. Among the many questions I've heard the following are just a few that have been answered honestly and never having caused offence.

- *How do you recognise each other when you're wearing a veil?*
- *Why do you eat bacon?*
- *What do Christians believe happens to people when they die?*
- *Have you ever got drunk?*
- *What do you believe about the Prophet Mohammed?*
- *Are terrorists true Muslims?*

4. It is useful for young people to be involved in interfaith encounters because they seem to have an ability to compartmentalise life more effectively than adults. The benefit of this is that they can hear things about Muslims or Christians in the media without allowing those ideas to impact negatively on their view of their friends from that faith. In my experience young people tend to be relatively adept at treating their friend as a person, not as a representative of their entire faith. They also seem less likely to blame their friends for things other people who share their friend's faith might do or say. This is quite a generalisation, so it needs to be understood cautiously, but peer relationships between young people appear to be far more directive in terms of their behaviour than might be found in adults.

Given the above, I believe young people have a vital role to play in Christian/Muslim dialogue, not as mini-adults in waiting, but as participants in their own right, with things to learn from adults but also things to teach adults.

GOOD PRACTICE

If we are going to work with young people with the aim of promoting Christian/Muslim dialogue and encounter, then we need to be effective youth workers. I've discussed above some of the differences between Muslim and Christian youth work, but teenagers themselves share a lot of things in common and any work with young people needs to take their needs, as young people, first and foremost (we owe them a duty of care beyond and between faith boundaries).

Good practice in inter-faith or dialogue work needs to be rooted in good practice in youth work. I've been to too many inter-faith events for young people where a series of elderly, usually male, speakers lecture a rather bored looking group of young people sitting passively on hard chairs. When I'm training new practitioners for this work I try to urge them to do good youth work with young people of different faiths in the room rather than run a traditional inter-faith conference with young people in the room.

One of the basic principles in working with young people and their 'gatekeepers' to overcome their concerns about meeting is to ensure, as much as is possible, that a 'safe space' is created for the encounter. By this I mean that each person can feel equally welcomed, will know that there has been an effort to try and cater for their needs and that they can feel physically, emotionally and spiritually safe. Endeavouring to ensure equality of experience is both vital and challenging. One thing that makes dialogue events tricky (risky) is where there is a significant imbalance between the numbers of different faiths; the larger group usually feel cheated that they haven't had greater opportunity to meet others and the smaller group can feel intimidated, having to work harder in any discussions.

I tend to run small events (up to 10 of each faith max) which have a greater impact on the young people who come than larger events, but this makes it easier to ensure equal numbers. I also try to choose a venue where everyone can feel comfortable; so we don't use churches or mosques, as although one group would feel comfortable the others would, potentially, feel uncertain as to the correct behaviour expected of them or might find their parents, guardians or wider family members are unhappy to let them visit that venue.

In order to do what you can to ensure that the young people feel safe during discussions we have developed a set of 'Guidelines for Dialogue' which set a framework for discussions (www. http://www.scriptureunion.org.uk/Uploads/Documents/guidelines_for_dialogue.pdf.)

These include:

- *We will be honest in what we say*
- *We will respect other people's views, even if we disagree with them*
- *We will not tell other people what they believe, but allow them to tell us*
- *We will acknowledge both similarities and differences between our faiths*
- *We can ask for a discussion to be stopped if we feel uncomfortable with what is being said*

This framework acts as a 'safety net' in the discussions, so that young people know that they are unlikely to be backed into a corner or feel that they have to agree with everything that's being said.

While much youth work practice recommends that the young people draw up their own rules, we at the Scripture Union decided to set these ourselves as we want to do what we can to make sure that the framework is in place. For those young people who haven't gone through this process it is possible that they won't know what their concerns will be until they are engaged in the dialogue. We want to pre-empt the concerns they, and their 'gatekeepers' might have so that they feel they are in a 'safe space' from the outset.

Creating a 'safe space' requires us to consider as many of the needs of all the young people as we can for each aspect of the day, which if the workers are from one faith means they need to spend time doing what they can to understand the needs of the others. So we need to provide space for Muslims to pray and timetable these in at the right time, but it is also important to provide space for Christians to worship. They might not have a set time, but may require music, Bibles or other items to help their worship and someone prepared beforehand to lead.

Providing halal food will, of course, be important, but some Christians feel uncomfortable eating halal food. Often the only option for them is vegetarian, but providing a non-halal meat dish might be useful in helping them to feel that their requirements are taken equally seriously as everyone else's.

Recently a youth worker challenged me when I was recruiting young people for an event. I was expressing my frustration that from a church with a large youth group very few young people were participating. 'The thing is' he said, 'you're asking the young people to do what none of the parents have ever done'. When I stopped and thought about it I realised the truth of what he was saying and, therefore, the on-going challenge of this work. Good practice in youth work also helps parents feel comfortable and that everything possible will be done for their children's safety at the event.

Having good consent forms, which explain clearly what is going on, and being able to give clear, succinct explanations as to why the event is happening are vital in reassuring parents. Often parent's and wider family concerns are as much about practicalities as about theology. They want to know where and when an event will be, who's in charge, will there be halal food, will it be single sex or mixed? Although it's important to develop a robust reason for why we are doing this work, that can be easily explained to parents and leaders from both faiths, we also need to keep remembering that it is fundamentally a meeting of young people and they need caring for as people, not as sample Christians or Muslims. It might feel like I'm labouring the point, but so often I've seen events struggle because people have failed to consider the youth work side of the engagement enough, being overly focussed on the inter-faith dimension; this is understandable but needs necessarily to be avoided.

After several years of this approach to youth work we are starting to move from one off events or events where groups meet infrequently (maybe 3 times a year) to more regular encounters. The impact of this is greater on the young people, as they get to know one another better and have the time to work on bigger projects and discuss a wider variety of issues. But the risks are greater as there is greater opportunity for witness and influence from the other. Some people are happy to let their children attend infrequently, but less happy for a more intense or lengthy engagement. This requires us to work hard with parents to promote understanding and for them to hopefully embrace the concept behind the work. Many of those who have reservations are parents of teenagers who mix daily with people of different faiths at school or college. The world is changing and, as youth workers, we often stand in the gap between the experiences and expectations of parents and those of young people. Our engagement with youth culture gives us the privilege and responsibility to be guided by young people but also be ready to respond to their requests for guidance where we can when it is appropriate. Often we can play something of the same role for parents as they sometimes struggle to make sense of the world their children inhabit. But we need to avoid thinking we know more about young people than their parents of family do; the result of a type of professional egotism that has no place in good practice but perhaps more particularly in faith related work.

Encounters between young people of different faiths and between young people of faith and those with no faith will increase as society changes. As youth workers we can put this issue to one side, view it as a luxury for specialists and consider talking about it sometime in the future. Or we can walk alongside young people as they negotiate this world, working with them to create relatively 'safe spaces' for them to meet people of other faiths and learn the attitudes, values and practices that will equip them to live out their faith in a multi-faith society.

As someone who has had the privilege of working with young people in this context I've seen how much they have to contribute and how it can transform their relationships, ideas and values in constructive ways. It has been said recently that many of our communities lead 'Parallel Lives' (Home Office 2001) where there is little interaction between members of the communities. This can lead to ignorance, suspicion, fear and occasionally violence. In the Bible, Matthew Chapter 5, Jesus is recorded as naming a number of groups of people who were to be considered as blessed. The 7th group he identifies in verse 9 are the peacemakers; he says that they will be called the sons of God. I suspect that all of us are peace supporters; we desire peace for ourselves, our families, our communities and the young people we work with. Working to bring young people of different faiths together in a constructive manner moves us beyond being a peace supporter; we become peace makers; a far harder task but, I believe, a far higher calling.

BIBLIOGRAPHY

al-Faruqi, I. (1998). *Islam and other faiths*. The Islamic Foundation.

Ansari, H. (2004). *The infidel within: The history of Muslims in Britain, 1800 to the present*. C Hurst & Co Publishers Ltd.

Board for Mission and Unity of the General Synod of the Church of England. (1984). *Towards a theology for inter-faith dialogue*. Church House Publishing.

Burney, S. (1999). Islam and Non-Muslims. *Reflect, 15*(1999), 16–17.

Community cohesion: A report of the independent review team chaired by Ted Cantle. Home Office.

Fowler, J. (1981). *Stages of faith: The psychology of human development and the quest for meaning*. Harper.

Maqsood, R. (1994). *For heaven's sake: A Muslim teenager's book*. Ta-Ha Publishers Ltd.

Smith, A. (2004). The role of young people in Christian Muslim dialogue. *The Journal of Youth Ministry, 2.2*, 89–96.

Smith, A. (2009). *My friend Imran: Christian-Muslim friendship*. Cambridge: Grove Books Limited.

Sudworth, T. (2007). *Mission-shaped Youth: Rethinking young people and the church*. Church House Publishing.

Talal, H. (2000). The future of Muslim-Christian relations: A personal view. *Islam and Christian-Muslim Relations, 11.2*(2000), 163–166.

Ward, P. (1996). *Growing up evangelical: Youthwork and the making of a subculture*. SPCK.

BRIAN BELTON

15. CONCLUSION - YOUTH WORK AND ISLAM (DOING IT)

FIRE

A while ago I was in Bradford. I was there as an external examiner at Bradford College for the youth work programme run by the University of Leeds. As I live in London, I got up to Bradford the afternoon before my day at the College. There was little for me to do by the evening, so I thought I'd go for a walk, to remind myself what the place was like.

I had been out for about 20 minutes when I saw a fire engine dealing with a burning car. As people do, I stood and watched the action. Suddenly a hail of broken bricks and bits of concrete came raining down on the fire officers. I looked at where the shower had come from and saw about 20 young men, I suppose aged between 12 and 15, picking up whatever they could find to bombard the fire officers and their engine.

The engine's crew tried to protect themselves by turning their hoses on the gang of lads, but as one of the men fell to the floor injured by what looked like a flying road sign, the fire officers retreated to the engine and fled the scene. The boys continued their assault. I saw the windscreen smash and one of the side mirrors shattered.

The fire blazed on.

WATER

O you are enveloped in your cloak!
Arise and warn!
Your Lord magnify,
Your raiment purify,
Pollution shun!
Qur'an IXXXIV:1-5
I read these words, not for the first time, on my first visit to Venice, whilst wandering around the Islands in the lagoon. Then, as now, I felt the verse is about the protection offered by the practice of a disciplined faith. But paradoxically, it is not a controlling imposition that is usually associated with the notion of 'discipline'.

B. Belton and S. Hamid (eds), Youth Work and Islam:
A leao of faith for young people,187–191.

It extols us to call on something that is within us; a human capability to discern; reject that which will hurt us and embrace 'magnify' the huge spiritual force that humanity both encompasses and is encompassed by.

The longest stay I had on any one of the islands was my visit to Torcello - I think it was the idea that it went back so far in the history of colonial Venice that attracted me (5th or 6th century I think). It has only a few dozen people living on it now and it is hard to see where the 20,000 or so population stayed when it was thriving.

The Byzantine Cathedral, Santa Fosca, is quite astounding. The basilica is over 1,000 years old - anything with that lineage is worth seeing, touching, smelling and in an odd way, listening to. The marble pulpit has bits that go back to the 7th century church.

I climbed to the top of the tower and looked out over the lagoon - it was quite a dizzying day and with a little imagination it could have been anytime in the last 1, 500 years . I roamed around the church and the central dome and the Museo dell Estuario for hours till the late afternoon then meandered along the canal that runs from the vaporetto stop to the basilica and back - there's a couple of little cafes along the way.

As dusk began to fall I got myself something to eat and sat outside a small restaurant. I had spoken to no one all day and that seemed kind of natural. I went back to Santa Fosca and on the edge of a field, just past the tower, I lay down, using my day sack as a pillow, and stared at the sky that seemed full of stars. I listened to the night. I guess I must have fallen asleep at about 2am and had a pleasantly incoherent dream about the greatness of time and creation that was full of a feeling of being lost in wonder, which was, strangely, orientating.

I awoke as the light broke over the lagoon. It was quite cold but the colours of the island, the sky and the lagoon were fascinating. I wondered if I had ever felt so free or if I ever would again. I walked to the mud shore and looked out towards Venice, sat down and slowly ate a chocolate bar and drank the water I had brought with me, that had pleasantly cooled overnight. I then strolled back to the vaporetto stop and took a slow boat back to St Marks.

Later I made my way to San lazzaro. I liked the idea of Byron going there. One of the monks told me that his great-grand father had met that infamous Lord - I also loved the idea of a press producing works in 36 languages 200 years ago...words tumbling loosely into the world - little droplets of light.

EARTH

I remember being alone in a police cell...they had turned the lights out...I could hear nothing but the beating of my own heart...I tried to recall when I had been more frightened...I knew they were going to come for me, that I was about to take a mighty beating...the loneliness of that moment can still be felt...how can you tell anyone about it? About how it is to be cut off from the world...the whole world and isolated in your fear...the fear that you might die having done nothing...there is an effort one makes to connect with creation after that and times and tastes like that. What makes the motivation to 'say', to 'speak' to find words and ways of connecting with everyone; finding a way back to everything? To discover things in your life that might connect you to others and try to say to them...to touch them...make connection with the wholeness of things more tangible...but it may be those who are cut off are just that...that the attempts at building bridges or crossing the lagoon of loneliness is no more than a kind of insubstantial nonsense...others are more able to do that or they don't have to or something...to be where others stand...ought we to be better than we are?

Fate and destiny are hard foes...it seems few of us make friends with those two towers. Perhaps that needs some certainly.

That boy in a cell is the reality - he should be embraced for the truth he is...the night draws in on him as the chatterers chatter about their world and worry about their chatter which reflects the world of loneliness...everything is outward looking - it is as if there is a vast void inside of us; the door to everything is closed by the obsessions with things that are nothing. There is no connection just the rumour of it...the relief is in the stop...the end of trying...

AIR

But right now, I'm still trying and that is partly because the great Absoluteness has, every now and then, been open to me. That revived the soul of the forgotten boy and the echoes of the unity of creation urge me to persist.

Love is an infinite ocean in which the heavens are no more than a flock of foam.

Know that it is the waves of Love which turn the wheels of heaven; without Love, the world would be without life.

Each atom is infatuated with this Perfection, and hastens towards it. Their haste says implicitly,

'Glory to God!'

(God says:) *If it were not by pure love, then how*
Would I have given existence to the heavens?
I raised up this sublime celestial sphere so that you
Might know how sublime is Love

Rumi and Sufism - Eva de Vitray-Meyervitch (from the Mathnawi, Jala al-Din Rumi Air)

We are all in reach of the resource of the 'infinite ocean' of love, the thing that might not be so obvious or even easy is the reaching out for this love, seeking it and of course giving it (love, that gives the world life) to others.

The capacity to perfect these related practices (which are in practice one organic process) is something that we do naturally; all of us want to give and get love, we only shun love when we are mentally or spiritually sick. I do not have to work hard to love my son, my daughter, my brother, my sister, my father, my mother.

Even if they have done something awfully wrong, my love for them persists. But extending this love and broadening my own access to the love of others, the world, takes both discipline and spiritual energy. The source of that divine power (I think by definition, because it is 'divine') can only be God. That power is obtained by the Word of God as given to us.

This is simple but complex, which is the nature of the sublime. However, what is clear is that in order to both get and give the great enriching life resource of love, we have to 'do' something; we cannot just get and be given love. The expectation of that happening is not only nonsensical it is destructively selfish in that it is achingly non-productive.

The tradition of Islam is the exact opposite of this. The life Islam offers is the outcome of sustained action emanating from belief - Islam is a faith that is 'practiced'. The sitting and waiting to get something, yet doing nothing, comes from another source entirely; it is the dream of an idiot whose only faith is in television commercials (they all promise something for nothing - but actually give nothing for something - route one to death).

It is in the traditions of Islam that we find a path to the 'practice' of love and as such the enhancement of our lives.

I once shared a flat with a man called Edward. He was from Tanzania. We were student youth workers and were both sent from London to work through a particularly cold winter in Hastings. This was a foreign place for me, being an 'East End' boy, but for Edward, born in the shadow of Mount Killmamjaro, that freezing, at the time, very white, very English place, must have been like another planet.

I used to run a lot, but that pass-time was not very appetizing given the bleak coastal winter weather. I used to ask Edward, 'Do you think I should go for a run' given it was raining or icy. He would nearly always reply; 'Just do it Brian. Just do it'. And for some reason, I nearly always did.

'Doing it' is harder than it sounds, particularly if it is something hard or something that we only half want to do. It might be that we just want the outcome without any effort at all. But if we don't 'do it' and come across people who are 'doing it' in one way or another, even the best of us are likely to feel a level of resentment towards them; they are doing what we can't or won't do.

The other side of resentment is nearly always blame. If you make someone feel bad about themselves, weather you mean to or not, the bad feelings that person might have may hurt them so much, they might want so much not to be reminded of not 'doing it', often you will be blamed for that hurt, because if the person blames themselves for the hurt, it might just be too much to handle.

When you do nothing or only that which is easy, that which you know you can do, firstly you do not develop; you remain immature, unskilled, ignorant etc. But in the universe nothing is like that, nothing stays as it is. Every thing is either growing or dying. The less we 'do it', the more we fail to nourish our internal world, the emptier we become. You can get drunk, or smoke a packet of cigarettes, or buy an album but these things will not fill you. The day after you've drunk you will feel a bit bad, no more; when you have smoked all the cigarettes you will just want more; when you have listened to the album twenty or thirty times, all you will want is a different album.

When I was at school, my religious studies teacher told me he thought hell was a place where there was no existence. For him there's literally nothing there. I think this is where those young men in Bradford were going. Watching them I could not help but feel their resentment, blame and emptiness. I felt they had never looked at the sky, felt the greatness of creation around them or ever 'done it'. They inhabited a cell of loneliness, resentment and fear, the midwives of blame and hatred.

As a youth worker I think that this situation is what I am dealing with. How can I be like Edward and say 'just do it'; fill and feel your life. How can I motivate or inspire someone to do that which is hard and/or something that they've never done before; promote growth and develop...ask them not die, not to go to that hell of emptiness?

I'd like to give an answer, but the reality seems to me to be that for every young person I've worked with, all over the world, the answer is always different. Each one is a unique and beautiful creation within the massive and unfathomable beauty of all creation; as such they deserve and require our nurture and care before our urge to educate or 'better' them; they are already all they need to be, even though who they are might just not ready to come out yet. They don't need my motivation, they have a motor. I can't help but ask if I risk be suffocated by my own ego if I aspire to inspire them. But hey, I might be able to be inspired and motivated by them; that is nearly always enough...and enough is enough...at least for now

This understanding of the extraordinary, divine exceptionalness of each individual helps us, because in this recognition we honour that which God has created and loves; we grasp that all of us cannot but develop and as we comprehend this we are able to reach out to and honour the integrity of those God has made.

This being the case, those lads stoning the fire fighters are a gift from God; they offer us a chance to 'do it', to give the acknowledgment of their nobility that is so clearly been denied, and in that giving grow ourselves in praise of God's creation and our appreciation of His love.

Lightning Source UK Ltd.
Milton Keynes UK

178300UK00001B/41/P